ISLAMIC FINANCE

Current Legal and Regulatory Issues

S. Nazim Ali

Editor

with an introduction by

Clement Henry

Published by the

Islamic Finance Project
Islamic Legal Studies Program
Harvard Law School

Cambridge, Massachusetts

Compiled in 2005 by the

Islamic Finance Project

ISBN: 0-9702835-5-5

Printed in the United States of America

Library of Congress Control Number 2004116625

Contents

Preface

This book is the first publication of the Islamic Finance Project (IFP) since we transferred to the Islamic Legal Studies Program (ILSP) at the Harvard Law School in January 2004. IFP's aim is to study the field of Islamic finance from the legal and shari`a points of view by analyzing contemporary scholarship, encouraging collaboration among scholars within and outside the Muslim world, and increasing the interaction between theory and practice in Islamic finance.

The Harvard University Forum on Islamic Finance continues to be one of IFP's principal activities. The authors included here originally presented their work at the Sixth Forum, held on May 8-9, 2004. Unlike previous years, we have published a volume of selected papers in lieu of complete Proceedings for the Forum. These papers are therefore only a fraction of the thirty-six papers presented at the Sixth Forum. The title reflects the theme of the Forum; the introduction has been provided by Clement M. Henry, to whom I am grateful.

It may be appropriate here to recall the senior addresses at the Sixth Forum, which have not been included in this volume. John B. Taylor, the Under Secretary for International Affairs in the United States Department of the Treasury, opened the Forum by expressing the U.S. Treasury's commitment to learning about and engaging with the Islamic financial services industry. He stressed the importance of transparency and disclosure and stated that, as with conventional financing, Islamic financing will benefit from transparency, good governance, and an internationally accepted regulatory framework.

Ahmad Mohamed Ali, president of the Islamic Development Bank (IDB) Group, emphasized effective supervision as a must for the success of the Islamic financial services industry. He identified risk management, disclosure and transparency, accounting and auditing, internal control systems, and corporate governance as areas where the formulation and adaptation of standards was required.

In his remarks at the Forum banquet, Nurcholish Madjid, Rector of Universitas Paramadina in Indonesia, elaborated on the morality and ethics of Islamic finance. He expressed the hope that the world community, in close global economic cooperation, would find a way to overcome injustices in the current financial system. He suggested that experimentation with Islamic finance based on the shari`a would allow Muslims to offer productive solutions to contemporary economic predicaments and thereby benefit humanity as a whole.

The Forum is one of a wider set of IFP efforts to study the field of Islamic finance. Since its transfer to the law school, we have also conducted research on the effects of 9/11 on the Islamic finance industry, have hosted a seminar featuring Jeffrey Sachs on the long-term economic prospects of the Middle East, and are in the final stages of preparation for what is perhaps the first seminar that brings together Islamic financial institutions and regulatory agencies in the Unites States.

A number of individuals have supported the project and worked together to enhance and increase its activities. Most notable among them are Frank E. Vogel, Director of the Islamic Legal Studies Program, Harvard Law School; Samuel L. Hayes, Professor Emeritus, Harvard Business School; and Thomas D. Mullins, former Associate Director, Center for Middle Eastern Studies. Peri Bearman, Associate Director of the ILSP, was particularly helpful in the organization of the Forum and review of papers.

IFP sponsors deserve special mention for the vision they show in promoting Islamic finance by means of independent academic inquiry. They are Arcapita Bank B.S.C.of Bahrain, Kuwait Finance House of Kuwait, and HSBC Amanah of United Arab Emirates.

A number of devoted Harvard students at different schools in the university were of great assistance to IFP in the compilation of the databank, organization of the Forum and seminars, and help with research and publications. The Project owes special thanks to them, particularly Mansoor Shakil LLM ’04; M. S. Shaheen JD ’06; M. A. Vaid MBA ’05; Aamir Rehman MBA ’04; and Abdur-Rahman Syed AB ’99.

I would like also to acknowledge the assistance provided by M. S. Shaheen JD ’06, in compiling these papers and Sina Muscati LLM ’05 in carrying out the preliminary editing. Special thanks go to Peri Bearman for reviewing papers and providing suggestions for improvement. And I should finally like to thank the copyeditor, Matthew Seccombe, for his assistance.

S. Nazim Ali
Director
Islamic Finance Project

Introduction

Clement M. Henry[1]

It is an honor to introduce this book of fine essays originally presented at the Sixth Harvard University Forum on Islamic Finance, May 8-9, 2004. Their focus on current legal and regulatory issues comes at a critical time in the history of the industry for three reasons. Since the year 2000, responding in part, perhaps, to high oil revenues flooding the economies of the Gulf Cooperation Council (GCC) states, Islamic financiers have devised an array of controversial new securities. Secondly, they have also in these years completed an institutional architecture designed to regulate the industry with common standards. Thirdly, international concerns about the stability of the international banking system led in 2004 to the Basel II Accord issuing new guidelines concerning the capital adequacy requirements of banks. Meeting the new guidelines poses special challenges for Islamic banks.

The essays reflect a current controversy over the future of Islamic finance. Barely three decades old, the industry is coming of age and is grappling with issues of regulation arising from its initial successes. Its entire financial surface – estimated at about $250 billion in total assets divided among 261 banks – is only about one-fifth the size of Citigroup, but, although minuscule by world standards, it is growing at an annual rate of at least 10 percent. Islamic finance is now "firmly established as a key regional industry and an interesting global niche industry,"[2] according to the Union of Arab Banks. It is also too large and visible, especially since 9/11, to avoid scrutiny on the part of international as well as national authorities by disappearing into a misty informal international economy. And just as high oil prices contributed to the original demand in the mid-1970s for

---

[1] Professor of Government and Middle Eastern Studies, Department of Government, University of Texas (Austin).

[2] Union of Arab Banks 2004. An announcement for the Fourth Annual Islamic Finance Summit sponsored in London by Euromoney claims that Islamic finance is growing 15 percent per year. See http://www.euromoneyseminars.com/pdfs/ELE667.pdf (last visited December 6, 2004).

Islamic banking, the new highs since 2000 seem to be stimulating another phase of rapid growth.

Islamic banks are rapidly gaining market share, especially in the Gulf Cooperation Council (GCC) countries. Conventional banks like the National Commercial Bank (NCB), Saudi Arabia's largest, are establishing Islamic windows.[3] Saudi American Bank (SAMBA) recently converted its Buraidah and Onaiza branches into "dedicated Islamic Banking locations," supervised like the NCB by an independent *shari'a* board. By 2004 interest ("commission")-free deposits and depositors' "investments" in Islamic banks and branches were probably accounting for close to half of the total market in Saudi Arabia.[4] In the smaller GCC countries the Islamic sector exceeded 15 percent, and it reached 10 percent in Jordan.

Its very successes have provoked much soul searching, as evidenced in Part III of this book. As originally conceived by some of its pioneers,[5] Islamic finance projected a distinctive ethic of risk-sharing, offering venture capital in the form of *mudaraba* and *musharaka* to small businesses.[6] Unlike conventional banks, Islamic banks were expected to engage in equity financing, sharing profits and losses with their clients. But venture capitalism was too risky, especially in Middle Eastern business environments, where the banks were also determined to compete with commercial banking systems. The transnational Islamic finance groups of Dar al Mal (headed by Prince Mohammed al-Faisal) and Al Baraka (headed by Saleh Kamel) quickly turned to less risky financial operations to compete with conventional banks. Even the less commercially driven Islamic Development Bank, a state-owned consortium, had to reduce its portfolio of *mudaraba* and *musharaka* to remain financially viable.

---

[3] In its 2003 Annual Report, the National Commerce Bank explains that its retail banking "provides banking services, including consumer lending, current accounts and investment management services to individuals and small sized businesses in addition to Islamic products in compliance with *Shariah* rules and supervised by the independent *Shariah* Board." See http://www.ncb.com.sa/fin/03/notes2.pdf (last visited December 6, 2004).

[4] Al Rajhi Banking and Investment Corporation alone had 14 percent of the kingdom's commercial banking deposits in 2000, and some 30 percent of all commercial banking deposits were non-interest-bearing in 2001. See Henry and Wilson 2004: 7, 109-114.

[5] Ahmad Najjar founded the first rural cooperatives in Egypt in 1963, modeled on German *Sparkassen* employing profit sharing techniques for financing small enterprises. To stay out of political trouble with Nasser, who had repressed the Muslim Brotherhood, he did not make any references to Islam. But he subsequently played an active role as an adviser to the transnational group of banks established by Prince Mohammed Al Faisal until the mid-1980s, when they split over ideological and business differences. See Clement M. Henry, *The Mediterranean Debt Crescent* (University Press of Florida, 1996), 269-275.

[6] See *infra*, pp. 19-21 for definitions of these terms.

Competing with conventional banks in fact required Islamic banks to mimic conventional practices. Their main customers are Muslim depositors who reject interest as *riba* (usury) yet wish to receive profits from their investments that meet prevailing interest rates of return on deposits. To generate the necessary profits for their depositors, the banks were obliged from their inception to invest their funds in less risky assets than those targeted by venture capitalists.

Their bread-and-butter instrument is the *murabaha*, a contract whereby the bank purchases a good for the client and sells it to him on a deferred payment basis at cost plus profit. Instead of sharing uncertain profits with the client as in a *mudaraba*, the bank is to receive a fixed payment by a certain time. The client agrees, for example, to pay the bank $22,000 a year later for a car that costs $20,000. Practices vary among Islamic banks but they seek to minimize any risk associated with owning the vehicle because they are competing with conventional banks. In most countries, especially those influenced by British or American banking practices, the commercial banks are supposed to specialize in finance and not be involved in other businesses such as car dealing. To compete effectively, the Islamic bank must also distance itself as much as possible from other businesses. Yet the bank must deal with the physical merchandise – and in the above example actually own the vehicle for at least a second or two – if its operations are to be deemed truly Islamic. In that example the *murabaha* is equivalent to a consumer loan of $20,000 at 10 percent interest. Despite taking on added risk, the Islamic bank cannot earn more "profit" than the going interest rate because the consumer will otherwise prefer to take out a conventional loan.

However closely it mimics the conventional bank, the Islamic one remains at a slight disadvantage because of the commercial risks and transaction costs associated with the *murabaha*. Yet the more effectively it mimics the conventional bank, the greater its vulnerability to the charge that it has compromised its Islamic identity – even to the point of appearing in the eyes of some Muslim critics as less truly Islamic and transparent than conventional banks!

Islamic finance is thus torn between the need to preserve its distinctive identity and the needs of the marketplace. Yet as recently as 2000 in his pioneering book on the subject, Ibrahim Warde highlighted difficulties even in demarcating Islamic finance, much less defining its identity:

> No definition … is entirely satisfactory. To every general criterion – a financial institution owned by Muslims, catering to Muslims, supervised by a Shariah Board, belonging to the International Association of Islamic Banks (IAIB) etc. – one can find some significant exception. Indeed, even the criterion of self-identification – i.e., an Islamic institution is one that calls itself Islamic – would leave out the Turkish Finance Houses or Saudi Arabia's Al-Rajhi Banking and Investment Company, which … do not refer explicitly

to their Islamic character. As for the principal focus on profit-and-loss sharing (PLS) activities, it remains more an ideal than a reality.[7]

The other major recent study of the subject is Frank E. Vogel and Samuel L. Hayes, III, *Islamic Law and Finance: Religion, Risk, and Return* (Kluwer Law International, 1998). They assert that "the structure of Islamic finance is firmly rooted in the Qur'an and the teachings of Muhammad, and the interpretation of these sources of revelation by his followers." They implicitly define the subject as "the application of Islamic law" to "an area of commercial life" or "a sector of modern commerce,"[8] but not specifically to the banking and finance sector. Presumably Islamic law cannot be applied to any conventional definition of this sector because, at least in their understanding, Islamic law is opposed to many conventional practices of banking and finance.

In effect, the Vogel-Hayes definition puts Islamic legal scholars in command of any further specification of a financial sector. Indeed, the body of their book deals with alternative legal rulings about various contracts that are central to the discipline of Islamic finance. The trouble with this approach, as Frank Vogel reveals in detailed analyses of cases and precedents, is that the legal scholars, including those on the various *shari'a* boards of the Islamic banks, disagree on many key points. A financial practice that one Islamic bank's *shari'a* board finds acceptable may be unacceptable to the board of another bank. Institutions with sufficient authority to make universally accepted definitions do not yet govern Islamic finance.

That is why the recent efforts to build a regulatory framework for Islamic finance are such a significant step forward. The Islamic Financial Services Board (IFSB), established in 2002 with sponsorship from the International Monetary Fund (IMF), is in effect mandated to define the industry by standardizing its products, and the International Islamic Rating Agency, established a year later, is to grade the financial management of its recognized agencies, the Islamic banks. These regulatory institutions have materialized just in time – amid an explosion of markets for new securities in response to booming demand from investors. But they are young, under-staffed and under-funded, more an expression of aspirations for Islamic financial order than an established industrial authority. The hope is that the IFSB can set and disseminate international standards for Islamic financial institutions. Its sixty members include fifteen central banks of predominantly Muslim countries, a variety of Islamic banks, and, as associate members, the IMF, the World Bank, the Bank of International Settlements, the People's Bank of China, and the Central Bank of the

[7] Warde 2000: 5.
[8] Vogel and Hayes 1998: 1-2, 19, 23.

Philippines.[9] The standard-setter behind the scenes that successfully lobbied for the creation of the IFSB is the Accounting and Auditing Organization for Islamic Financial Institutions (AAOIFI), founded in Bahrain in 1991. To date it has issued fifty-seven standards on accounting, auditing, governance, and ethical and *shari'a* standards, most of them within the past two or three years.[10]

Were the IFSB to gain the full international authority required to define Islamic banking practices, however, they would still be subject to religious or ethically inspired objections to their "Islamic" identity. The present book goes over some of these objections, as well as the varying responses of different authors. Although we cannot resolve the authors' disagreements, a careful reader can acquire an objective understanding of the issues at stake. The practitioners tend to focus on operational interpretations of fourteen centuries of *fiqh* law, whereas the theorists, including some lawyers (Hegazy) as well as economists (El-Gamal and Siddiqi), contrast what they consider to be the spirit of the law with prevailing Islamic banking practices. It is encouraging to note at the outset that all of the authors appreciate the logic of the other parties to the debate.

In Part I of this book Ibrahim Warde offers the necessary background about the basic instruments of Islamic finance for understanding what follows. He introduces us to many of the early, still unresolved problems of corporate governance in the Islamic banking sector. "Moral hazard" applies as much to religious or ethical organizations as to conventional businesses: indeed regulation may be even more necessary here, Warde notes, because some crooks tend to seek cover in ethical or religious shelters – and this tendency is by no means confined to Muslims! Warde takes us to the crux of the special problem facing Islamic banks: they operate under conflicting logics. "Unlike secular systems, the legal system of Islam incorporates both an economic and a religious logic." The conflict will be further analyzed in Part III, but first it is useful to examine a sample of the explosive new developments in Islamic finance, which are displayed and analyzed in Part II.

Islamic banks faced growing problems of excess liquidity and mismatched maturities in their first two decades of operations. They could not by definition park funds in conventional interest-bearing financial instruments unless they were ready to commit financial suicide by forgoing the interest payments. They were in need of functional equivalents of T-bills and other tradable securities, overnight interbank instruments, and other facilities available as a matter of course to their conventional commercial bank competitors. Finally, in 2000, the Bahrain Monetary

---

[9] The current members are listed on the IFSB website at www.ifsb.org/index.php?ch=3&pg=7&ac=10 (last visited December 6, 2004).

[10] See the AAOIFI website at http://www.aaoifi.com/ (last visited December 6, 2004).

Agency introduced the first Islamic T-bill, a non-tradable *sukuk al-salam*. The following year Bahrain pioneered a way of bundling Islamically acceptable leases into the first tradable Islamic debt security, a *sukuk al-ijara*. Malaysia followed suit in 2002, this time creating an internationally tradable *sukuk* that met U.S. regulatory requirements for conventional global bonds and was rated by Standard & Poor's and Moody's. The Islamic Development Bank, Qatar, Kuwait, Dubai, and the German state of Saxony-Anhalt subsequently issued a succession of Islamic bonds. Dubai formally launched its $750 million *sukuk al-ijara* on October 10, 2004, in partnership with the Hong Kong Shanghai Banking Corporation (HSBC) and other major international and regional banks, and our first contributor to Part II, who works for HSBC, explains the financial architecture supporting these new instruments.

Mohamed Rafe Md. Haneef, with law degrees from both the International Islamic University, Malaysia and Harvard Law School, applies his formidable cross-cultural legal skills to the analysis of the *sukuk*. Qualified both by the Malaysian and the New York Bar Associations, he was associate director of the HSBC Amanah, Dubai and evidently has hands-on experience with these Islamic bonds. His chapter here dissects the structure of the *sukuk al-ijara* and also the slightly more complex *sukuk al-istithmar* issued by the Islamic Development Bank. The structures, centered on a Special Purpose Company or Vehicle (SPC or SPV), effectively insulate Islamic investors from interest-bearing instruments, while retaining fixed payouts like the *murabaha* or more complex variants thereof to the Islamic investor. The reader may follow Haneef's argument step-by-step, looking at the variety of contracts between the complex of partners that constitute the deal. At each step in describing the components relevant to the Islamic investors, *shari'a* law precedents are cited. Generally the Malaysians accept the relatively "liberal" (for these purposes) interpretations of the Shafi'i school of law.

Haneef's paper will fascinate financial engineers but it will also appeal to Islamic legal scholars because he is careful not to overlook the opposing arguments from Shafi'i and other schools of Islamic law. Although other authors directly criticize the legal dexterity illustrated in these case studies of financial engineering, Haneef anticipates the attacks and admits that there can be honest disagreements. His paper also points to certain traits of *shari'a* law that are more consonant with the Anglo-Saxon common law tradition than with civil law, and indeed invites scholars steeped in Western civil law traditions – as in Jordan and much of the GCC – to better appreciate their own Islamic traditions.

The following paper by Kilian Bälz develops this theme. Common law tends to share more affinities than civil law with Islam's "common law" tradition of *fiqh*. In particular, the Islamic banks' bread-and-butter instrument of *murabaha* finds closer family resemblances in British common law than in German civil law. Bälz focuses on the treatment of the

Islamic contracts in these two legal traditions. The bottom line is that they are enforceable in both systems if they are suitably worded. This chapter does not deal explicitly with *sukuk* but points to legal methodologies that should work in enforcing these new instruments as well as the more traditional ones. The underlying importance of these findings cannot be underestimated because much, probably the majority, of Islamic finance involves overseas investment, subject to litigation in London and other Western capitals rather than in Bahrain, Cairo, Jedda, or Kuala Lumpur.

Michael McMillen takes Islamic overseas investment a step further. McMillen is a trained obstetrician as well as a New York and London-based lawyer, but after delivering dozens of babies he is now midwife to controversial new Islamic financial instruments in consultation with top-of-the-line *shari'a* lawyers and scholars. In his paper he takes us through the steps, methodically building a brilliant, complex instrument whereby the junior bonds financing up to 30 percent of a South Korean real estate project comply with the *shari'a* and thus with the needs of an Islamic investor. McMillen backs up much of his analysis of the various contracts with the *shari'a* law codified by the *Majelle* of the British colonial administration in Palestine in 1933, but he also has the advice of many active scholars. Rather than resorting to conventional Islamic standbys of *murabaha* or *ijara* (leasing), he sanitizes the junior debenture by pointing to the *shari'a*'s recognition of the residual use of property. The rents acquire an equity component that legitimates the fixed rate of return on the bonds. Analyses along these lines open the way to many further innovations that may help Islamic finance to catch up with its conventional competitors.

Indeed, one aspect of the transaction described by McMillen involves an Islamic option, which fortuitously meets a desire expressed by Haneef in his chapter for *shari'a*-compatible derivatives.[11] McMillen concludes that *sukuk*, while promising and innovative, are not the only way that Islamic finance can diversify its instruments. With more creativity and "reconsideration," not in the sense of rejection but rather of bringing back the full range of Islamic jurisprudence, he thinks Islam can continue to redefine finance in ways that will vastly expand the range of *shari'a*-compliant financial products.

---

[11] McMillen notes, "It is assumed for purposes of this essay that the *Shari'a*-Compliant Investor desires to achieve a specific internal rate of return (the '*Target IRR*') on its investment and is willing to participate at a level of risk that is generally associated with equity capital investments. It is further assumed that the *Shari'a*-Compliant Investor is willing to forgo returns in excess of the Target IRR." Those returns could be viewed as an option. Note Mahmoud Al-Gamal's observation: "Protected capital mutual funds marketed in Saudi Arabia tend to rely on non-Islamic partners or advisers to receive an option-like payment as management or advisory fees (e.g. by capping investor returns at some percentage, and giving the partner/adviser all excess returns above that level as fees, i.e. paying with a call option)."

Looking to the long-term future of Islamic finance, it may be significant that, as noted above, the People's Bank of China joined the Islamic Financial Services Board as an associate member, along with the World Bank and the IMF. But full integration of Islamic finance into the global economy also rouses fears among some theorists and practitioners of Islamic banking that the spirit of Islam is being lost along the way. The contributors of Part III articulate some of these fears in their debates about the ethical issues and concern that Islamic finance retain its cultural and religious authenticity.

M. Nejatullah Siddiqi recalls the basic outlines of the ethical debate introduced by Ibrahim Warde. For Siddiqi the religious logic is expressed by the injunction against *riba*, any hint of which leads down a slippery slope. He conflates *riba* with social injustice and considers its prohibition to be "the first threshold in deterring injustice and unfair practices." Yet, as a former economics professor and president of the International Association for Islamic Economics, he also recognizes international market forces and the profit motives of commercial banks, Islamic as well as conventional. He re-examines two perennial problems faced by Islamic banks: (1) coping with delays in repaying *murabaha* debts, and (2) the permissibility of securitizing *murabaha* and other Islamically acceptable contracts. Each case illustrates conflicts between "jurists bent on ensuring justice by avoiding anything similar to *riba*/interest and the economists keen to maintain efficient markets."

Siddiqi objects, however, to the handling of certain legal issues by the *shari'a* boards of "an industry in a hurry" under market pressures from conventional banks. He is not convinced, for instance, that the analogies that some boards make between certificates of ownership in a company and shares in *murabaha* assets really justify the securitization of debt. Instead of manipulating legal interpretations to meet economic pressures, he argues for public recognition and debate over the conflicting ethical and economic priorities in light of a deeper understanding of Islam.

Mahmoud A. El-Gamal, who is the Chair Professor of Islamic Economics, Finance, and Management at Rice University, sharpens the debate by not only reaffirming Siddiqi's concerns but also implicitly attacking the Vogel-Hayes conception of Islamic finance:

> … By approving and eventually codifying (through AAOIFI, IFSB, OIC *Fiqh* Academy, etc.) legal stratagems to replicate conventional financial practices, jurists and bankers eventually drown the substance of Islamic law in their contemporary reconstructions of medieval forms of classical jurisprudence. …
>
> By focusing on medieval juristic forms rather than eternal legal principles of Islam, the industry may in fact violate those principles and become less Islamic than prudent utilization of conventional financial products.

Furthermore, El-Gamal outlines a model of "*shari'a* arbitrage" that suggests how Islamic finance may be losing its identity in the reams of arcane contracts illustrated by Haneef and McMillen. *Shari'a* arbitrage is a variant of regulatory arbitrage whereby a financial practice allowed in country B is not allowed in country A. The country B product is restructured offshore in a manner acceptable to country A. Now imagine instead that the countries are SPVs and other entities depicted in Haneef's or McMillen's complex diagrams of the new Islamic securities. The interest-based contracts required by conventional bank regulators can be hived off from the *shari'a*-based contracts required by Islamic investors.

El-Gamal illustrates the logic of this form of arbitrage by examples of simple back-to-back contracts for the purchase of a stapler. Virtually any conventional financial instruments can be mimicked by various degrees of separation insulating Islamically acceptable contracts from other contracts that may be Islamically unacceptable. He presents an abstract set of tools for securitizing debt and even generating Islamic put or call options, which El-Gamal, unlike Haneef, apparently deplores, because the Islamic investor is not permitted to control the risk by hedging. Virtually anything goes, as long as the *shari'a* boards of the banks selectively confine their attention to certain contracts within a project rather than analyzing the entire set of contracts and its underlying intentions.

El-Gamal joins Siddiqi in invoking "the spirit of Islam" to warn against these practices, and he goes so far as to compare the lawyers' artifices with those used in money laundering. His principal concern seems to be that instruments advertised as "Islamic" may engender among Muslims a greed for credit characteristic of American consumers. In a way he is echoing a concern expressed by Haneef, who viewed an Islamic mortgage instrument as acceptable for financing one's year-round home but not a summer place in southern France (or presumably a South Korean real estate project).

Just as it is refreshing to read economists voicing ethical concerns, it is interesting to read a lawyer, not an economist, exposing the political economy of *shari'a* arbitrage. Walid Hegazy, with law degrees from Harvard and Paris IX, is a member of both the Egyptian and American bar associations. In his paper he reinforces El-Gamal's reservations about Islamic legalisms by raising serious questions about conflicts of interests of the legal scholars who serve on the salaried *shari'a* boards of Islamic banks and make the rulings *(fatwas)* concerning their financial practices.

He also critically examines their "circumventive methodologies" for interpreting the *shari'a*, namely the *hila* (juristic stratagem, pl. *hiyal*) and *talfiq* (biased amalgamation of previous opinions to circumvent a prohibition). The *hila* is "a juristic trick that aims at circumventing the legislative intent behind a certain rule." As Ibn Khaldun[12] and many other scholars point out, however, not all *hila* are illegal, depending on the purpose behind circumventing a regulation. But Hegazy marshals many examples in which the underlying intent is merely to circumvent the law so as to indulge in *riba*. He casts doubt on a number of key building blocks of the complex bond issues discussed in Part II.

Talfiq is the other legal methodology he deplores. It is a patching operation that also in his eyes compromises the legitimacy of the financial muftis' rulings. One of his illustrations is the *fatwa* issued in 1978 and reconfirmed in 1988 that ensured the economic viability of the banks' bread-and-butter *murabaha*, representing over 70 percent of their financial transactions. Hegazy's analysis implies that Sayyid al-Tantawi, the Egyptian Shaikh al-Azhar, may have been pretty much on target in 1988 when, then serving as Mufti of Egypt, he issued a *fatwa* to the effect that conventional banks were legal whereas so-called "Islamic banks" were not.

As if Islamic finance does not face enough challenges on the home front, the banks are also especially vulnerable to the new capital adequacy measures set forth in the Basel II Accord. In Part IV of this book Mansoor Shakil and Kristin Smith examine the external threats and opportunities.

Shakil's paper presents the relevant aspects of Basel II. The good news for Islamic finance is that measures of capital adequacy may be more carefully tailored to the risk profiles of individual banks and thus take certain specificities of Islamic financial houses into account. The bad news is that Basel II discriminates in favor of large banks that have the resources needed to analyze their risk profiles. Further, assets of non-OECD countries are graded as riskier than OECD-based assets and consequently require greater capital backing. Although greater disclosure requirements probably favor Islamic banks, their small size and location may put them at an ever-greater disadvantage against their commercial competitors. To level the playing field, Shakil suggests dissociating the banks from their investment accounts and reducing the capital requirements from the latter. New securities companies or a second tier of Islamic investment banks would then have separate, lower capital adequacy requirements. They would include the bulk of the present balance sheets of Islamic banks.

Indeed, Smith's paper reports that a compromise may be in the works that would split the difference. In 2001 the Bahrain Monetary Agency (BMA) already accepted the argument that investment accounts were not normal bank deposits and that half their value could be subtracted from

[12] In *The Muqaddimah* (Bollingen edition, Princeton University Press, 1967), p. 300, Ibn Khaldoun observes that "Commerce is a natural way of making a living. However, most of its practices and methods are tricky and designed to obtain the (profit) margin between purchase prices and sale prices. This surplus makes it possible to earn a profit. Therefore the law permits cunning [hiyal] in commerce … [as long as it does not] mean taking away the property of others without giving anything in return."

risk-weighted assets in assessing an Islamic bank's capital adequacy. The chairman of the Islamic Financial Services Board (IFSB), who as secretary general of AAOIFI had originally negotiated the agreement with the BMA, is currently negotiating Islamic banking compliance with Basel II along similar lines with the international financial institutions.

Smith's paper goes well beyond Basel II, however, to present a concluding overview of the "harmonization" of Islamic finance with the global order. The reader may well be advised, in fact, to jump directly from Warde's introduction to Smith's paper so as to get the global picture before entering into the details of financial rulings and interpretations discussed in the other chapters. Smith does not go into the details but she presents institutional developments that may cut through the legal quagmires. As Walid Hegazy, the sternest of the critics in these pages recognizes, a proper institutionalization of Islamic finance may counteract the tendency of *shari'a* arbitrage to undermine its Islamic identity.

As a political scientist who has done extensive fieldwork in Kuwait and other GCC countries in the Islamic financial sector, Smith has examined the synergies between the bankers and Islamist politicians.[13] In the present volume she spells out the surprising political strategy employed by the bankers to pressure their national regulatory authorities: utilizing the affinities noted by Bälz and others between Anglo-American law and Islamic finance, they appealed directly to international financial institutions, dominated by Anglo-American traditions of banking, to lobby on their behalf. They gained influential international allies, notably in the IMF, and enlisted them to sponsor the IFSB and other transnational Islamic institutions that mirror conventional standard setting authorities. Smith tells the fascinating story of Islam's new financial architecture along with visions, since 9/11, of shifting the Islamic investment flows from West to East.

Between Warde and Smith, the two political scientists who introduce and conclude the discussion, the other contributors can be seen to represent an unruly "civil society" of OECD-based lawyers and bankers scrutinized by critical theorists. Collectively they express the remarkable power of the international civil society that underlies Islamic finance and that is pressing for its integration with conventional finance, and they also articulate major ideological contestation. The hope, shared by the entire sample of "civil society" represented in this volume, is that the new regulatory authorities may work to institutionalize the ongoing debate.

Such institutionalization, let me suggest by way of concluding this introduction, may carry broader political implications in the wake of 9/11. Islamic finance is giving rise to a new transnational political space in which a distinctively Islamic dialectic of globalization can be articulated. Even as the Bush Administration's responses to 9/11 have intensified Muslim

[13] See her chapter on Kuwait in Henry and Wilson 2004: 168-190.

perceptions of a clash of civilizations and provoked defensive jihad among growing numbers of Islamists,[14] other Islamists are redefining globalization in the financial sphere. Most of their respective states do not offer adequate political space for actors to articulate their theses and antitheses; indeed, authorities tend to skirt around the economic and political ("governance") reforms associated with globalization as well as repressing the related discourse about them. But the transnational financial sphere offers a new arena in which to play out the dialectics of globalization and overcome moralistic identifications of globalization with imperialism—by Islamizing the economic forces at work. Conversely, however, unless the United States adjusts its foreign policies, the forces of imperialism and anti-imperialism may destroy the fragile freedom of Islamic finance.

---

[14] The "must-read" analysis of the phenomenon is Anonymous (Michael Scheuer), *Imperial Hubris*: *Why the West is Losing the War on Terror* (Washington, D.C.: Brassey's, Inc. 2004).

Part I

Introducing the Challenges of Regulation

Corporate Governance and the Islamic Moral Hazard

Ibrahim Warde[1]

Corporate governance, defined as "the whole system of rights, processes and controls established internally and externally over the management of a business entity with the objective of protecting the interests of all stakeholders,"[2] has taken center stage in the past few years. The initial impetus came in the wake of the 1997 Asian financial crisis, when "bad governance" was designated as the primary culprit in the sudden collapse of economies that appeared healthy on the surface. The interest in the subject has not abated, as a steady stream of corporate scandals in the United States and Europe—involving companies such as Enron, World Com, Global Crossing, and Parmalat—has kept the preoccupation with corporate governance in the limelight.[3]

The Islamic world has in that regard been the subject of special scrutiny. Since the attacks of September 11, 2001, there is a wide consensus about the need for democratic reform and institution-building in the "greater Middle East."[4] Financial institutions, and especially the Islamic ones, have for a variety of reasons (such as their importance within national and regional economies, their inscrutability to outsiders, their rapid growth, the lack of universally accepted norms, etc.) been urged to take the issue of corporate governance particularly seriously.[5]

This paper focuses on the need to integrate moral hazard in the debate on the governance of Islamic institutions. The abundant literature on corporate governance has an ethnocentric character. It assumes U.S. style practices and norms, and places heavy emphasis on checks and balances and the creation of committees to monitor compensation, conflicts of interest,

---

[1] Reseach Affiliate, Center for International Studies, Massachusetts Institute of Technology (Cambridge, Massachusetts).

[2] Lannoo 1995: 5.

[3] See Warde 1998 and 2002.

[4] The "Greater Middle East" initiative was, for example, at the center of the June 2004 meting of the G8 meeting in Sea Island, Georgia.

[5] See the issues raised in Taylor 2004.

and the like. As in all one-size-fits-all approaches, it ignores the different institutional frameworks and regulatory cultures within which Islamic institutions operate. More specifically, being essentially secular, the corporate governance canon pays no attention to the religious element, which of course is at the core of Islamic finance.

At the same time, the Islamic finance literature resolves by assumption the issues raised by the corporate governance and moral hazard debates. A pioneer in the field explains what is expected of employees: "The staff in an Islamic bank should, throughout their lives, be conducting in the Islamic way, whether at work or at leisure."[6] By the same token, clients are expected to be people of impeccable character. Overall, "Islamic banks have a major responsibility to shoulder. . . . [A]ll the staff of such banks and customers dealing with them must be reformed Islamically and act within the framework of an Islamic formula, so that any person approaching an Islamic bank should be given the impression that he is entering a sacred place to perform a religious ritual, that is the use and employment of capital for what is acceptable and satisfactory to God."[7]

In addition, good governance happens to represent one of the ideals of Islamic finance, which is all about fairness, transparency, accountability, and social responsibility. Thus the Islamic concept of "trust" *(amana)*, which requires financial institutions to manage the funds entrusted to them in an effective, efficient, and responsible manner, corresponds almost exactly to that of corporate governance.

From the early days of Islamic finance in the 1970s, the ideal was not easy to put in practice. Problems of moral hazard, and by extension of corporate governance, proved endemic. Over time, Islamic institutions dealt with them in a number of ways—from devising contractual safeguards to avoiding certain transactions altogether—which resulted in diluting their Islamic character. The Islamic moral hazard has nonetheless seldom if ever been analyzed in any systematic way. However, as this paper will show, eliminating it or at least reducing it would be an essential step toward good governance. The paper consists of three parts: the first discusses the moral hazard issue, the second explains how it has been addressed by Islamic institutions, and the third attempts to identify the roots of the Islamic moral hazard.

MORAL HAZARD

Moral hazard refers to a range of perverse incentives and unintended consequences. It exists whenever a contract changes the risk-taking

---

[6] Janahi 1995: 28.
[7] Janahi 1995: 42.

behavior of one party to the detriment of the other, or whenever a party can gain from acting contrary to the principles implied by the agreement. In the financial world, perverse incentives and unintended consequences include excessive risk taking, unwise investments, reneging on commitments undertaken, and outright fraud.[8]

For example, an insurance policyholder may have a financial incentive to wreck his car or burn down his house. This is why insurance companies devise ways (for example, by imposing costs on the policyholders, such as deductibles) to minimize such occurrences. Similarly, in the financial industry, loose credit, lax controls, and implicit or explicit guarantees of bailout can create moral hazard. The collapse of U.S. savings and loans in the 1980s has generally been attributed to the moral hazard created by the combination of sudden deregulation and generous deposit insurance. Indeed, just as savings and loan companies, whose activities were once confined to the financing of single-family homes, were allowed almost overnight to invest in virtually anything, the ceiling on deposit insurance was raised from $40,000 to $100,000. In a freewheeling environment, unscrupulous entrepreneurs gambled on risky construction projects or junk bonds with the assurance that the government would bail them out. From their standpoint such gambling was always rewarded, since they would keep whatever profits they made while the deposit insurance would cover their losses.[9] Profits were thus privatized and losses socialized, at an eventual cost to American taxpayers of over $300 billion.[10] Throughout the 1990s, a succession of bail-outs of countries (Mexico, Russia, etc.) and companies (such as Long Term Capital Management), have perpetuated the moral hazard problem by rewarding reckless lending.

THE EARLY EXPERIENCE OF ISLAMIC BANKS

Though seldom addressed as such, the moral hazard problem was evident from the early years of Islamic finance. Since it was assumed that participants in Islamic finance were righteous, questions of governance and moral hazard were by definition resolved. As noted by Hamid Algabid: "At the beginning, confidence was the rule. The good faith of the participants could not be questioned since it was identified with religious faith. Since spiritual and temporal matters could not be dissociated, a pious man could only act in good faith. Experience has since shown that banking operations

[8] See Allen 2001: 13, and Temple 2001: 73.

[9] Another thing made possible by deregulation was that investment bankers could group deposits into insurable $100,000 bundles and place them in savings and loans offering high returns.

[10] Vickers 1997: 98.

could not be established on that assumption, and particularly that guarantees could not be limited to the affirmation of one's Islamic faith."[11]

After a few years, Islamic institutions discovered that perverse incentives were at play, and dealt with those incentives in a variety of ways. This section considers the cases of late fees, *murabaha*, profit-and-loss sharing, and investment accounts.

Late Fees

For most religious scholars, late fees are analogous to *riba*, and thus forbidden. In the early years of Islamic finance, late fees were seldom charged. This had an impact on the behavior of debtors who "know that they can pay Islamic banks last since doing so involves no cost."[12] Over time, Islamic institutions realized that such behavior had a real impact on their management, and often a real cost. Although there are differences across institutions, most consider that late fees are necessary as a "disciplining mechanism," forcing borrowers to pay on time. At the same time, because of theological considerations, late fees are typically treated differently: after deducting actual costs, income derived from late fees goes to charity.

Murabaha

Mark-up transactions are by far the most common Islamic financial products.[13] The best-known is the *murabaha*, a cost-plus contract in which a client wishing to purchase equipment or goods requests the financial provider to purchase the items on his behalf and sell them to him at cost plus a declared profit. It is thus a financing-cum-sale transaction: the bank purchases the required goods directly and sells them on the basis of a fixed mark-up profit, agreeing to defer the receipt of the value of the goods.

Two of the main theological sticking points concern the actual "ownership" of the goods by the financial institutions, and the implications of the "promise" to purchase. In theory, the deal involves two sales transactions (one involving buying the goods from the manufacturer, the other involving selling them to the "borrower"). There is thus a period during which the financial institution owns the goods. During that time the bank bears the risk that the goods will be damaged or destroyed, or that the client may go bankrupt, or otherwise reject the goods as unsatisfactory.

[11] Algabid 1990: 182.
[12] Vogel and Hayes 1998: 139.
[13] al-Harran 1995: xi and 135.

Shari'a scholars in the early days of Islamic finance were keen, in the name of the risk-sharing logic of Islamic finance, to place a significant burden on the financial institutions. There were also intense debates among *shari'a* scholars as to what the promise *(wa'd)* entailed, or whether a promise was binding or not.[14]

A few institutions introduced *murabaha* contracts that were in effect revocable, insofar as they resulted in the actual, though of course temporary, ownership of the goods by the bank and did not consider the promise to purchase binding. In effect, such contracts allowed the buyer under many circumstances to renege on the deal. Not surprisingly, quite a few clients abused the privilege—leaving the financial institution with an unanticipated headache. Put differently, there was a clash between the risk-sharing logic of Islamic finance and the prudential rules of bank management. It did not take long for financial institutions to discover that it was neither their role nor part of their expertise to act as potential merchants for whatever products their clients had ordered.

Thus the practice of *murabaha* changed over time. Today, in most cases, the period of ownership by the financial institutions will be more symbolic than real. The duration could theoretically be of just one second. Hence the notion of "synthetic *murabaha*." Frank Vogel wrote about the commonly-used trade financing deals: "many doubt the banks truly assume possession, even constructively, of inventory, a key condition of a religiously acceptable *murabaha*. Without possession, these arrangements are condemned as nothing more than short-term conventional loans with a predetermined interest rate incorporated in the price at which the borrower repurchases the inventory."[15] In sum the moral hazard problem was resolved, albeit at the expense of the principle of correspondence of risk and reward. Indeed, the risk incurred by the bank is minimal, whereas the profit margin is determined in advance and usually pegged on interest-based benchmarks such as Libor. As a result of criticisms by Islamic scholars, many financial institutions have vowed to start phasing out certain types of *murabaha* transactions—though in practice this remains to be seen.[16]

Islamic Profit-and-Loss Sharing

The basic principle of profit-and-loss sharing is that instead of lending money at a fixed rate of return, the banker forms a partnership with the "borrower," sharing in a venture's profits and losses. The partnership can be of one or two types: *mudaraba* (finance trusteeship) and *musharaka*

[14] Vogel and Hayes 1998: 125-128.
[15] Vogel and Hayes 1998: 9.
[16] Vogel and Hayes 1998: 143.

(longer-term equity-like arrangements). In both cases, the financial institution receives a contractual share of the profits generated by business ventures.

In the early days of Islamic finance, a lot of enthusiasm was generated by the prospect of implementing the ideal of profit-and-loss-sharing finance. It was at once the most "authentic" form of Islamic finance since it replicated transactions that were common in the early days of Islam,[17] the one that was most consistent with the value system and the moral economy of Islam, and the most "modern" one. Indeed, venture capital and merchant banking—both among the fastest growing segments of contemporary finance—were the conventional equivalents of profit-and-loss sharing arrangements.

One of the criticisms of collateral-based lending at a fixed, predetermined interest was that it is inherently conservative. It favored well-established businesses and was only marginally concerned with the success of the ventures it financed. In contrast, under profit-and-loss sharing, Islamic institutions as well as their depositors linked their own fate to the success of the projects they were financing. The system allowed a capital-poor but promising entrepreneur to obtain financing. The bank, being an investor in the venture, had a stake in its long-term success. The entrepreneur, rather than being concerned with debt-servicing, could concentrate on matters of business growth, which in turn would provide economic and social benefits to the community.

Under *mudaraba*, one party, the *rabb al-mal* (beneficial owner or the sleeping partner), entrusts money to the other party called the *mudarib* (managing trustee) who is to utilize it in an agreed manner. After the operation is concluded, the *rabb al-mal* receives the principal and the pre-agreed share of the profit. The *mudarib* keeps for himself the remaining profits. The *rabb al-mal* also shares in the losses, and may be in a position of losing his entire investment. There are a few other basic principles: The division of profits between the two parties must necessarily be on a proportional basis and cannot be a lump-sum or guaranteed return; the *rabb al-mal* is not liable for losses beyond the capital he has contributed; the *mudarib* does not share in the losses except for the loss of his time and efforts. Such a financing system was common in medieval Arabia where wealthy merchants financed the caravan trade. They would share in the profits of a successful operation, but could also lose all or part of their investment if, for example, the merchandise was stolen, lost, or sold for less than its cost. *Mudaraba* contracts were codified by medieval jurists and could take on extreme complexity.

Musharaka is similar in its principle to *mudaraba*, except for the fact that the financier takes an equity stake in the venture. It is in effect a joint-venture agreement whereby the bank enters into a partnership with a client

---

[17] Udovitch 1970: 170-248.

in which both share the equity capital, and sometimes the management, of a project or deal. Participation in a *musharaka* can either be in a new project, or in an existing one. Profits are divided on a pre-determined basis, and any losses shared in proportion to the capital contribution.

Islamic profit-and-loss sharing has been a major disappointment. Today it only accounts for barely 5 percent of Islamic banking assets. The moral hazard problem between the entrepreneurs and their lenders is one of the many reasons for the failure. Under profit-and-loss sharing, although the financier shares in the risk, he does not share in the management, and this creates the potential for conflicts of interest, as well as managerial and regulatory complications that have yet to be fully mastered. For instance, the *mudarib* can ask for more money than he needs, or he can engage in high-risk endeavors, knowing that he will not be committing his own money. The bank can also take advantage of a *mudarib* who is pressed for cash, or of holders of investment accounts who know little about the deal. More generally, there is the possibility of structuring the transaction in such a way as to transfer the risk onto the other participants.[18]

Moral hazard issues are at the core of the failure of profit-and-loss sharing. In explaining why his bank was no longer involved in profit-and-loss sharing, Hassan Kamel, chief executive of the (now-defunct) London branch of Al-Baraka, (PLS) operations addressed the issue: "The depositors wanted an Islamic deal without risk. They liked, at least, to guarantee their capital. The problem with PLS is that (the Islamic economists) assume the scenario of the entrepreneur being a good Muslim."[19] After suffering losses, many banks left profit-and-loss sharing activities altogether. Others have tried, not always successfully, to devise appropriate safeguards. But decisions to exert due diligence thorough checks on *mudarib*s and striving for transparency and the avoidance of negligence, mismanagement, or fraud were not easy to put in practice.[20]

Investment Accounts

The distinctive feature of Islamic institutions on the liability side of their balance sheet is their reliance on investment accounts, which allow the customers to share in the profits of the bank. Because of the ban on interest *(riba)*, an Islamic bank is not supposed to commit to any fixed return in advance. Unlike a conventional bank which is basically a borrower and lender of funds, an Islamic bank theoretically operates on the basis of "double *mudaraba*"—one with its "depositors," the other with "borrowers"

---

[18] See for example Ziaul Haque, *Riba: The moral economy of usury, interest, and profit* (Lahore: Vanguard 1985), 190-214.
[19] al-Omar and Abdel-Haq 1996: 43.
[20] Parigi 1989: 137.

in need of financing. Investment accounts come in a variety of forms: "depositors" can share in the profits of certain instruments only (for example "special investment accounts" dealing with, say, a specific real estate fund, or a broader class of investments) or of the bank as a whole.

Many of the observations made in the previous section in connection with the latter form of *mudaraba* also hold true in connection with the former, where the bank is the *mudarib* and the depositor acts through his investment account as the *rabb al-mal.* Such partnership entails fundamentally different relations with the financial institution than under conventional banking. The distribution is done according to a certain ratio. For example 80 percent of the net profits may be distributed to the depositors, and 20 percent to the shareholders. Empirical surveys have shown that banks often arbitrarily change distribution ratios. When profits decline, depositors often still expect a competitive rate of return, or else they may take their savings to another Islamic institution, or to a conventional bank. Thus in Egypt, from the mid to the late 1980s, the International Investment Bank for Investment and Development (IIBID) distributed all its profits to investment account depositors, while the shareholders received nothing. In 1988, the bank even had to distribute to its depositors an amount exceeding its total net profit. The difference appeared in the bank's account as "loss carried forward."[21] Clearly such practices fly in the face of sound banking management practices, and cannot be sustained for long, yet the competitive logic of financial markets makes such behavior likely in the absence of strict regulatory controls.

ISLAMIC FINANCE AND THE MORAL HAZARD ISSUE

Many of the well-publicized cases of fraud or abuse could be traced to the righteousness assumption. Following the collapse of the Bank of Credit and Commerce International (BCCI) in 1991, it appeared that at least a couple of Islamic banks had failed to exercise proper scrutiny and due diligence. Although not itself an Islamic bank, BCCI had set up in 1984 an Islamic Banking Unit in London, which at its peak had $1.4 billion in deposits, and had generally made heavy use of Islamic rhetoric and symbolism. The Price Waterhouse report commissioned in the wake of the bank's closure revealed that of BCCI's $589 million in "unrecorded deposits" (which allowed the bank to manipulate its accounts) the major part—$245 million—belonged to the Faisal Islamic Bank of Egypt (FIBE). This amount was supposed to be used for commodity investments, though there was no evidence that such investments were ever made.[22] Similarly, the Dubai Islamic Bank (DIB) had

[21] Kazarian 1993: 179.
[22] Potts et al. 1992: 77-78.

placed $86 million with the bank. Although neither FIBE nor DIB was suspected of wrongdoing, the scandal highlighted the problems of control and due diligence. In 1998 two major swindles, one involving bank employees, the other involving a client, occurred at Dubai Islamic Bank, causing runs on deposits and necessitating the Dubai Central Bank and the United Arab Emirates' authorities to ride to the rescue.[23]

While it is undeniable that religious fervor was for many people a reason to work for an Islamic bank, or conduct business with it, it was soon discovered that religion could be a double-edged sword. The religious character of certain institutions could turn certain institutions into a magnet for dubious characters. And indeed, a number of bank executives have acknowledged that they had trusted people who did not deserve their trust.[24] Since time immemorial, con artists have used the cover of religion as a means of rapid enrichment. Countless financial scandals have involved religious figures.[25] Even when the overwhelming majority of people are honest, all it takes is a few bad apples—a few dishonest customers or employees—for banks to incur serious difficulties. Indeed, one big swindle can bring a financial institution down.

A broader issue is that of the ambiguity of norms. Unlike secular systems, the legal system of Islam incorporates both an economic and a religious logic. In the words of Noel Coulson: "Commercial law . . . in the West is orientated towards the intrinsic needs of sound economics, such as stability of obligation and certitude of promised performance. In the religious law of Islam, on the other hand, equitable considerations of the individual conscience in matters of profit and loss override the technicalities of commercial dealings. It is the harmonization of these two very different approaches which poses the real challenge for developing Islamic law today."[26]

This dual logic can account for a variety of dysfunctions. Religion can make certain institutions immune to scrutiny or criticism. In Iran, for example, a whole sector of the economy has been able to operate outside of any regulatory framework, allowing financial abuses to persist and go unsanctioned.[27] Then there is the question of forbearance. Like other religions, Islam recommends forbearance and even loan forgiveness to borrowers in difficulty.[28] Unlike secular bankers, who can use a whole array of tools to protect their interests as lenders (and at times take advantage of borrowers who have fallen on hard times), Islamic institutions are expected

---

[23] Warde 2000: 84.
[24] Algabid 1990: 182.
[25] DiFonzo 1983.
[26] Saleh 1986: preface.
[27] Zubeida 1997: 113.
[28] "If the debtor is in difficulty, grant him time till it is easy for him to repay. But if you remit it by way of charity, that is best for you if you only knew." (Qur'an: 2:280)

to take into account the borrower's circumstances. Those who are unable to pay for reasons beyond their control are treated differently from those who are able but unwilling to fulfill their financial obligations.

The dilemma of Islamic financial institutions is that although they are profit-making enterprises, as opposed to charities, they are bound by religious precepts. Moral hazard issues appear whenever customers take advantage of dilatory legal and religious devices to renege on their obligations. Invoking religious principles, forum-shopping, or otherwise taking advantage of dual or multi-layered systems that are common in the Islamic world has been a problem for Islamic banks. In Pakistan, where the banking system was (in theory though not really in practice) Islamicized in 1979, and where a complex legal system includes special banking tribunals and *shari'a* courts, this happened quite frequently.[29] Many businessmen who had borrowed large amounts of money over long periods of time seized the opportunity of Islamicization to claim that the accumulated interest on their debt was now voided, leaving them liable only for the principal owed—usually only a small part of the total amount due.[30]

Saudi Arabian banks commonly encounter comparable problems. Peter Wilson observed that "Saudi Arabia's bad loan problem is as old as the country's banking system, given the doctrinal dilemma of having an interest-based financial system in a country that officially prohibits interest."[31] More specifically: "The Kingdom's law courts reflect the uneasy balance in the country. There are Islamic or *shari'a* courts that fall under the jurisdiction of the cleric-dominated Ministry of Justice and special commercial committees under the sway of the more progressive finance and commerce ministries. Enforcement, however, remains the domain of the Interior Ministry and each province's governor. The result is a legal quagmire, as the country's economic development has overwhelmed the abilities of the existing courts."[32]

CONCLUSION

The preoccupation with the corporate governance of Islamic institutions has largely left out moral hazard issues that, as argued in this paper, should be an important preoccupation of both students and practitioners of Islamic finance. Those issues, which stem from the hybrid nature of the Islamic finance industry—its being subjected to both secular and religious norms—have been addressed piecemeal.

---

[29] Warde 2000: 112-117.
[30] al-Omar and Abdel-Haq 1996: 101.
[31] Wilson 1991: 109.
[32] Wilson 1991: 8.

This paper has looked at the early experience of Islamic finance in connection with late fees, *murabaha*, profit-and-loss sharing, and investment accounts. In dealing with these issues, many Islamic institutions have either created theologically dubious solutions (as was the case with the "synthetic *murabaha*") or abandoned altogether distinctive instruments such as *mudaraba*. In both cases, it confirmed the view of critics of Islamic finance who say that it replicates, albeit under different names, the main conventional instruments.

This paper suggests that by systematically and thoroughly addressing the question of moral hazard, more creative solutions can be found. It is useful to recall that Islamic financial institutions only came into existence in the mid-1970s, and are still experiencing growing pains. At a time of rapid growth, and as a number of organizations (among them the Accounting and Auditing Organization for Islamic Financial Institutions [AAOIFI] and the Islamic Financial Services Board [IFSB]) are attempting to create transnational industry norms, thinking about adequate solutions to the moral hazard problem holds the promise of revitalizing original Islamic instruments.

Part II

Forging New Financial Instruments

Recent Trends and Innovations in Islamic Debt Securities: Prospects for Islamic Profit and Loss Sharing Securities

Mohamed Rafe Md. Haneef[1]

INTRODUCTION

The twentieth century witnessed the revival of Islamic finance in various parts of the Muslim world as an alternative mode of financing that is in compliance with *shari'a*. From its mundane beginnings, when Islamic financiers were mainly providing Islamic trade financing solutions, the Islamic finance industry today offers a wide range of products and services including personal finance, corporate finance, project finance, equity funds, property funds, and private equity. All these products and services are structured in accordance with *shari'a* principles as interpreted in their respective jurisdictions. The existing product range, which is often priced competitively, provides Muslims with a viable option to manage their financial matters Islamically.

With the dawn of the twenty-first century, we are witnessing the Islamic finance industry constantly venturing into new and exciting areas of finance. One of the important recent endeavors is the development of Islamic debt securities commonly known as *sukuk*. Most Islamic financiers often end up with high levels of liquidity due to various reasons. The Islamic finance industry also lacks *shari'a*-compatible derivative products that could mitigate any asset-liability mismatch risks. The high levels of liquidity often led to inefficiency in the Islamic finance market and the industry leaders actively sought solutions. The *sukuk*, which is a tradable and potentially liquid investment, was seen as a possible avenue for the Islamic financiers to invest their surplus liquidity.

---

[1] Head of Islamic Finance, ABN AMRO (Dubai, UAE).

HISTORY OF ISLAMIC DEBT SECURITIES

Interestingly, *sukuk* or *sakk* is not a new invention of the Islamic finance industry. The concept of *sukuk* has been with the Islamic world since the early days of Islamic civilization. Malik has recorded the first historical account of *sukuk* in his famous treatise *al-Muwatta.* It is stated that in the first century Hijri (corresponding to the seventh century AD) the Umayyad government would pay soldiers and public servants both in cash and in kind. The payment in kind was in the form of *sukuk al-badai,* which has been translated as "commodity coupons"[2] or "grain permits."[3] The holders of the *sukuk* were entitled to present the *sukuk* on its maturity date at the treasury and receive a fixed amount of commodity, usually grains. Some of the holders used to sell their *sukuk* to others for cash before the maturity date. Although the validity of such trade was been questioned by scholars of that period, it shows that the concept of *sukuk al-badai* as a tradable instrument has been known to the Islamic world for a very long time.

The word *sakk*, though it may sound unfamiliar, is astonishingly well known to all of us. The origin of the word *check*, ubiquitous in the modern financial world, is from the Arabic word *sakk.* It is well known that many of the commercial practices and customs of the Muslim world were transmitted to medieval Europe through Islamic Spain, and *sakk* is one of them.[4] However, like many other inventions of Islamic civilization, the concept of *sukuk* was not exploited to its full potential by the Muslims. The financial community in the West adopted and refined the concept of *sukuk* and expanded its scope of use to a wide range of commercial and financial activities. Today, we see the Islamic financial world adopting the practices of Western finance and adjusting them to meet the requirement of *shari'a.*

In 2001, almost fourteen centuries later, the *sukuk* re-emerged in Bahrain as an Islamic alternative to conventional debt securities.[5] The State of Bahrain[6] offered its inaugural *sukuk al-ijara* issue in the domestic market. The issue amount was USD250 million and had a tenor of five years. The *sukuk al-ijara* concept was derived from the prevailing practices of "lease ending with purchase" *(ijara muntahia bi-tamlik)* which is commonly known in conventional finance as "finance lease."[7] The *sukuk* carried six-monthly lease rentals that were fixed at the lease inception and

---

[2] *See* Kamali 2000 for more details.
[3] *See* Ibn Anas 2000: 296.
[4] Schact 1982.
[5] In 2000, the State of Bahrain led the way by issuing the innovative *sukuk al-salam* but these securities were non-tradable.
[6] As it was then known; now the Kingdom of Bahrain.
[7] For a detailed exposition of *ijara muntahia bi-tamlik, see* Standard no. 9, *Shari'a* Standards of the Accounting and Auditing Organization for Islamic Financial Institutions (1424-5 Hijri / 2003-4 AD).

paid in arrears during the lease term. The *sukuk* offering was highly successful. The Bahrain *sukuk* issue was a major milestone in Islamic finance as it marked the birth of an Islamic capital market where Islamic equity and debt-based instruments are issued and traded.

In 2002, the Federation of Malaysia created another landmark by issuing the first Islamic securities that complied with the U.S. Regulation S and Rule 144A formats that are used for conventional global bonds.[8] The Malaysian *sukuk al-ijara* was the first *sukuk* to be listed in the Luxembourg Stock Exchange and rated by Standard & Poor's and Moody's. The USD600 million *sukuk* was offered globally to Islamic and conventional investors including "Qualified Institutional Buyers" in the United States. The issue was hugely successful and was twice oversubscribed. The Malaysian *sukuk* was a significant development because it was able to successfully fuse the concept of *sukuk al-ijara* with conventional bond practices such as listing, ratings, dematerialized scripts, and centralized clearance.

Subsequently, there have been a number of successful *sukuk* issues in Regulation S format, including the Islamic Development Bank's offering of USD400 million *sukuk* in 2003, the State of Qatar's debut USD700 million *sukuk al-ijara* issue in 2003, and the Kingdom of Bahrain's USD250 million *sukuk al-ijara* issue in 2004. These successful issues have created a lot of excitement in the Islamic finance markets and more issuers are looking at the *sukuk* option as a viable and attractive alternative source of funds. This paper will examine some of the key *sukuk* products currently available in the Islamic finance markets and analyze the structure of each product. It will highlight the salient features of each product and examine the various *shari'a* innovations and the legal aspects of the structures. The paper will also look at the prospects for Islamic profit sharing products[9] and the current impediments to the growth of such products.

SUKUK AL-IJARA

A *sukuk al-ijara* issue is typically structured as follows:

---

[8] Prior to that, in December 2001, Kumpulan Guthrie Berhad, a Malaysian public listed company involved in the plantation and construction sectors, has offered a *sukuk al-ijara* issue in the U.S. Regulation S format. The company offered a USD150 million *sukuk* issue with a floating rate return and the tenor was divided into three years (USD50m) and five years (USD100m). The *sukuk* was listed on the Labuan International Financial Exchange.

[9] The term "Islamic profit sharing product" refers to a product or security that is structured on the principle of profit and loss sharing based on *mudaraba*, *musharaka,* or similar concepts.

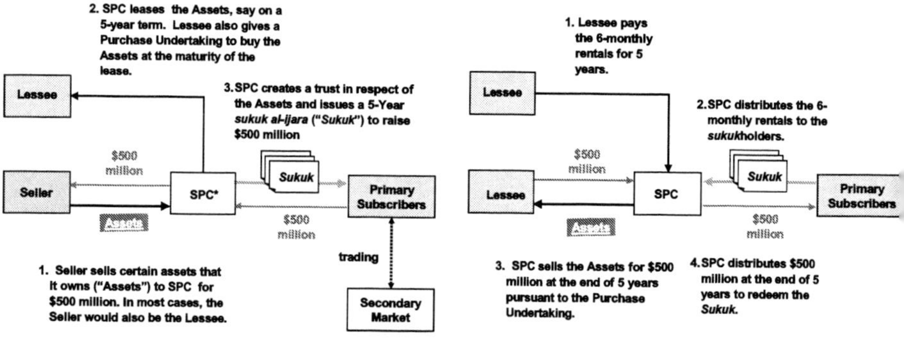

** A special purpose company established solely for the purpose of facilitating the issuance of the Islamic securities.*

Figure 1. A Typical *Sukuk al-Ijara* Structure

The above structure was used, with minor modifications, in the USD250 million Kingdom of Bahrain *sukuk al-ijara* issue, the USD600 million Federation of Malaysia *sukuk al-ijara* issue, and the USD700 million State of Qatar *sukuk al-ijara* issue. The underlying assets were bought from the seller and immediately leased to the lessee based on the principle of *ijara muntahia bi-tamlik* (lease ending with purchase). The SPC will act as the trustee for the *sukuk* holders and will distribute to the *sukuk* holders the rental proceeds of the leased assets in accordance with the terms of the trust. At the end of the lease period the SPC will sell the assets to the original seller for a sum equal to the original sale price, which the SPC will distribute to the *sukuk* holders to redeem the *sukuk*. Some of the salient features of the *sukuk al-ijara* are discussed below.

Sukuk Characteristics

One of the fundamental requirements of *shari'a* for a security to be tradable is that the security must reflect or evidence the security holder's share in an underlying asset or enterprise.[10] For example, contemporary *shari'a* scholars have allowed investment in equity or share in a company on the basis that the security reflects the holder's ownership of the underlying assets of the company. Through the ownership of the company the shareholders are deemed to indirectly own the assets held by the

---

[10] The asset or enterprise itself has to be *shari'a*-compatible. Hence, an enterprise involved in alcohol or gambling is not compatible with *shari'a*.

company.[11] By making a link between the ownership of the company with the ownership in the company's assets, the *shari'a* scholars have been able to allow "the buying and selling of these securities on the model not of partnership in the enterprise,[12] but of undivided co-ownership of the company's assets."[13] If the company as a going concern makes a profit by trading in goods, assets, or services the shareholders are entitled to receive from the company a share in the profit through dividends.

A conventional bond, on the other hand, typically confers on the bondholder a contractual right to receive from the issuer of the bond certain interest payments during the life of the bond and the principal amount at the maturity of the bond. The bondholders themselves are deemed as creditors to the issuer of the bond and are ranked as senior unsecured and unsubordinated creditors of the issuer in priority to the shareholders.[14] The juridical nature of a conventional bond is clearly contrary to *shari'a.*

The major challenge was to structure a *shari'a*-compatible instrument that embodies the ownership characteristic of an equity instrument as well as the priority status and the fixed income characteristics of a bond instrument. In addition to those, the *shari'a*-compatible instrument also has to be transferable, rated by recognized rating agencies, listed on major securities exchanges, cleared through major clearinghouses, and documented, in terms of legal documents and disclosures, on par with the prevailing standards in the conventional bond market.

After much concentrated effort, a *shari'a*-compatible solution was finally found, interestingly, with the aid of the common law of trust. At common law, when a person holds an asset on trust for another, the latter can be construed as the beneficial owner of the asset held by the former. The relationship between the trustee and the beneficiary is evidenced by a trust deed executed (often unilaterally) by the settlor. The trust deed can

---

[11] At one time the common law also used to treat the shareholders as having some sort of equitable interest in the assets of a company. The company itself was deemed as holding the assets as trustee for the shareholders. However, the prevailing common law position is that a share is a chose in action which confers on the shareholders the contractual right to vote, to receive dividends, return of capital upon winding up, and other rights except that it does not confer a right to possess any physical assets. *Gower's Principles of Modern Company Law* (Paul L. Davies ed., 6th ed. 1997), 299-302.

[12] It is important to note that, from a *shari'a* perspective, if the shares in a company are construed as co-ownership in an enterprise only, the shareholders will then be construed as partners in an enterprise like *mudaraba* and the strict rules of *mudaraba* will come into play. But when the link is made with the ownership in the assets owned by the company, the shareholders will be treated as co-owners of an asset or *shirkat al-milk* and this will allow a co-owner to freely sell his share without the consent of the other co-owners. *See* Vogel and Hayes 1998: 175-176.

[13] *See* ibid., 175.

[14] *See* generally, Ravi C. Tennekoon, *The Law & Regulation of International Finance* (1991), 161-176.

also be documented to allow the relationship between the trustee and the beneficiaries to be created through the issuance of a trust instrument by the trustee to the beneficiary or class of beneficiaries. For instance, a settlor can create a trust over, say, a house pursuant to a trust deed and appoint a trustee to issue trust instruments to a class of beneficiaries. The class of beneficiaries will be limited to the investors who purchase the trust instruments offered by the trustee for a certain consideration. The investors who purchase the trust instruments will automatically become the beneficiary of the trust and be construed as pro-rata owners of the house held on trust by the trustee. The trust deed can also be structured to allow the holders of the trust instrument to transfer the trust instruments to others on a willing-buyer and willing-seller basis. If the trustee leases the house to a tenant for a fixed or variable rental term, the holders of the trust instrument will be entitled to a pro-rata share of the rental income derived from the house held on trust.[15]

These characteristics of the trust instrument squarely meet the requirements of *shari'a*. The trust instruments were aptly named in Arabic as *sukuk* or *sukuk al-ijara* because the trust assets were leased out to produce a lease income. The holders of the *sukuk* will be construed under *shari'a* as co-owners of an asset, although held on trust, similar to a *shirkat al-milk*. As a co-owner of an asset, each co-owner is entitled to sell his share in the asset without the consent of the other co-owners at whatever price he can command in the market. When the trustee receives the variable rentals from the lessee, the *sukuk* holders will receive a proportionate share in the rental proceeds. At the maturity of the lease, which corresponds to the redemption date of the *sukuk*, the trustee will sell the trust asset to the lessee for a price equal to the original acquisition cost of the trust asset.[16] With the proceeds of the sale, the trustee will redeem the *sukuk* and the *sukuk* holders will receive their principal investment. The payment profile of the *sukuk* is thus comparable to a conventional bond or a floating rate note.

The lessee's obligation to pay the lease rentals and the purchase price will be ranked as a senior unsubordinated debt obligation of the lessee toward the trustee, as lessor. This ranking in priority is also comparable to the ranking of a conventional bond instrument.

The concept of trust instrument is also familiar to the conventional investors. In the United States, for example, Equipment Trust Certificates or ETCs have been widely used since the time of the railway boom. A railway company will order the rolling stock from the manufacturer and request the manufacturer to sell the rolling stock to a trustee company set up by the

---

[15] See Pettit 1997: 14-17.

[16] This aspect of the transaction is structured as an *ijara muntahia bi-tamlik* in line with the Standard no. 9, *Shari'a* Standards of the Accounting and Auditing Organization for Islamic Financial Institutions (1424-5 Hijri / 2003-4 AD).

railway company.[17] The railway company will then agree to lease the rolling stock from the trustee for an agreed period. The trustee will then issue trust certificates to the investors to raise the funds required to pay the manufacturer. From the proceeds of the lease collected from the railway company, the trustee will pay the periodic interest and the principal amount to the trust certificate holders. Since the trustee will own the rolling stock, it will be able to repossess the rolling stock if the railway company defaults on the lease and re-lease it to other railway companies. Because the rolling stock was quite standardized and there was a deep secondary market for it, the trustee was able to obtain the lowest rates in the bond market.[18]

The commonality between the *sukuk* and the trust instrument, such as the ETC, is a key factor because it made the *sukuk* familiar and easily acceptable to the conventional investors, the leading rating agencies, the major securities exchanges, and the leading clearinghouses. The *sukuk* issues by the Federation of Malaysia, the Islamic Development Bank, and the State of Qatar were all rated by international rating agencies like Moody's, Standard & Poors, or Fitch. The *sukuk* issues were also successfully listed on leading exchanges such as the Luxembourg Stock Exchange, the Labuan International Financial Exchange, and the Bahrain Stock Exchange. The *sukuk* were also cleared through Euroclear and Clearstream. These features made the *sukuk* a truly tradable security that met the requirements of *shari'a* as well as the expectations of the conventional bond investors in line with the bond market norms.

Legal and Beneficial Ownership

In the Malaysian *sukuk* issue, one of the *shari'a* concerns was that the trustee was only acquiring the beneficial ownership of the assets held on trust. Usually, when a seller sells a landed property to the buyer, the buyer will acquire the legal ownership of the property when the seller transfers the title to the property to the buyer after receiving full payment from the buyer. In the Malaysian *sukuk* issue, the seller[19] sold the landed assets to the trustee but did not transfer the title to the landed assets to the trustee in order to avoid payment of certain charges and taxes. Instead, the seller declared that it was holding the landed assets on trust for the buyer. The concern from a *shari'a* perspective was whether such a transfer is valid under *shari'a*.

The position under Malaysian law, which is quite similar to the position at common law, is that when the buyer pays the full consideration

[17] The trustee company will be an orphan entity with no corporate relationship with the railway company.
[18] Fabozzi and Modigliani 2002: 515-516.
[19] The Federal Land Commission, a statutory body that holds all federal lands in Malaysia.

for a landed asset, the seller becomes a bare trustee and the buyer[20] becomes the beneficial owner of the landed assets.[21] As a bare trustee the seller cannot dispose the land to another without the consent of the beneficial owner. From a legal perspective, the law considers the beneficial owner as the true owner with the power to possess and dispose the landed assets.[22] To protect the rights of the beneficial owner against any third party who may claim any interest on the landed assets held on trust, the bare trustee was required to procure a trust endorsement on the land title held at the land registry.[23] The trust endorsement will give a clear notice to third parties of the beneficial owner's right in the landed assets and will avoid the bare trustee from inadvertently transferring the landed assets to any third party.

The distinction between legal and beneficial ownership was initially not familiar to most *shari'a* scholars particularly those who come from civil law jurisdictions.[24] There is no concept of beneficial ownership in civil law. Through fresh interpretations, the contemporary *shari'a* scholars were able to extend the scope of ownership in *shari'a* to include the concept of beneficial ownership when, as illustrated in Malaysia, the true owner in the eyes of law is the beneficial owner and the seller remains only as a bare trustee.

Unilateral Undertaking to Buy the Assets

The issue of whether a unilateral purchase undertaking given by the lessee to the trustee is a binding promise has been debated among the contemporary *shari'a* scholars. Some scholars are of the view that a unilateral purchase undertaking or promise does not create a legal obligation at all but only a moral obligation on the part of the promisor. The proponents of this view rely on the opinions of Abu Hanifa, Shafi'i, Ahmad, and some Maliki jurists. The opponents of this view, however, argue that unlike a bilateral contract of deferred sale,[25] all unilateral undertakings or

---

[20] The buyer, however, has to be a bona fide purchaser for value without notice of any prior third party rights attached to the landed asset.

[21] This principle was firmly laid down in the Malaysian case of *Borneo Housing Mortgage Finance Bhd v. Bank Bumiputra Malaysia Bhd*, [1991] 2 MLJ 261.

[22] Such a disposal, however, has to be made through the bare trustee who will have to comply with the instructions of the beneficial owner.

[23] This endorsement is done under section 344 of the Malaysian National Land Code, 1965. For more details *see* Mary George, *Malaysian Trust Law* (1999), 11.

[24] Most of the countries in the Gulf Cooperation Council are civil law jurisdictions.

[25] The concept of unilateral undertaking or promise has a unique existence in Islamic law because Islamic law prohibits an agreement to sell in future (i.e. a deferred sale) and only allows a sale contract where the property in the goods is transferred to the buyer at the time of contract. Most Muslim jurists argue that for a valid sale under *shari'a*, at least one of the counter values, either the purchase price or the goods, has

promises to do something in the future are valid arrangements that are binding on the promisors. The opponents rely on the authority of a prominent companion of the Prophet and the opinions of other renowned scholars including al-Bukhari. Some other scholars, particularly from the Maliki school, have taken the middle view that a unilateral undertaking is only binding on the promisor if "the promisor has caused the promisee to incur some expenses or undertake some labor or liability on the basis of [the] promise."[26] It has been argued elsewhere[27] that the proponents of the view that a unilateral undertaking is not binding at all have not been able to successfully attribute their views to Abu Hanifa and Malik. As mentioned below, both the Hanafi and Maliki jurists have recognized the validity of the promise to effect a sale in future made by the buyer in a *bay'al-wafa'* contract. Furthermore, there is also evidence in the primary sources of *shari'a*, the Qur'an and the *Sunna*, to imply that a promise is binding on the promisor. It is mentioned in the Qur'an: "O ye who believe! Why say ye that which ye do not? Grievously odious is it in the sight of God that ye say that which ye do not."[28]

There are also compelling social and economic arguments to support the view that a unilateral purchase undertaking or promise should be binding. Imagine someone promising to another that if the latter goes and buys certain goods from the market, the promisor will buy the goods from him at a specific price. If the promisor is allowed to repudiate his promise and decline the goods, the promisee will be left exposed to the risk of liquidating the goods without any remedy against the promisor. The promisee may suffer economic losses due to the breach of promise. For example, the promisee may end up selling the goods to another at a discounted price. This will seriously hinder the development of various economic activities such as the *murabaha* contracts where the financier will be relying on the promise of the client when it purchases the goods ordered by the client.

---

to be delivered at the time of contract. Deferring both counter values at the time of contract vitiates the contract. *Murabaha* contracts, for instance, have been allowed because only one of the counter values, i.e. the purchase price, is deferred. Another example is the *salam* contract, where only the commodities are deferred while the purchase price is paid at the time of contract. The only exception seems to be the *istisna'* contract, where both counter values are allowed to be deferred based on the prevailing custom *(urf)*. For a detailed discussion on the *shari'a* treatment of deferred sale, *see* Kamali 2000: 131. For a comparative analysis of the common law position, where both a deferred sale and a sale contract are allowed, *see* Goode 1995.

[26] Usmani 2002: 122.

[27] Ibid., 123.

[28] Qur'an: 61:2-3 (Abdullah Yusuf Ali translation).

Based on these grounds and the views taken by many prominent scholars, the Islamic *Fiqh* Academy resolved[29] that a promise made in a commercial transaction, like a *murabaha* contract, is binding on the promisor subject to the following conditions:

1. the promise should be unilateral;
2. the promise must have induced the promisee to incur some liability;
3. if the promise is to purchase something in the future, the parties must enter into the actual sale contract at the appointed time; and
4. if the promisor breaches his promise, the promisee can seek legal remedy in a court of law for specific performance or damages.[30]

Contemporary scholars have extended the above ruling to the *sukuk al-ijara* issue and ruled as valid the unilateral purchase undertaking given by the lessee to buy the assets at the maturity of the lease.[31] This was a significant development that made the *sukuk* issue economically feasible. Otherwise, it would lead to an inequitable result where the lessor would be exposed to the economic losses that may result from the breach of promise while the promisor would be absolved of any liability.[32]

---

[29] Islamic *Fiqh* Academy 1988.

[30] Actual damages are confined to "actual monetary loss suffered by [the promisee], but will not include the opportunity cost." Usmani 2002: 126.

[31] It has been argued elsewhere that the scope of the Islamic *Fiqh* Academy resolution should not be extended beyond the ambit of *murabaha* transactions and an example was given of a *salam* transaction involving unilateral promise that could lead to "anomalous and radical" results from a *shari'a* perspective. Vogel and Hayes 1998: 126-128. While there is some merit in limiting the scope of the resolution in cases where it may lead to inconsistent results, this should not in itself be taken as a ground to bar the extension of the resolution to cases where if the promisor is allowed to repudiate his promise it would lead to an inequitable situation.

[32] It is interesting to note that this development in the contemporary *fiqh* has some resemblance to the development of the principle of promissory estoppel at common law. The common law had for a long time taken the stand that a promise made in a commercial transaction is only binding if there was consideration for it. In the celebrated English case of *High Trees*, [1947] 1 KB 130, Denning J., changed the course of common law by ruling that when a person makes a promise and knows or reasonably should know that the promisee will rely on his promise, the promisor will be bound by his promise if the promisee has actually relied on that promise and acted upon it. The court ruled that it would otherwise be inequitable to the promisee if the promisor is allowed to dishonor his promise in such circumstances. This is a classic instance where equity has come to remove the rigors of common law, which would have allowed to the promisor his strict right to retract his promise. Since *High Trees*, there has been a plethora of cases reaffirming the principle of promissory estoppel.

Sale of Assets to the Original Seller

Another concern among some *shari'a* scholars was the issue of the trustee selling the assets back to the lessee (being the original seller) at the original cost. Their view was that this arrangement resembles the contract of *bay'al-wafa'* which has been prohibited on the basis of *riba* by the Maliki and Hanbali schools as well as the earlier generation of scholars from the Hanafi and Shafi'i schools. *Bay'al-wafa'* is a contract usually involving a landed asset where the seller will sell the landed asset to the buyer for an agreed price and subsequent to the sale the buyer will promise to sell the landed asset back to the seller whenever the seller pays an amount equal to the original purchase price paid by the buyer. The later generation of scholars from the Hanafi and Shafi'i schools, including the prominent Hanafi scholar Ibn Abidin, however, have allowed this type of contract provided that the promise is made after the sale has been concluded and the promise itself is not made a condition of the sale contract.[33] They took the opposite view that such a transaction actually prevents one from getting involved in *riba* and therefore should be allowed.[34] Some Hanafi scholars have even allowed a *bay' al-wafa'* transaction where the promise has been given prior to the sale itself.[35]

Historically, *bay'al-wafa'* arrangements have been widely practiced in Central Asia and South East Asia for a very long time and they have been recognized as valid by many Islamic scholars.[36] In a *sukuk* issue the sale of the assets to the trustee is made independent of the purchase undertaking given by the lessee to the trustee and the undertaking itself is not made a condition to the sale contract. Based on this arrangement contemporary scholars have allowed the sale of the assets back to the original seller.

Sale of Assets at Market Value

Some scholars took the view that the sale of the assets to the lessee should be at market value determined at the time of actual sale.[37] From a

[33] Nyazee 1995: 74.
[34] *See* Malaysian Securities Commission 2002: 26-28.
[35] Usmani 2002: 87-89 and 123.
[36] In Malaysia, there is ample evidence that such arrangements have been in practice for decades and they have been recognized as valid contracts under *shari'a*.
[37] It is important to observe that, like the issue revolving unilateral undertakings, the issue of selling back the asset to the original seller at the original price goes to the root of *ijara muntahia bi-tamlik* where the lessee will invariably undertake to buy the assets from the lessor at the original cost. Such practice has been in vogue for a long time and has been endorsed by Standard no. 9, *Shari'a* Standards of the Accounting and Auditing Organization for Islamic Financial Institutions (1424-5

classical *fiqh* perspective, the predominant view is that the sale price has to be known to both the seller and the buyer in advance in order to make the contract valid. The Shafi'i and Maliki schools have both maintained that any ambiguity and ignorance of the price will vitiate the contract and that uncertainty or *gharar* is removed only by determining a specific price.[38] The Hanbali scholars Ibn Taymiyya and Ibn Qayyim, however, have taken a more liberal view by stating that the price can be determined by assigning a fixed amount or by reference to a certain convention, for example, "the price which other people pay; or the market price, provided that the parties find [that] agreeable and is clear enough to avoid disputes."[39] These opinions, when extended to the unilateral purchase undertaking given by the lessee, mean that the price of the asset can either be determined as a fixed sum at the inception or at the time of actual sale based on the market practice. Since both these options were validly recognized under *shari'a*, the unilateral purchase undertaking given by the lessee in the Malaysian *sukuk* issue to buy the assets at a specified amount based on the original purchase price paid by the trustee is a valid arrangement under *shari'a*. This was in fact in line with the majority view that required a fixed sum to be determined by the parties at the inception of a bilateral or unilateral arrangement in order to avoid any *gharar*.

Late Payment Treatment

Another contentious issue in contemporary *fiqh* is whether a creditor is entitled under *shari'a* to charge a late payment to a debtor who has either delayed or defaulted on a payment obligation. The general principle of *shari'a* is that any additional amount charged to a debtor for any late payment is *riba* and is clearly prohibited. This form of *riba* is commonly known as *riba al-jahiliyya*.[40] Accordingly, in the early days of Islamic finance, the *murabaha* and *ijara* contracts did not contain any provision allowing the Islamic financiers to charge any late payment amount from the purchasers or the lessees. This practice naturally resulted in some debtors abusing the system by delaying, often willfully, the payments due to the Islamic financiers while making every effort to make their payments on time to their conventional lenders. The conventional lenders will invariably impose on the debtors late-payment charges, which are sometimes

Hijri / 2003-4 AD). This matter therefore should not be confined to *sukuk* issues alone. If the practice is acceptable in *ijara muntahia bi-tamlik* transactions, it should be automatically applicable to *sukuk al-ijara* since the underlying transaction evidenced by the *sukuk* is *ijara muntahia bi-tamlik*.

[38] Kamali 2000: 95.

[39] Ibid., 95.

[40] To connote a type of *riba* widely practiced during the pre-Islamic days in Arabia.

compounded on a daily basis. The strong moral basis behind the prohibition of *riba al-jahiliyya* is that a debtor in difficulty should be given a respite until he can improve his financial conditions instead of imposing on him further hardship in the form of late payment charges. The prevailing practices, however, led to a moral hazard whereby the Islamic financiers, and their depositors, were exposed to hardship caused by the willful delays of the debtors.

A fresh *shari'a* interpretation was required to address the contemporary problem faced by the Islamic industry. The scholars who favored the late payment compensation to be charged to the debtor relied on the well-known *hadith* that "a wealthy person who delays the payment of his debts, subjects himself to punishment and disgrace."[41] It is not uncommon for a wealthy person to be short of liquidity due to excessive leverage or a lavish lifestyle and based on the above *hadith* he should not be excused for delaying a payment obligation to another. He should be penalized for the delay and for causing the hardship to the creditor. The form of punishment includes payment of monetary compensation to the creditor. Therefore, late payment charges can be validly imposed on a willful defaulter.

The opponents of the above view, however, contend that any penalty on the defaulter can only be imposed by a competent judicial authority or by arbitration. *Shari'a* does not allow a creditor to decide unilaterally that the debtor has willfully defaulted and also impose the quantum of compensation payable by the debtor. Unless a creditor brings a legal action against the debtor to prove the willful default, the creditor cannot claim compensation from the debtor.

The middle view is that a creditor can validly procure the debtor to irrevocably undertake that if he delays any payment due to the creditor, he will donate to a charity nominated by the creditor a specific amount of money. Since the creditor does not receive the late payment amount or benefit from it, the scholars have allowed such an undertaking without any need for the creditor to bring a legal action. If the debtor fails to honor his undertaking, the creditor can enforce the undertaking in a court of law.[42] The scholars hope that this mechanism will eliminate or reduce the moral hazard faced by the creditor. This method was accordingly adopted in the Qatar *sukuk* issue.

For practical purposes, the scholars have also allowed a debtor who delays any payment to pay the late payment amount directly to the creditor who will then donate the late payment amount to charity after deducting any

---

[41] *See* Usmani 2002: 134.

[42] Whether such an action will be enforceable in a court of law will depend on the respective legal jurisdiction. Under English law, the current view is that such an undertaking will be enforceable by the creditor although the creditor is not the recipient of the payment.

administrative expenses that the creditor has incurred in monitoring and recovering the delayed payment. This method for recovering a late payment amount was adopted in the Malaysian *sukuk* issue.

SUKUK AL-ISTITHMAR

The USD400 million *sukuk* issue by the Islamic Development Bank (IDB) was based on the following structure:

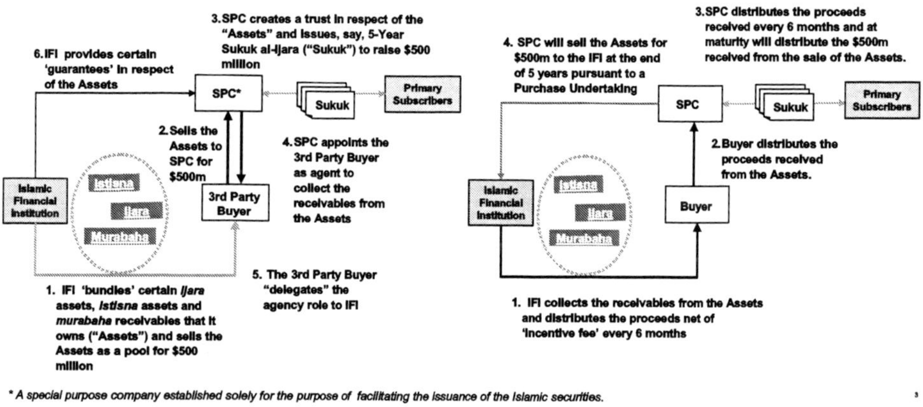

Figure 2. Structure of the USD400 Million *Sukuk* Issue by the Islamic Development Bank

The IDB *sukuk* issue was highly structured and a detailed elucidation of the structure is beyond the scope of this paper. Some of the key characteristics are discussed below.

Mixed Portfolio of Assets

One of the most innovative *shari'a* features in the IDB *sukuk* is the extension of the *khulta* principle to the field of commercial transactions like the sale of a mixed portfolio of assets consisting of tangible assets and receivables. The validity of sale of receivables or debt, known in *fiqh* as *bay'al-dayn* or *bay' al-kali' bi-al-kali'*, has been a contentious subject among contemporary scholars. The majority of scholars in the Middle East have taken the view that the sale of debt or receivables is not allowed under *shari'a* because it is tainted by *riba*. This ruling severely constrains the Islamic financial institutions from securitizing the receivables due from their *murabaha* facilities, which form the bulk of their assets. However, utilizing the principle of *khulta*, the Islamic financiers can now create a mixed portfolio or a mixed fund[43] by pooling together the receivables *(dayn)* with tangible or physical assets *('ayn)* and then sell the mixed portfolio. The important criterion from a *shari'a* perspective is that the percentage of tangible assets in the mixed portfolio has to be at least 51 percent.

When an object consists of two substances and one of those is prohibited under *shari'a*, the object can still be construed as *shari'a*-compatible if the quantity of the non-compatible substance is insubstantial. For example, if a ring is made of gold and silver, it is permissible for a Muslim male to wear it if the quantity of the gold substance is insubstantial. Opinions differ among scholars as to what amounts to an "insubstantial" quantity. Most scholars have taken the view that the non-compatible substance will be regarded as insubstantial if the quantity of the *shari'a*-compatible substance is at least 51 percent.[44] Some Hanafi scholars have taken a more liberal view of the *khulta* principle. They have not allocated any fixed percentage or quantity but have left the matter to be decided on a case-by-case basis. Hence, there may be circumstances where even if the non-compatible component is more than 50 percent, the object can still be considered to be *shari'a*-compatible as a whole.

In the IDB *sukuk*, the mixed portfolio consisted of *ijara* assets comprising 65.8 percent of the portfolio and *murabaha* and *istisna'* receivables comprising 34.2 percent. The 65.8 percent of *ijara* assets is comprised of certain physical assets owned by the IDB and which have been leased out to various counter parties. Since the *ijara* assets can be freely transferred at any price by the IDB, by mixing the *murabaha* receivables *(dayn)* with *ijara* assets *('ayn)* the IDB was able to transfer the *murabaha* receivables as well.

Replacement of Maturing Assets

Since the receivables in the mixed portfolio will mature during the life of the *sukuk*, the *sukuk* structure has to accommodate two changes in circumstances. First, the composition of the portfolio will evolve into a

[43] The concept of a mixed fund has been espoused for some time by prominent scholars like Sheikh Taqi Usmani and the IDB *sukuk* has caused the concept to gather wider acceptance. *See* Usmani 2002: 218.

[44] Based on the bare or simple majority rule. A similar rule was used in screening *shari'a*-compatible equities: only equities of companies having not more than 45 percent account receivables were accepted as *shari'a*-compatible. *See* the Methodology Overview of Dow Jones Islamic Market Indexes (visited April 10, 2004) at www.djindexes.com/jsp/imiMethod.jsp.

mixed portfolio of *ijara* assets, *murabaha* and *istisna'* receivables, and cash from the matured receivables. In this scenario, the cash will be re-invested in new *ijara* assets or new *murabaha* trades to be sourced by the IDB. The key aim is to ensure that the cash is not held idle and is promptly invested in *shari'a*-compatible assets.

Secondly, some of the *ijara* assets in the portfolio may be redeemed from the portfolio prior to the *sukuk* maturity. In the event, the composition of the mixed portfolio will change and the percentage of *ijara* assets may fall below the 51 percent requirement and may taint the *shari'a*-compatibility of the whole portfolio. The *shari'a* scholars have tackled this matter quite ingeniously. They have allowed the percentage of the *ijara* assets in the mixed portfolio to temporarily drop to the level of 25 percent of the total portfolio during the interim period when the cash is being re-invested into new *ijara* assets. The key objective is to give sufficient time for the cash to be re-invested in *ijara* assets so that the makeup of *ijara* assets can be increased back to the level of at least 51 percent. However, if the level of *ijara* assets falls at any time below the threshold of 25 percent, the level of *shari'a* tolerance comes to an end and the portfolio has to be promptly unwound. The IDB will then be bound to buy the mixed portfolio of assets at a price equal to the original price paid by the *sukuk* holders.

Net Asset Value Computation

Another important principle laid down by the contemporary scholars in the IDB *sukuk* is that the value of the *murabaha* and *istisna'* receivables to be included in the mixed portfolio can be based on their net asset value (NAV). The pricing model for both the *murabaha* and *istisna'* financing consists of two components: the cost and the agreed profit margin. The *shari'a* scholars have allowed the NAV for the *murabaha* and the *istisna'* receivables to be calculated net of all agreed profit margin. In the past, it was unclear whether the value of the *murabaha* and *istisna'* receivables can be computed based on an NAV basis. The NAV computation method as adopted in the IDB created a strong precedent and is more pragmatic and in line with the needs of the industry.

The same computation method has been adopted for the NAV of the *ijara* assets that were computed on the basis of the net lease rentals after deducting the profit margin component. It is a well-entrenched principle that an *ijara* asset, being a tangible *('ayn)* asset, can be sold at whatever price that the parties may mutually agree including on an NAV basis. The NAV computation method for *ijara* assets in the IDB *sukuk* was therefore in line with the prevailing practice.

Seller's Guarantee

Another significant principle applied in the IDB *sukuk* issue is that the seller of an asset can independently guarantee the performance of the end-user of the asset or the payment obligations of a third party emanating from the asset. For instance, the seller of a house subject to a lease can guarantee to the buyer that if the lessee defaults on the lease payment obligations, the seller will indemnify the buyer. The key conditions for the validity of the guarantee are: (1) that the guarantee should be independent of the sale of the house and should not be made a condition to the sale contract; (2) the guarantor should not charge any consideration for the guarantee; and (3) the guarantor should not act as agent or *mudarib* of the person whose liability is being guaranteed.[45]

To meet all the three conditions above, the mixed portfolio was sold by the IDB to a third party[46] and the third party then sold the mixed portfolio to the issuer. The IDB then provided the guarantee directly to the issuer covering the payment obligations of all the lessees and the *murabaha* and the *istisna'* counter parties. There was no consideration paid by the issuer to the IDB. The issuer then appointed the third party as its agent to administer and service the mixed portfolio.[47] Without the third party's involvement, the issuer would have to directly appoint the IDB as its administrative and servicing agent. This would then mean that the IDB would not be able to provide the guarantee to the issuer because it also has to act as the agent of the issuer.

Liquidity Facility

In the IDB *sukuk,* there is a likelihood of a timing mismatch between the time for receiving the proceeds due from the underlying lessees and the *murabaha* and *istisna'* counter parties and the prescribed dates for payment

---

[45] It is important to note that the above principle does not extend to the seller guaranteeing the performance of the asset itself. For example, the seller of an equity or share in a company cannot validly guarantee that the equity will yield a certain amount of dividends (e.g., if the share does not yield the dividends as guaranteed, the seller will then indemnify the buyer to the extent of the deficit). The ambit of the guarantee as used in the IDB *sukuk* is only confined to the obligations of an end-user of the assets.

[46] Islamic Corporation for the Development of the Private Sector ("ICD") was involved as the third party in the IDB *sukuk* issue.

[47] The third party then delegates the administration and servicing obligation to the IDB. From a *shari'a* perspective, this arrangement does not create a link between the issuer and the IDB. There is no contractual nexus between the issuer and the IDB and thus the IDB is not treated as the agent of the issuer.

of the periodic distributions by the issuer to the *sukuk* holders. The issuer may only receive the proceeds a few weeks after the prescribed dates for payment. Technically the issuer is only obliged to make the periodic distributions after it has received sufficient proceeds due from the mixed portfolio. This will mean that the periodic payment dates cannot be set in advance, which will in turn lead to other logistical problems for the issuer and the investors. To mitigate the timing mismatch difficulties, the *shari'a* scholars have allowed the IDB to provide an interest-free liquidity facility to the issuer whereby if there is a shortfall in the proceeds on the prescribed distribution date, the issuer can draw an amount equal to the shortfall from the liquidity facility. The issuer will then be able to make the full distribution payment on the prescribed distribution date. When the issuer finally receives the proceeds, the advance made by the IDB through the liquidity facility will be repaid in full.[48] This unique *shari'a* innovation was able to resolve the issues raised by the potential timing mismatch and facilitate the successful issuance of the IDB *sukuk*.

BAY' BI-THAMAN 'AJIL BONDS

Bay' bi-thaman 'ajil (BBA) bonds are the most popular form of Islamic debt securities in the Malaysian domestic debt capital market and in recent years have accounted for almost half of the total new debt securities issued in the domestic market. The structure of the BBA bonds, which is fairly simple, is set out below:

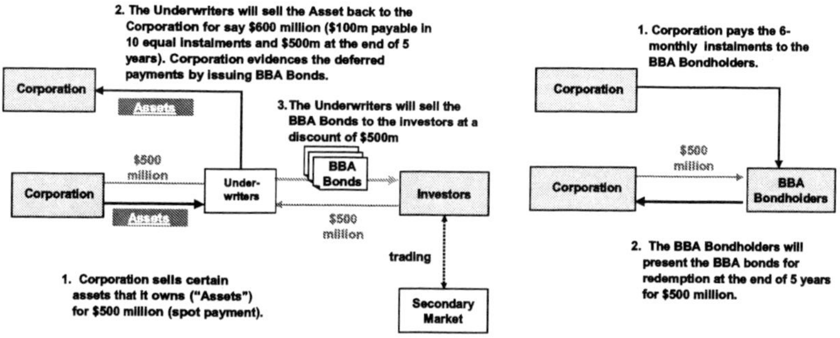

Figure 3. *Bay' bi-Thaman 'Ajil* Bond Structure

---

[48] Alternatively, the advance received by the issuer can be repaid when the portfolio is sold back to the IDB under the purchase undertaking. The exercise price for the portfolio will include an amount equal to the outstanding advances.

The BBA bond structure is built upon the principles of *bay'al-'ina* and *bay' al-dayn*, which are briefly discussed below.

Bay' al-'Ina

A transaction involving two sales where the seller sells an asset to the buyer on a spot payment basis and the buyer then immediately sells it back to the seller at a higher price on a deferred payment basis is known in *fiqh* as *bay'bi-thaman 'ajil*[49] or *bay' al-'ina*. The term *bay' al-'ina* also includes a transaction where the seller sells an asset to the buyer on a deferred payment basis and the buyer then immediately sells it back to the seller at a lower price on a spot payment basis. Both parties end up executing two contemporaneous contracts, one for spot payment and another for deferred payment, without taking any delivery or possession of the underlying asset.

The contemporary scholars who support the validity of *bay'al-'ina* rely on the views of Shafi'i and Zahiri schools.[50] They maintain that the validity of contracts is to be examined only through their external manifestation. The motive of the parties to the contract is immaterial and it does not invalidate the contract. Hence, the motive of the parties in entering into the two sales in a *bay' al-'ina* arrangement is irrelevant. The argument goes that only God knows the motive of man and man judges only the external deeds. The motive is left to God. These scholars rely on a *hadith* that states that in certain areas of human affairs, such as marriage, divorce, and manumission, motive or intention of the parties is irrelevant.[51]

The opponents of *bay' al-'ina* strongly contend that the *hadith* relied on by the proponents do not establish a general rule that in matters of personal affairs such as marriage, divorce, and commercial transactions one should not look at the intention of the parties. The well-established rule in Islam, they contend, is that all actions are judged by the intention of the parties. The *hadith* cited by the proponents merely lay down an exception to the general rule in certain limited circumstances. The reason for the exception, as pointed out by Ibn Qayyim, is that the acts of marriage, divorce, and manumission involve the right of God *(haqq Allah)* and it is not desirable for humans to act in jest with God. The Prophet, due to the

---

[49] The term *bay` bi-thaman 'ajil* (similar to *bay' al-mu'ajjal)* is used mainly in Malaysia.

[50] Malaysian Securities Commission 2002: 21.

[51] The *hadith* relates to the pronouncement of *nikah* or *talaq* in jest. It has been recorded that the Prophet said: "He who jests with the words that will make a binding contract of marriage, or with the words that pronounce a divorce or declare a slave free, shall be taken to have meant the words seriously." *See* Malik Ibn Anas, *al-Muwatta*, Book 28 (Aisha Abdarahman at-Tarjumana & Yaqub Johnson translation).

magnitude of the acts involved, had imposed the strict obligation on those who make statements in jest. This exception is only confined to marriage, divorce, and manumission and accordingly the *hadith* clearly mentions only these three circumstances. If it had been meant to include all types of commercial contracts the Prophet would have expressly mentioned it. Since no such express statement was made, the *hadith* should only be confined to areas of marriage, divorce, and manumission and there is no justification to extend it to commercial transactions.

The proponents also rely on another *hadith* regarding a case of adultery and the issue of *li'an*.[52] In this case, there was a strong possibility that the accused was taking a false oath, but despite that the Prophet decided that she was not guilty based on her oral statement and her external conduct. This *hadith* was relied upon to prove that motive or intention is not relevant in personal matters that include commercial transactions. The opponents strongly deny this by submitting that the Prophet in hearing the dispute was weighing between two probabilities: the probability that the charge against the accused was true and the probability that her oath denying adultery was truthful. The Prophet acting as a judge had to weigh both probabilities and deliver a just ruling. Based on the peculiar facts of that case, the Prophet decided that the probability of the truth of an oath was stronger. The *hadith*, therefore, does not support the proposition that one is always judged by one's external deeds rather than one's intention or motive.

The majority of the scholars have therefore decided that *bay'al-'ina* is not a valid contract under *shari'a* and regard it as a *hila* or *hiyal* (legal fiction) to practice *riba*.[53] The Malaysian scholars, however, have adopted the minority opinion and allowed it as a valid *shari'a* transaction.

Bay' al-Dayn

The debt arising out of the two contracts of sale or exchanges *(awad al-muawadhat)* as described above are securitized using the concept of *bay'al-dayn*. Pursuing the above example, the corporation will evidence its debt (i.e., the sale price payable on deferred terms) to the underwriters by issuing debt securities known as *shahadat al-dayn* and these are comparable

[52] The *hadith* relates to *li'an* and the wife of Hilal bin Umaiyyah. The wife of Hilal was charged with adultery and she denied the charge by taking the oath. Before taking the fifth oath, she faltered. It seemed for a moment that she might admit adultery but then she said that she was not going to dishonor her tribe by admitting adultery and took the fifth oath denying adultery. Here, there was a strong possibility that she was taking a false oath, but despite that the Prophet decided that she was not guilty based on her external deed (oral statement); *see* Muhammad Al-Bukhari, Sahih al-Bukhari, Volume 6, Book 60 (M. Muhsin Khan translation).

[53] Malaysian Securities Commission 2002: 21.

to zero coupon securities. The debt securities or BBA bonds are issued to the underwriters at par. The underwriters will then offer the securities in the primary market at a discount similar to a primary offering of zero coupon bonds.

The subject of *bay' al-dayn* is still being debated by contemporary *shari'a* scholars. The majority of the scholars in the Middle East have prohibited *bay' al-dayn* on the basis of an *ijma'* (consensus of opinion) among the scholars. Ahmad has recorded that such an *ijma'* has taken place. These scholars also rely on a *hadith* where it is reported that the Prophet has expressly prohibited *bay' al-kali' bi-al-kali'*.[54] Others argue that if the exchange of $100 today for $110 payable in cash one month later is considered as *riba*, it is inconceivable that *shari'a* would allow an exchange of $100 today for $110 worth of receivables that will accrue one month later. The "prohibition of *bay' al-dayn* is a logical consequence of the prohibition of *riba* or interest. A 'debt' receivable in monetary terms corresponds to money, and [in] every transaction where money is exchanged for the same denomination of money, the price must be at par value. Any increase or decrease from one side is tantamount to *riba* and can never be allowed in *shari'a*."[55]

The proponents of *bay' al-dayn,* however, contend that there is no evidence to support the existence of an *ijma'* on the issue of *bay' al-dayn*. They also maintain that the various schools have different views on what constitutes *bay' al-dayn* or *bay' al-kali' bi-al-kali'* and it is impossible for an *ijma'* to materialize with such a divergence in views. They also rely on prominent scholars like Ahmad, Ibn Qudama, and Ibn Taymiyya who have refuted the validity of the *hadith* prohibiting *bay' al-kali' bi-al-kali'*. They conclude that since there is no clear evidence in the *shari'a* that prohibits *bay' al-dayn,* the guiding principle should be that it is a permissible transaction.[56] However, they have not been able to respond to the argument of the opponents that the debt, being traded for money, should also be treated as money and consequently money traded at a discount is tainted with *riba*.

The scholars in Malaysia have adopted the minority view and using the concept of *bay'al-'ina* and *bay' al-dayn* were able to permit the issuance of *bay' bi-thaman 'ajil* bonds.[57] Both these contracts have been prohibited by scholars in the Middle East.

---

[54] Kamali 2000: 128 (citing the *hadith* reported by Musa ibn Ubayday on the narration of Abd Allah ibn Umar).

[55] Usmani 2002: 217.

[56] Kamali 2000: 125-130.

[57] Malaysian Securities Commission 2002: 16-19.

PROSPECTS FOR ISLAMIC PROFIT SHARING PRODUCTS

The common thread permeating all the three *sukuk* structures discussed above is that all these structures share a close resemblance to conventional debt securities. In particular, their economic profile is often identical to that of a conventional bond. All of them have a fixed income component, either in the form of a fixed profit margin or variable lease rental. Like conventional debt securities, all of them have a redemption feature where the principal investment is returned at the maturity date of the *sukuk*. These features have inevitably led to the criticism that the Islamic alternatives are merely alternatives in form and not in substance. They argue that if in substance the Islamic alternatives are not dissimilar to their conventional counterparts then the Islamic products are merely another type of product within the broad range of conventional products. The argument does hold certain weight when one looks at it from purely an economic perspective. For customers who seek Islamic alternatives, often the paramount consideration is whether the Islamic products offered are competitively priced. The yardstick used for measuring the competitive pricing for Islamic products is unfortunately the pricing prevailing in conventional finance. For example, when a customer walks into an Islamic bank seeking Islamic home finance, one of the key considerations for the customer is whether the pricing of the Islamic product is on par with the conventional mortgage products available in the market. Hence, if the pricing for a fixed rate 20-year mortgage is 10 percent par, the customer will invariably demand the same pricing for the Islamic product. While the majority of the customers seek Islamic finance solutions to satisfy their religious convictions, the economic reality is that the pricing consideration often prevails over their religious convictions. If the pricing of the Islamic product is more expensive, then there will be less demand for the Islamic alternative. It appears that only a handful of customers will be prepared to pay a premium for an Islamic solution.

Pricing an Islamic Debt-Based Product

Faced with this reality, the Islamic finance providers are compelled to structure the Islamic products in a manner so that the risk profile of the Islamic alternatives is as close as possible to their conventional products. For instance, if we look at the *murabaha* home financing solutions available in the market it will be evident that the risk profile of the *murabaha* is not dissimilar to the risk profile of a conventional mortgage. The Islamic financier will buy the property chosen by the customer and immediately sell the property to the customer for a fixed price payable over a period of, say, ten years pursuant to a *murabaha* arrangement. To secure the deferred payment obligations of the customer the Islamic financier will take a mortgage over the property. What is the risk profile of this transaction? The Islamic financier is exposed to the credit risk of the customer and this risk is secured by the value of the property held on mortgage. Isn't this risk profile identical to the risk profile of a conventional mortgage? The law of one price[58] would dictate that in an efficient market similar products must be priced alike; otherwise it would create riskless arbitrage opportunities. It follows from this principle that an Islamic home finance product, which shares a similar risk profile to a conventional mortgage, must share the same pricing as the conventional mortgage product. The stark reality is that Islamic finance providers, being driven by the customers to price their products competitively with the conventional products in the marketplace, are compelled to structure the Islamic alternatives with a comparative risk profile. If a 20-year fixed rate conventional mortgage is priced in the market at 10 percent pa, a 20-year *murabaha* financing will inescapably also be priced at 10 percent pa. This then raises the question of whether the similarity in risk and pricing profile makes the products like *murabaha* or *ijara* doubtful in the eyes of *shari'a.*

Fortunately, the Qur'an has addressed this very question where the text states: "they (non-believers) say: 'Trade is like usury, but God hath permitted trade and forbidden usury.'"[59] According to the renowned commentaries of the Qur'an,[60] this verse was revealed to address the confusion among the non-believers regarding a particular type of transaction prevailing at the time of the Prophet. It was common at that time for people to buy goods and commodities on credit or deferred payment terms and the sellers would charge a higher price for the credit sale. For instance, if the cash sale price is $10, the price for a deferred sale payable in one month might be $12. If at the time of payment, the buyer requests an extension of one month, the seller would increase the price to $14 and then grant the extension. The Prophet has prohibited any increase in the debt in return for an extension of time and such increase is known in *fiqh* as *riba al-jahiliyya.* The non-believers "used to say that it is all equal whether we increase the price in the beginning of the sale, or we increase it at the time of maturity. Both are equal."[61] To them the $2 increase at the time of sale is the same in substance as the $2 increase at the time of extension. Why should the first $2 be allowed as sale and the second $2 prohibited as *riba*?

---

[58] A well-entrenched principle of economics which states that the same item or closely equivalent item must sell for the same price or related prices in an efficient marketplace. The principle also shows that financial products with similar cash flows or payoffs should command the same price thereby denying the arbitrageurs the opportunity to profit from riskless arbitrage opportunities.
[59] Qur'an: 2:275 (Abdullah Yusuf Ali translation).
[60] Usmani 2000b: 36-37.
[61] Ibid., 37.

This complex issue was resolved by the Qur'an in very simple terms: "God hath permitted trade and forbidden usury." According to a prominent jurist:

> The Holy Quran could have mentioned the difference between interest and profit in pure logical manner, and could have explained how the profit in a sale is justified while the interest is not. The Holy Quran could have also spelled out the evil consequences of *riba* on the economy. But this line of argument was intentionally avoided. . . . The hint given is that the question whether these transactions have an element of injustice is not left to be decided by human reason alone, because the reason of different individuals may come up with different answers and no absolute conclusion of universal application may be arrived at on the basis of pure rational arguments. . . . [O]nce a particular transaction is held by Allah to be haraam, there is no room for disputing it on the basis of pure rational argumentation because Allah's knowledge and wisdom encompasses all those points which are not accessible to ordinary reason.[62]

The above verse and commentary clearly lend support to the view that the similarity from a risk and return profile between a *murabaha* sale and a conventional loan financing does not necessarily mean that the *murabaha* sale is tainted with *riba*. From a *shari'a* viewpoint, the similarity in risk and pricing profile does not affect the *shari'a* authenticity of these products.

The Role of Debt in Islam

One could then argue that the above conclusion would mean that the Islamic finance industry could be built on the basis of *murabaha, istisna'*, *ijara* and other similar debt-oriented products, all of which would have risk and return profiles comparable to conventional financial products. We have already seen the economic resemblance between a *murabaha* and a loan transaction. An *ijara muntahia bi-tamlik* transaction, where the lessor leases an asset with an option to sell to the lessee, also has some resemblance to a conventional finance lease. An *istisna'* arrangement, where the Islamic financiers will finance the construction of an asset and then sell the completed asset to the customer, also shares common features with a conventional construction loan facility. In all these Islamic transactions the customers incur debt obligations, either in the form of installment payments or lease rentals or purchase consideration payable under a purchase undertaking.[63] This then attracts the criticism that Islamic finance, as currently practiced, is actively promoting debt transactions in the society instead of promoting the Islamic profit sharing products. If, for the sake of argument, a financial system moves from a conventional debt-based

---

[62] Ibid., 87.
[63] Particularly in an *ijara muntahia bi-tamlik* transaction.

financing model to an Islamic debt-based financing model, will the ills of a debt-driven financial system be removed from the Islamic model? According to a prominent jurist, when "the whole economy turns into a debt-oriented economy. . . . [It] not only dominates over the real economic activities and disturbs its natural functions by creating frequent shocks, but also puts the whole mankind under the slavery of debt."[64] One then wonders whether the Islamic finance model based on predominantly debt-based solutions will end up experiencing the same problems encountered in the conventional finance model.

The above criticism does have some merit when one looks deep into the wisdom or *hikma* behind the prohibition of *riba*. One of the values behind the prohibition is to discourage Muslims from incurring debt without a reasonable need. For example Muslims are discouraged from incurring debt for "living beyond one's means or to grow one's wealth." It has been said elsewhere that "[t]he well known event that the Holy Prophet refused to offer the funeral prayer *(salat al-janaza)* of a person who died indebted was, in fact, to establish the principle that incurring debt should not be taken as a natural or ordinary phenomenon of life. It should be the last thing to be resorted to in the course of economic activities."[65] If one wants to grow one's wealth through commercial and other revenue-generating activities, Islam actively promotes financing through equity participation and profit and loss sharing mechanisms such as *mudaraba* or *musharaka*. It follows from this analysis that a debt incurred through *murabaha*, *ijara,* or other comparable products will be discouraged under *shari'a* if the debt has been incurred without a reasonable need. The key issue for consideration, then, is what is a "reasonable need"?

When analyzing a reasonable need, the scholars usually look at various factors including, among others, the nature of the need, the economic conditions of the debtor, and the prevailing conditions in the country of the debtor. The scholars are not oblivious to the reality of the prevailing economic conditions in the world today. For instance, they clearly understand that under the current economic conditions it is extremely difficult for many individuals to acquire a house without incurring a debt. For many individuals, even a lifetime of savings may not be sufficient to achieve their aspiration of owning a home. In many markets house prices keep increasing at an alarming pace and one may not be able to rely on savings alone to purchase a house. And no one will deny the fact that owning a house for self-occupation has become an indispensable

---

[64] Usmani 2000b: 101 (citing the existing state of economic affairs in the world where many countries, including those in the developed world, are over-burdened by excessive domestic and foreign debts, which in some cases even exceed the country's total GDP). *See* also Tarek El Diwany, *The Problem with Interest* (1997), 61-74, 115-122.

[65] Usmani 2000b: 100.

requirement. It can therefore be strongly argued that if one can only acquire a house through incurring a debt, then such a debt is a just and reasonable need. The *shari'a* should therefore allow the individual to incur a debt provided there is no element of *riba* involved. The homebuyer can seek Islamically structured home financing based on, say, *murabaha*, *ijara*, or *musharaka mutanaqisa*. Conversely, if someone wants to incur a debt to acquire a house in the south of France for his family to use during the summer break, most scholars may conclude that such a debt is for an unreasonable or excessive need and should be discouraged.[66]

The *shari'a* scholars believe that, by screening the use of Islamic debt-oriented products through the filter of reasonable need, the Islamic products will not be used to proliferate the spread of debt in the society. Such a safeguard will hopefully prevent the Islamic finance model from inheriting the kind of problems encountered in the conventional finance world. Like many other predicaments faced by the contemporary Muslim world, the hurdle lies in the implementation. Islamic finance is currently being used to finance almost all the needs of the society, from financing a home to financing a holiday. In its zeal to compete with the conventional finance world, the Islamic finance industry is constantly innovating to produce various Islamic alternatives to match the conventional product range. While innovations are certainly healthy and always welcomed, the Islamic finance industry should be careful to avoid being used as a medium to proliferate debt in society. Various safeguards should be built in to screen the type of debt that can be incurred Islamically. Indiscriminate extension of credit without the safeguards provided by *shari'a* will eventually lead to the Islamic finance industry facing the same problems that are faced by the conventional finance industry.

Impediments to the Growth of Islamic Profit Sharing Products

If the Islamic finance industry is aware of the potential hazards linked to debt-based products, why is the industry not actively promoting or offering more Islamic profit sharing products? The Islamic finance industry is constrained by several factors in seeking to do this and some of them are highlighted below.

[66] Some contemporary scholars argue that the issue of reasonable need is very subjective and should be left to the individual incurring the debt. If the debtor decides that it is a reasonable need for him, he can incur the debt through Islamically structured financing.

1. Mindset in the industry

In any given industry the most important factor for its success is its human resources. The Islamic finance industry is no exception. Since the Islamic finance industry is relatively new, most of the Islamic finance practitioners have been appointed from the conventional finance market. It is inevitable that most of the practitioners, having been brought up in the conventional banking environment, will find it difficult to shift from the conventional finance mindset to an Islamic finance mindset. Due to the familiarity with conventional debt products, the practitioners often tend to perceive Islamic products purely from a debt perspective. Often the key focus and energy is concentrated on finding Islamic substitutes to the conventional products that the practitioners are familiar with. For example, a practitioner with a corporate loan origination background may, consciously or subconsciously, end up designing an Islamic product comparable to the conventional counterpart. Often an Islamic product is offered to the customer in the same way as a conventional product, without taking the extra effort to explain the rationale behind the Islamic structure or to explain the pricing justification. Many a time we hear the simplistic response: "The Islamic product is the same as the conventional product. Instead of paying interest you pay a profit or rental." This type of approach and mindset is injurious to the industry and a paradigm shift is urgently required. The industry leaders should promptly look into this issue and develop training programs and workshops to inspire an indigenous culture and frame of mind in the Islamic finance industry. In particular, the programs should focus on the development of real alternatives, based on profit and loss sharing mechanisms, for suitable commercial or productive activities.[67]

2. Customers' reluctance to share the economic upside

The customers who seek Islamic finance solutions also view Islamic products through the spectacles of conventional finance. Most of the customers, being familiar with conventional finance products, expect to see in the Islamic structure some resemblance to the conventional counterpart particularly in terms of pricing and security. If the customer can get a clean corporate loan at say 5 percent p.a., it expects the same terms for the Islamic

[67] Not all financing needs are suitable for profit-sharing mechanisms. For instance, consumption-related transactions like home and car financing are not suitable for profit-sharing modes of financing. Although home financing products have been structured through *musharaka mutanaqisa*, the underlying transaction is still based on *ijara*.

facility. If the corporation is offered an alternative Islamic financing structure based on a profit and loss sharing mechanism, most often the offer is declined. From a conventional finance perspective, the corporation's key aim is to maximize profits for its shareholders.[68]

If, say, a corporation obtains a loan of $100 at 5 percent p.a. and is thereby able to generate a profit of $10, the corporation has maximized its profit by $5 after paying the $5 interest. And if the profit generated is $15, the corporation has maximized its profit by $10. If the same corporation were to take an Islamic profit and loss sharing facility with a profit ratio of, say, 50:50, in the first scenario where the profit generated is $10, the company will increase its own profit by $5. The remaining $5 will be distributed as profit to the Islamic investors. In the second scenario, however, the corporation only gets $7.50 because it has to share the profit of $15 with the investors in the ratio of 50:50. This scenario makes the profit and loss structure less appealing to most of the customers. The following third scenario, however, is beneficial to the customers if they were to take the Islamic alternative. Assuming the profit generated is only $3, the corporation will still make a profit of $1.50 because it only has to distribute $1.50 to the Islamic investors as their share of the profit. Under the conventional loan, the corporation would have suffered a $2 loss since it has to pay a fixed interest amount of $5. But in reality, the well-established corporations are not prepared to share the economic upside. Often they are tempted by the best-case scenarios where they can maximize their profits manifold and the worst-case scenarios are disregarded as remote.

The above example, although rather simplistic, shows that profit and loss sharing solutions do not generate much appeal, particularly among the well-established corporations. Newly established companies, who often find debt financing too costly or limited, however, may be attracted by the profit and loss sharing solutions, but, unfortunately, very few investors will have an appetite for such type of credit risks. This anomaly is likely to remain so long as the corporations have access to conventional debt solutions at competitive rates. We hope, however, that one day a paradigm shift will occur among the Muslim corporations and they realize that Islam provides only a limited role for leverage and they reorganize their financing requirements through profit and loss sharing means. Contemporary scholars, realizing the problems faced, have even allowed the financiers to agree on "capping" their potential returns on their investment with the corporation. If the investment generates profit beyond the agreed cap, the financiers will distribute the upside to the corporation as an "incentive fee." It is hoped that this mechanism will persuade the well-established corporations to accept Islamic profit sharing products.

---

[68] Islam also encourages the maximization of profit but within the framework of *shari'a* that, among other things, discourages leverage and encourages growth through profit and loss sharing mechanisms.

3. Investors' aversion to sharing the economic downside

On the other side of the coin, some Islamic investors are risk-averse and reluctant to share the economic downside of the Islamic profit and loss sharing mechanisms. These investors are used to investing in Islamic investments with a fixed income profile like *murabaha*, *ijara*, and *istisna'*. Their investment strategy is often conservative and has little room for taking equity-type risks where the investors are also exposed to the economic downside of the investment. This mindset again inhibits the development of Islamic profit sharing products. Frequently, the investment strategy is designed by practitioners who come from conventional commercial banking backgrounds. Most of these practitioners have little exposure to profit and loss participation investments and lack the necessary skill sets. Investing in profit and loss sharing ventures requires a different type of (and more onerous) due diligence exercise and investment analysis compared to debt-based investments. These investments also require the investors to regularly monitor the performance of the business. Occasionally it may require the investors to take over the conduct of the business and appoint their own management to replace the defaulting entrepreneur. These tasks require resources with a wide range of skills including corporate finance and private equity expertise. The Islamic investors must therefore employ more people with such backgrounds to enable the shift from debt-based products to the Islamic profit sharing products.

The industry is not expecting all the investors to convert overnight their investment strategy to one entirely based on profit and loss sharing investments. The Islamic investors must gradually revise their investment strategy in line with the ideals of Islamic finance and give priority to Islamic profit sharing products. This will certainly take time and needs the critical support of all the corporations and entrepreneurs who seek Islamic financing. If the entrepreneurs are hesitant to take Islamic profit sharing products, then there will be less interest among the Islamic investors. Conversely, if the Islamic investors are reluctant to invest, there will certainly be less interest among the entrepreneurs. It is encouraging to note that some Islamic banks have been strongly advised by their *shari'a* committees to develop and invest more in Islamic profit sharing products.[69]

[69] All Islamic banks offer profit and loss sharing investment accounts where the depositors share the profits and the losses with the Islamic banks. But these funds are invested in mainly *murabaha*, *ijara*, and *istisna'* products.

4. Moral hazard

Another reason for the slow development of Islamic profit sharing products is the minimal level of corporate transparency and corporate governance prevailing in most Muslim countries. Some Muslim countries also lack a well-defined property rights law, which is critical for profit and loss sharing mechanisms to work.[70] The investors also fear the lack of transparency and good corporate governance among the entrepreneurs *(mudarib)*. There is always the concern that the entrepreneurs may conduct the business dishonestly and may disclose a lower profit. All these concerns, added to the lack of accountability on the part of the entrepreneurs who violate these obligations, result in the Islamic investors shying away from Islamic profit sharing products. To alleviate these moral hazards, Islam advocates the importance of good corporate governance and transparency in all dealings including commercial transactions. The Qur'an unequivocally states:

> O ye who believe! When ye deal with each other, in transactions involving future obligations in a fixed period of time, reduce them to writing. . . . Let him who incurs the liability dictate, but let him fear his Lord Allah, and not diminish aught of what he owes. . . . And if one of you deposits a thing on trust with another, let the trustee (faithfully) discharge his trust, and let him fear his Lord. Conceal not evidence; for whoever conceals it—his heart is tainted with sin. And Allah knoweth all that ye do.[71]

These Qur'anic injunctions highlight the duty of the entrepreneur who is entrusted with the trust obligations to exercise proper care and due diligence and conduct the business (for example, a *mudaraba* business) in a transparent manner. The *mudarib* is obligated to conduct the business profitably within the boundaries of *shari'a* and to truthfully make a full disclosure of the business profits and distribute the due share of profits to the *rabb al-mal* (investors). The *mudarib* is also fully accountable for any breach of trust including any negligence in carrying out the terms of the investments or willfully defaulting in his duties. Since Islam firmly advocates the importance of good corporate governance and transparency, it is obligatory upon all Muslims to implement them in their daily activities.

The industry leaders, realizing the importance of implementing these safeguards, have established the Islamic Financial Standards Board (IFSB) that will, among other things, promulgate standards for corporate governance and transparency for the Islamic finance industry. The IFSB,

---

[70] In some countries ownership in a company and landed property has to be effected through a local sponsor and the enforceability of the contractual arrangement between the investors and the local sponsor is often hazy.

[71] Qur'an: 2:282-283 (Abdullah Yusuf Ali translation).

based in Malaysia, is expected to issue standards that meet the international prudential standards and comply with the principles of *shari'a*. The Muslim countries will then adopt these standards and proper sanctions will hopefully be put in place by the respective countries for any breach or violation of these standards. These standards and sanctions, once in place, will create a conducive platform for Islamic profit sharing products to flourish and reform the current landscape of the Islamic finance industry.

5. No level playing field

Another barrier to the entry of Islamic profit sharing products is the uneven tax treatment currently in place for equity-based products. Interest payment, and correspondingly profit payment in *murabaha* and rental payment in *ijara*, are all tax deductible on the ground that they constitute cost items. A profit distribution under a *mudaraba* or *musharaka* is, on the other hand, not tax-deductible. The distribution is made net of tax. This unfair tax treatment frequently makes the Islamic profit sharing products more expensive for the corporations. The existing tax environment inevitably makes leverage and gearing more attractive to the corporations.[72] Assuming the corporate profit tax rate is 30 percent and a corporation, with say $100 equity, borrows $900 at 10 percent p.a. and makes a profit of 20 percent, then the leverage will produce a return on equity of 77 percent for the corporation.[73] Conversely, if the corporation raises the $900 in equity instead of debt and still makes a profit of 20 percent, the return on equity is merely 14 percent.[74] The existing environment creates an uneven playing field for the Islamic investors who are keen to offer Islamic profit sharing products. The economics of the profit and loss sharing mechanism simply makes it less appealing for the corporations. The industry regulators must take urgent steps to reform the tax system in their respective countries and to create a level playing field for the Islamic profit sharing products. Perhaps, with equal tax treatment, the interest among corporations to seek profit and loss sharing solutions may increase and promote less reliance on the Islamic debt-based products. Obviously, more research has to be done in this area before it can be successfully implemented.

[72] For an interesting discussion on the negative impact of leverage to the economy and the limited role of leverage in an Islamic economy, *see* Tarek El Diwany, *The Problem with Interest* (1997), 167-172.
[73] ($200 profit minus $90 interest minus $33 tax) / $100 (equity) = $77.
[74] ($200 profit minus $60 tax) / $1,000 (equity) = $140.

CONCLUSION

The various *sukuk* products discussed above have opened up to the Islamic finance market a new and attractive asset class with a fixed income profile and tradability feature. This asset class will hopefully be able to consume the huge surplus liquidity existing in the Islamic finance market. The credit goes to contemporary *shari'a* scholars who were able to inspire and guide the industry in producing the various *shari'a* innovations that made the *sukuk* a reality today. The *sukuk* product, however, should be employed judiciously to ensure that it is not used as an avenue to proliferate debt in society. The Islamic finance practitioners should channel their focus and energy in spreading the growth of Islamic profit sharing products. There are various hurdles but these are not insurmountable. History speaks for itself. Three decades ago, very few would have believed that the *sukuk* would be a reality. Perhaps, three decades from now, the Islamic profit sharing products will be the mainstream products in the Islamic finance market.

Islamic Financing Transactions in European Courts

Kilian Bälz[1]

INTRODUCTION

This paper explores the enforcement of Islamic financing transactions in European courts, an issue that is of particular relevance to any practitioner involved in the structuring and drafting of Islamic financing transactions. The use of Islamic financing techniques is no longer confined to the original Islamic banking strongholds of the Middle East and South Asia. Many, perhaps most, Islamic financing transactions today are implemented in Europe, with London and Geneva in particular having earned a reputation as Islamic banking hubs. In addition, the globalization of Islamic financing transactions seems to encourage corresponding litigation. Lenders default and Islamic banks sue and enforce their rights, once Islamic finance is disengaged from the cultural context of Islamic societies and freed from the shackles of communal ties.

The first part of this paper will discuss two recent English cases of relevance. The second part will address the issues discussed in these cases from the perspective of German law, thus complementing the common law perspective with that of the civil law tradition. The third part will proceed to discuss how to draft *shari'a* compliant agreements, which can also be enforced in a European court. The discussion will focus on *murabaha* agreements, since it is transactions of that type that have been litigated the most. Some of the more general questions discussed in this paper, however, will also be relevant to other Islamic financing structures, in particular *sukuk* and *ijara* transactions.

---

[1] Partner, GLEISS LUTZ (Frankfurt, Germany). The author specializes in international corporate and M&A work with a particular focus on the MENA region.

THE COMMON LAW APPROACH: RECENT DECISIONS OF ENGLISH COURTS

Islamic Financing Transactions in the English Courts

English law has become the standard for international financing transactions, at least in Europe, Africa, and the Middle East. It provides professionals with wide discretion in establishing law through practice, which suits the needs of the international business community.[2] Furthermore, the London High Court is a popular venue for commercial disputes of all sorts, including many cases geographically unrelated to the United Kingdom. It is no surprise, therefore, that most Islamic banking cases in Europe have so far been of English origin. As a general rule, the (English) common law approach to commercial agreements, in particular the obsession with a literal interpretation that construes clauses close to their wording, is sympathetic toward Islamic financing agreements, provided the agreements are properly drafted. However, the English courts tend to be at odds with issues of Islamic law, if they arise, and are reluctant to enter into discussions related to *shari'a* matters.

Symphony Gems

The first time an English court was concerned with an Islamic banking transaction[3] was in *Islamic Investment Company of the Gulf (Bahamas) Ltd. v. Symphony Gems N.V. and Others*, in the High Court of London.[4] The case illustrates the global reach of Islamic banking transactions and the resulting challenges for the Islamic finance industry. In the case the claimant, an Islamic bank incorporated in the Bahamas, had entered into a contract described as "*Murabaha* Finance Agreement" with the defendant. Upon instruction of the defendant, the claimant purchased two deliveries of precious stones from a diamond broker in Hong Kong. The precious stones allegedly never reached the defendant. When the claimant brought a claim

[2] Goode 1995: 162.

[3] Market Intelligence, cf. for example, www.islamic-banking.com/conference/conf-documentation-report.php. For a more comprehensive analysis of the case, see Umar F. Moghul and Arshad A. Ahmed, "Contractual Forms in Islamic Finance Law and *Islamic Investment Co. of the Gulf (Bahamas) Ltd. v. Symphony Gems & Ors.*," *Fordham International Law Journal* 25 (2003): 150, and Bälz 2004b: 117-134.

[4] February 13, 2002. To my knowledge, the case has not been published. The following quotations are taken from the transcript provided by Beverly F. Nunnery & Co.

for the balance due, the defendant argued, inter alia, that the transaction was a contract of sale, under which the defendant's obligation to pay was conditional on delivery of the goods. The defendant also alleged that the contract was void altogether, on grounds that it contravened the principles of the Islamic *shari'a*.

The loss of goods in transit is among the typical legal risks attached to a *murabaha* transaction.[5] In this event, the question arises whether the *murabaha* is to be treated as a sale of goods, which an analysis of traditional *fiqh*-rules may suggest, or whether it is to be treated as a financing transaction, which would conform to its contemporary use in trading practice. Islamic banks tend to mitigate the risk of a loss of the goods through detailed contractual provisions, making payment of the balance independent from any delivery of the supplies. In the present case, the agreement provided:

> 4.2 When the Seller shall have purchased Supplies, the Purchaser shall be absolutely, unconditionally and irrevocably obliged to purchase such Supplies from the Seller and to pay (a) all sums as mentioned in the Acceptance relating to such Supplies and (b) all other sums expressed or agreed to be payable hereunder in respect of such Supplies, in all cases notwithstanding any defect, deficiency or any loss or any other breach of any Supply Contract relating thereto by the Supplier or any other matter or thing whatsoever.[6]

This principle is reiterated in a subsequent clause in the agreement as follows:

> 4.4 The relevant instalments of the Sale Price in respect of each Purchase Agreement shall be payable by the Purchaser to the Seller on the due dates therefor, whether or not: (a) any property in the Supplies has passed to the Purchaser under the relevant Purchase Agreement and/or to the Seller under the relevant Supply contract ... and such payment shall not be conditional upon the happening of any event, in recognition by the parties of the facts that the source of the supply of the Supplies is selected by the Purchaser [...][7]

When interpreting these clauses, the High Court first highlighted the choice of law clause contained in the agreement, which stated that the "Agreement and each Purchase Agreement shall be governed by, and construed in accordance with, English law."[8] On this basis, the Court declined to be drawn into any discussions regarding the nature of *murabaha* under Islamic law. Instead, the Court interpreted the respective contractual clauses in accordance with English legal principles, holding that:

---

[5] Vogel and Hayes 1998: 141.
[6] *Islamic Investment Company of the Gulf v. Symphony Gems*, 4-5.
[7] Ibid., 5-6.
[8] Ibid., 12.

> What clauses 4.4, 5.1, 5.2 and 5.6 demonstrate is that all of the arrangements concerning the acquisition of the goods by the seller from the supplier fall to be made by the purchaser, for the very good reason that this is a financing agreement facilitating or apparently facilitating the purchase of the goods of the supplier. If therefore there has been no delivery of the goods from the supplier to the seller and thus from the seller to the purchaser, that can only be because the purchaser has not made the necessary arrangements. ... Clause 4.4 provides that the instalments are payable whether or not the seller is in breach of any of its obligations under the relevant purchase agreement, which must include failure to deliver.[9]

On this basis the High Court concluded that "delivery of goods is not a prerequisite to recovery by the seller of the relevant instalments of the sale price from the purchaser"[10] and held that the agreement was no orthodox contract of sale. The Court found that the *murabaha* was a financing transaction and that the defendant remained under the obligation to pay the purchase price even in the event of failure by the claimant to deliver the goods.

In addition, the Court saw no basis for the argument put forth by the defendant that the contract was altogether void on the grounds that it contravened Islamic law. Although it is debatable whether the allocation of risk under the transaction conformed to a more orthodox interpretation of traditional *shari'a* law and relevant expert evidence had been submitted in the proceedings, the Court declined to look into this issue. It held instead that these questions were irrelevant in the case in light of the express choice of law and the lack of any relationship with an Islamic legal order. As a result, the contract was construed as an English agreement and the defenses were altogether dismissed.

The *Symphony Gems* case was received with much relief by the international Islamic banking community. In essence, it affirmed that a *murabaha* agreement, if properly drafted, may be enforced in an English court, if and to the extent that the agreement is governed by English law. The same applies to contractual structures whose permissibility is, from a more orthodox *shari'a* standpoint, at least questionable.

---

[9] Ibid., 22-23.
[10] Ibid., 23.

Beximco

This issue was then taken up in *Shamil Bank of Bahrain v. Beximco Pharmaceuticals Ltd. and Others.*[11] The *Beximco* case was based on a similar set of facts, at least to the extent that it concerned a defaulting debtor under a *murabaha* agreement who raised, inter alia, the defense that the agreement did not comply with Islamic legal principles. When the claimant brought an action over the amount of the balance due in the London High Court, the defendant argued that the transaction was altogether void, alleging it was only dressed up as a *murabaha* agreement, but was in fact an interest bearing loan. Thus it violated the Islamic prohibition of *riba* and was unenforceable.

Given its facts and in light of the *Symphony Gems* case, it may be surprising that this case actually made it to the Court of Appeal. The reason is that the agreement in the *Beximco* case contained a choice of law clause which, unlike the one in the *Symphony Gems* agreement, also made explicit reference to Islamic law. The relevant clause reads: "Subject to the Principles of the Glorious *Shari'a*, this Agreement shall be governed by and construed in accordance with the laws of England."[12]

This choice of law is rather ambiguous, to say the least, and raises a whole set of questions.[13] One is whether and to what extent the parties can validly agree on Islamic law as the governing law of a financial transaction. This is a question that has not been fully resolved so far.[14] In view of the interpretative pluralism in Islamic law, both past and present, and the extensive controversies regarding financial innovations among Islamic scholars, it seems a difficult if not impossible task for any court to come up with an interpretation of Islamic law that will satisfy all circles concerned. Moreover, as far as English private international law is concerned, it is questionable whether the parties can validly opt for a choice of law other than that of a particular national jurisdiction. According to the prevailing opinion, it is only permissible to opt for the law of a particular country to govern the contract.[15]

---

[11] January 28, 2004, [2004] EWCA Civ 99. The following quotations are taken from the transcript by Smith Bernal Wordwave Ltd.

[12] Ibid., no. 1

[13] For a more comprehensive discussion, see Bälz 2004a. Among these questions are whether the parties indeed intended to subject the agreement simultaneously to two legal orders (Islamic and English Law) or at least, in effect, subject the exercise of rights granted under the agreement to the mandatory principles of Islamic law. Further, one may raise the question of whether the parties did intend to determine a proper law of the contract pursuant to which the transaction contemplated in the agreement may be deemed void.

[14] For a more detailed discussion see Bälz 2001: 73-85.

[15] Collins 2000: 1223.

In the end, therefore, both the London High Court and the Court of Appeal declined to attribute any legal effect to the reference to Islamic law contained in the agreement. First, it was argued that pursuant to the applicable conflict rules the choice of any non-national legal order—such as the *shari'a*—was irrelevant. Art. 3(1) of the Rome Convention provides:

> A contract shall be governed by the law chosen by the parties. The choice must be expressed or demonstrated with reasonable certainty by the terms of the contract or the circumstances of the case. By their choice the parties can select the law applicable to the whole or a part only of the contract.

Both the High Court and the Court of Appeal held that this provision permits only the selection of a specific national law as the governing law of the contract. Any reference to transnational legal principles such as the *lex mercatoria* or the Islamic *shari'a*, understood as the historic (but living) legal order of Islam, is no valid choice of law. Second, and maybe more important, the courts also decided against an incorporation of Islamic legal principles into the contract (being in principle governed by English law). The doctrine of incorporation is acknowledged in English law, and it is thus possible to make selected foreign legal principles part of an English law agreement. The courts held, however, that such incorporation requires that reference be made to a specific "black letter" rule (be it of a foreign legal order or of a set of international principles). In the words of the Court of Appeal:

> The doctrine of incorporation can only sensibly operate where the parties have by the terms of their contract sufficiently identified specific "black letter" provisions of a foreign law or an international code or set of rules apt to be incorporated as terms of the relevant contract such as a particular article or articles of the French civil Code or the Hague Rules. By that method, English law is applied as the governing law to a contract into which the foreign rules have been incorporated. In such a case, in construing and applying those rules, where there is ambiguity or doubt as to their ambit or effect, it may be appropriate for the court to have regards to evidence from those experts in foreign law as to the way in which the provisions identified have been interpreted and applied in their "home" jurisdiction.[16]

The Court of Appeal held that the reference to the "Glorious *Shari'a*" was too vague to have any legal meaning:

> The general reference to principles of *shari'a* in this case affords no reference to, or identification of, those aspects of *shari'a* law which are intended to be incorporated into the contract, let alone the term in which they are framed. It is plainly insufficient for the defendants to contend that the basic rules of the

[16] *Shamil Bank v. Beximco*, no. 51.

> *shari'a* applicable in this case are not controversial. Such "basic principles" are neither referred nor identified. Thus the reference to the "principles of ... *shari'a*" stand unqualified as a reference to the body of *shari'a* law generally. As such, they are inevitably repugnant to the choice of English law as the law of the contract and render the clause self-contradictory and therefore meaningless. ... The words are intended to simply reflect the Islamic religious principles according to which the bank holds itself out as doing business rather than a system of law to be applied in ascertaining the liability of the parties under the terms of the agreement.[17]

In addition, in light of the interpretative pluralism in Islamic law, it would be an impossible task for the court to determine the applicable principles, as there are, in the words of the Court of Appeal, "indeed areas of considerable controversy and difficulty" in ascertaining the applicable *shari'a* rules.[18] Furthermore, the Court of Appeal argued that it is doubtful whether the parties intended to confer the authority to decide such questions on an English court. The Court supported this interpretation by arguing that the parties, who were fully aware of the economic realities of the transaction, could not possibly have intended to subject the agreement to legal rules invalidating the transaction.

As a result, both the High Court and the Court of Appeal declined to interpret *shari'a* principles, the strict application of which may well have resulted in sincere doubts as to the validity of the transaction. The transaction resembled a so-called "synthetic *murabaha*," carrying an allocation of risk comparable to a conventional financing transaction.[19] Instead, the Courts interpreted the agreement applying English legal principles only and confirming the validity of the agreement from the perspective of English law, but not opining on it from the viewpoint of the Islamic *shari'a*. The latter task is left to the Islamic financial community.

Islamic Financing Transactions under English Law

On the basis of the case law analyzed, it seems fair to conclude that an English court will enforce a *murabaha* agreement based upon a literal interpretation of its wording, provided that the mechanics of the transaction are intelligible and the agreement is properly drafted. In doing so, however, the court cannot be expected to enter into any discussions relating to the *shari'a*. Put differently, in the case law, however limited it is up to now, the courts have shied away from entering into any such analysis. An English

---

[17] Ibid., no. 52.
[18] Ibid., no. 55.
[19] For a more detailed discussion of this type of transaction, see Vogel and Hayes 1998: 142-143.

court will be prepared to assist an Islamic bank in collecting the balance outstanding under a *murabaha* agreement when due. However, it cannot be expected to also guarantee *shari'a* compliance.

THE CIVIL LAW APPROACH: HOW GERMAN COURTS WOULD DECIDE

Civil Law—An Altogether Different Approach?

Much has been written about whether the civil law approach is all that different from the common law approach. In fact, in many areas of law, the convergency thesis seems compelling and any juxtaposition of a civil law legal culture with a common law legal culture is, in light thereof, rather artificial. This, however, is not true for all areas of law. This paper argues that there is indeed a substantial difference between the English approach on the one hand and the German approach on the other, at least as far as non-national norms and the doctrine of incorporation is concerned. Unlike in England, there appears to be no relevant German case law relating to *murabaha* transactions. As a consequence, the following is something of a Continental European exercise in legal realism, a prophecy of what the German courts might decide when concerned with the choice of law clause of the kind included in the agreement in the *Beximco* case.

Choice of Law

With respect to the question of whether the parties may select the principles of Islamic law as the proper law of the contract, the situation under German private international law is somewhat similar to the English approach. Section 27(1) of the German Introductory Law of the Civil Code (*Einführungsgesetz zum Bürgerlichen Gesetzbuch—"EGBGB"*), which contains the applicable conflict rules, is based on the Rome Convention and reads:

> The contract is governed by the law chosen by the parties. The choice of law must be explicit or must be derived with sufficient certainty from the terms of the contract or the circumstances of the case. The parties may agree on a choice of law to comprise the entire contract or a part thereof.[20]

[20] English translation by the author.

This provision allows the parties to determine the law applicable to an international contract (and thereby reflects the international standard in that field). Moreover, according to the predominant opinion in German legal literature, only the law of a national legal order is a valid choice.[21] However, this opinion is not universally accepted and, by comparison to English legal writing, German lawyers seem more sympathetic toward non-governmental rules, such as the *lex mercatoria*, the UNIDROIT principles, or the principles of European contract law. In light of the increasing importance of private standardization in international commerce on the one hand, and the decreasing significance of the nation-state as legislator on the other, it has been argued that it is erroneous to limit the choice of law to national law; instead, there should be the possibility to select a particular set of non-national rules.[22] Accordingly, it should also be possible to select Islamic legal principles as the proper law of the contract.

Even following the predominant opinion, the selection of Islamic legal principles must be permitted if the dispute is submitted to arbitration. In relation to the substantive law applicable in arbitration proceedings, the German Code of Civil Procedure (*Zivilprozessordnung—"ZPO"*) provides in Section 1051(1) that the tribunal shall decide pursuant to the "legal rules" determined to be applicable by the parties.[23] This wording is understood by prevailing opinions to allow also for the selection of non-national rules.[24] As a consequence, it should be possible to select Islamic law as the proper law of contract if and to the extent that the agreement contains an arbitration clause. It follows that if the parties insist on defining the Islamic *shari'a* as the proper law of the contract, they should also be advised, if German conflict rules apply,[25] to include an arbitration clause in the contract. An arbitration tribunal is likely to respect such a choice of law. However, it is highly recommended to provide in the contract that the arbitrators will have the required knowledge of Islamic law and, more importantly, Islamic banking practice. It follows that at least some of the arbitrators should be required to have the appropriate qualifications, i.e., be well-versed in *shari'a* matters and experienced in the current Islamic banking practice. The effect of the choice of law will in practice depend on the wording of the arbitration clause.

---

[21] This opinion is forcefully put forth, e.g., by Von Bar and Mankowski 2003: 87-88. It conforms to the predominant, albeit not entirely uncontested opinion in German legal literature (see the references ibid.).

[22] Wichard 1996: 262-302; Berger et al. 2002: 12-37. Both authors emphasize the importance of non-governmental rule-making from an empirical/sociological perspective.

[23] English translation by the author.

[24] Wagner 2002: 791 with further references.

[25] Which is, practically speaking, the case if the venue or place of arbitration, as the case may be, is located in Germany.

Incorporation of Islamic Legal Principles into a German Law Agreement

German law acknowledges the doctrine of incorporation and the parties may, by reference to a defined set of rules or standards, make them part of their agreement. This is true even if the rules are of a non-national nature and would therefore not qualify as law in the positivist sense.[26] Thus, this approach allows one to make reference to Islamic legal principles even though the contract is otherwise governed by German law. This situation, with respect to the underlying principle, is not all that different from the position of English law. One exception may be that the German courts are likely to be somewhat more lenient with respect to the formal requirements of such an incorporation. As a general rule, German courts will be less obsessed with the wording of a particular contractual clause and more likely to investigate what the parties actually intended (or, alternatively, what the court believes the parties should have written in the contract).[27] In practice, this can make a significant difference, and a German court may well have interpreted the choice of law clause in the *Beximco* agreement to the effect that the parties had indeed intended to subject the exercise of their rights to the Islamic *shari'a*. According to this interpretation, the exercise of any rights may be limited by its permissibility according to *shari'a* principles. Therefore, the claimant in the *Shamil* case may have faced difficulties in collecting the monies due, if and to the extent that the defendant was in a position to ascertain that the agreement did in fact contravene Islamic *shari'a*.[28]

In addition, and perhaps more important, German courts have in the past interpreted certain agreements pursuant to Islamic legal principles even without any explicit reference to *shari'a* law. This approach has, in particular, been followed with Islamic marriage contracts that are formally governed by German law pursuant to the applicable conflict rules, but based

---

[26] Von Bar and Mankowski 2003: 87-88.

[27] For a critical discussion from a comparative perspective, see Zweigert and Kötz 1987: 433-434.

[28] One can only speculate about the outcome. The agreement at hand, which resembled a synthetic *murabaha*, may well be contrary to a more orthodox interpretation of *shari'a* principles. The possible consequences, however, are not very clear. One approach would be to hold that the agreement is void only as far as the payment of "interest" is concerned. Based on such an understanding the bank would be able to collect the principal without, however, being entitled to the mark-up. If and to the extent one holds that the agreement is void altogether, the question arises whether the bank may nevertheless collect the principal pursuant to the rules of unjustified enrichment (which would be the position under German law; see Bundesgerichtshof, judgments of July 29, 1989, *Wertpapiermitteilungen* 1083 and June 15, *Neue Juristische Wochenschrift* 1993, 2108).

on and inspired by traditional Islamic structures. Here, the German Federal Court has explicitly referred to the concept of a *mahr* under Islamic law when dealing with an Islamic marriage contract that was entered into between two German residents, dressed up as a prenuptial agreement governed by German law, and notarized by a Bavarian notary public.[29] A German court is likely to adopt a similar approach with *murabaha* agreements governed by German law. In this case the court may investigate in further detail whether the *murabaha* is in fact a sale of goods or a financing transaction; it may also look into the details of whether the purchaser is under any obligation to repay the "loan" if the goods are lost in transit. The court may also ask whether parties intending to transact in "the Islamic way" can be barred from exercising certain rights formally granted to them under the agreement, if this contravenes fundamental *shari'a* principles.

Islamic Financing Transactions under German Law

Compared to the English courts, it is likely that a German court would pay more attention to Islamic legal rules. It is unlikely that a German court would dismiss outright any reference to the Islamic *shari'a* or a traditional Islamic contractual model by arguing that German law governs the agreement. It is more likely that a German court would try to give the agreement a specific Islamic interpretation (or, more precisely, whatever the court would assume such an Islamic interpretation to be). It should be emphasized that this may at times, from the point of view of the Islamic financing industry, be a problematic approach. The legitimacy of some widely spread contractual structures, such as the synthetic *murabaha*, is still being debated among Islamic scholars. A German court concerned with such agreements may well take defenses derived from Islamic law more seriously than the English courts have done. This may ultimately hinder enforcement of at least some of the rights under such an agreement.

---

[29] Bundesgerichtshof, judgment of October 14, 1998, *Neue Juristische Wochenschrift* 1999, 574 f.

LESSONS FOR THE STRUCTURING AND DRAFTING OF ISLAMIC FINANCING AGREEMENTS

Generating Islamic Legitimacy in a Secular Legal Environment

Ensuring *shari'a* compliance in a secular legal environment is not an easy task, and Islamic financial institutions employ various techniques to assure their customers that their dealings are Islamic (and thereby generate the Islamic legitimacy on which their business model is based). On an institutional level, most Islamic financial institutions rely upon a *shari'a* board entrusted with advising the institution's management in connection with Islamic questions and ascertaining that the business transacted complies with *shari'a* principles.[30] In addition, and more debatable from a legal perspective, some Islamic financial institutions also include a reference to Islamic legal principles in the agreements themselves (as, for example, in the *Beximco* case). In this case, the Islamic orientation of the transaction is not merely expressed by a general policy statement in the institution's articles of association or the use of Islamic contractual structures. The claim to abide by Islamic legal principles is also expressed through a choice of law clause establishing Islamic law as the proper law of the contract. Such an approach most clearly reflects the business policy of Islamic financial institutions being guided by the Islamic *shari'a*. In light thereof, it is only consistent to include a provision in the agreement providing for a choice of Islamic law. The case law of the English courts discussed in this paper demonstrates the difficulties of such an approach. I would like to make two specific suggestions as to how these difficulties might be overcome, both on a substantive and on a procedural level.

Defining Applicable *Shari'a* Rules

One of the key difficulties for any court concerned with applying *shari'a* law to an agreement is determining the substance of the relevant rules. The attitude of many English courts regarding the alleged vagueness of *shari'a* law, and the notion that it is more of a moral code than a legal system, is unfair and indicative of a persistent orientalist bias. It must be conceded, however, that in light of the diversity of opinion among Islamic scholars, it is not always easy to resolve a specific issue on the basis of Islamic law, particularly when financial innovations are concerned.

As a starting point, any reference to Islamic legal norms, be it a choice of law proper or by way of incorporation into the agreement, must be

---

[30] Saeed 1999: 108-118.

specific and must allow a third party interpreting the agreement to ascertain its content. This requires precise definition and description of the sources of such rules. One approach may be to refer to a specific *madhhab*, or even more precisely, a specific work of *fiqh*, defined as the authoritative source of Islamic law for the purpose of the agreement. Both techniques are known approaches in family law reform. They could be extended to the realm of financial transactions as well. However, the downside of this approach is that if a certain *madhhab* is selected, it will not exclude but in the best scenario only narrow down ambiguities and differences in opinion. As for the selection of certain authoritative *fiqh* books, it must be noted that even contemporary expositions of Islamic contract law do not focus on modern financial transactions and leave many intriguing questions open. It follows from this that even if a certain *madhhab* or treatise of law is specified, this will provide only limited certainty with respect to the outcome of a potential dispute.

In my experience, the most advisable reference is to the AAOIFI *shari'a* standards. AAOIFI is a non-governmental organization based in Bahrain, which is active in the definition of the best practice applicable to Islamic financial institutions.[31] AAOIFI also has promulgated a set of *shari'a* standards that, currently in their second edition,[32] provide guidance for most Islamic financing transactions (and, furthermore, are deemed to represent the middle ground position for many disputed questions). The standards are a restatement of *shari'a* principles relevant to Islamic banking transactions, formulated in a language and manner intelligible even to lawyers without formal training in *shari'a* law. Therefore, if it is intended to incorporate *shari'a* principles into the contract, a reference to the AAOIFI standards is a workable solution. These principles are widely accepted among *shari'a* sholars, they focus on the areas of law relevant to financial transactions, and are formulated in a reasonably precise manner. From a practical point of view, however, it is not advisable to refer to Islamic legal principles without precisely defining what this will imply in the event of a dispute.

Dispute Resolution: Division of Labor Between Courts and Experts

Even if the relevant *shari'a* norms are precisely defined, their application to a specific transaction will easily give rise to ambiguities. This, to be fair, is not due to the nature of *shari'a* law, but is rather an unavoidable consequence of any legal interpretation. Consequently, the

---

[31] For details see www.aaoifi.com.
[32] Accounting and Auditing Organization for Islamic Financial Institutions 2003.

appointment of the authority on which this task is to be conferred may, in practice, be even more important than the selection and definition of the rules as such.

If Islamic legal rules are properly incorporated into an agreement, they will bind a court, which must then apply these rules. There is always a possibility that the court will treat these rules as a choice of foreign law, even if they are integrated into the agreement by incorporation. In this event, determining the substance of such rules will ultimately depend on relevant expert opinions. English and German approaches to that question will differ in detail. Whereas in Germany the expert will be appointed by the court and investigate the issues of foreign law *ex officio* and impartially, an English court will treat a question of foreign law as a factual question, left to the parties to ascertain. In any event, the involvement of foreign law experts can substantially slow down the proceedings, particularly if these experts are appointed *ex officio*, as would be the case in a German court. From a practical perspective, therefore, it is advisable to avoid, to the extent possible, the involvement of court appointed experts. This will hold true particularly when advising an Islamic bank.

One possible additional remedy to this situation is to determine in the agreement itself who shall have the authority to interpret the relevant *shari'a* rules in the event of a dispute. This can easily be done by providing that the institution's *shari'a* board shall also have the last word on such questions. Once a typical transaction has been sanctioned by the *shari'a* board, there will effectively be no further dispute with respect to their *shari'a* compliance. In such a case, however, the reference to Islamic legal principles will be more of a tautology that does not add anything substantive to the agreement. Another possibility, representing a compromise position, would be to name in the agreement an independent institution or a third party to exercise the function of the expert. This technique is fairly widespread in complex commercial agreements, where often specific questions relating to technical and accounting matters are referred to an institution other than the normal dispute resolution body. The expert decides a particular aspect of the dispute based on special expertise.[33] Such a structure can also be used where issues of Islamic law arise, and the questions could then be referred to an expert appointed pursuant to the agreement.

[33] For a more comprehensive discussion, see Bälz 2004a.

CONCLUSIONS

Based on the limited case law available, it is fair to conclude that *murabaha* agreements are enforceable under both English and German law, provided they are drafted in a professional manner that makes their underlying structure intelligible to a non-Muslim court. Any reference to *shari'a* norms should be precisely defined, and such references should also establish an authority other than the court entrusted with the interpretation of Islamic principles. A European court can be expected to enforce a commercial agreement according to its terms and conditions. It cannot, however, be expected to express any opinions on *shari'a* law.

Structuring a Securitized *Shari'a*-Compliant Real Estate Acquisition Financing: A South Korean Case Study

Michael J. T. McMillen[1]

INTRODUCTION

Securitization in Islamic finance is becoming a reality, as evidenced by the recent *sukuk* offerings by national governments and Islamic investment banks and the *sukuk* offerings presently being structured for municipalities, regional governmental entities, and private commercial entities. The primary foci of *sukuk* structures implemented to date have been on pooled lease *(ijara)* securitizations and securitizations of pools of *murabaha* payment obligations. The conventional wisdom in the Islamic finance field has been that there cannot be a securitization of obligations, in compliance with the principles and precepts of Islamic *shari'a* (the "*shari'a*"), in transactions where the financing for the transaction is primarily conventional interest-based debt and there is no *shari'a*-compliant lease or similar *shari'a*-compliant obligation.

---

[1] Partner, King & Spalding LLP. The author is resident in the firm's New York and London offices. All intellectual property rights, including copyright, are retained by Michael J. T. McMillen. The author expresses his gratitude to the *shari'a* scholars who considered the many complicated aspects of the South Korean transaction that forms the basis of this case study and to the entities involved in that transaction. Confidentiality considerations prevent the identification of those scholars and entities, but do not diminish the author's gratitude. The author also expresses his gratitude to other *shari'a* scholars who consulted on many of the complicated *shari'a* questions and issues raised by the structuring of this transaction, most notably Mohammed Ali Elgari, Sheikh Nizam Yaquby, and Sheikh Yusuf Talal DeLorenzo. For the same confidentiality reasons, the author could not describe to these scholars all aspects of the South Korean transaction, nor could he identify the transaction or the participants in the transaction to these scholars, when discussing aspects of the transaction with them. Nevertheless, as always, these gentlemen were generous with their thoughts, their wisdom, their criticism, their humor, their time, and their creative suggestions.

This essay is intended to focus discussion on the basis for that conventional wisdom by examining, through a case study, the fundamental conception of securitization in Islamic finance. It is intended to challenge the widespread assertions that the presence of conventional interest-bearing debt in a transaction necessarily prohibits the application of the securitization model to that transaction. It is also intended to illustrate how careful and creative transactional structuring can be used to develop a *shari'a*-compliant transaction that opens new markets to Muslim investors.

Thus, this essay will focus on the fundamental nature of structuring an individual transaction involving primarily conventional interest-based debt financing, and no *shari'a*-compliant *ijara* or *murabaha* obligation, so as to permit securitization of that transaction in compliance with the *shari'a*. The focus is on the individual transaction:[2] a case study of a single real estate acquisition financing transaction in South Korea where financing is mandatorily subject to the South Korean securitization laws and is thus comprised of conventional interest-bearing debt (the "Securitized Acquisition Financing Transaction").[3] The critical inquiry is whether a transaction such as this can be structured so that it can be securitized in a manner that is compliant with the *shari'a*.[4]

A GENERIC OVERVIEW OF SECURITIZATION

Before examining the Securitized Acquisition Financing Transaction, it is essential to have a framework understanding of the general nature and process of securitization. The New Basel Capital Accord of the Basel Committee on Banking Supervision of the Bank for International Settlements broadly defines securitization as follows:[5]

---

[2] This essay will not focus directly on asset-based securitizations of the type evidenced by the recent *sukuk* issuances. Nor will this essay focus on the pooling and related statistical concepts that underpin the predictability concepts that are essential to securitization.

[3] The description of the transactional case study set forth in this essay departs from the actual facts of the South Korean transaction in various particulars. Those departures are intended to highlight certain issues pertaining to *shari'a* compliance as well as to protect client confidences.

[4] Any departures from compliance with the *shari'a* that may be perceived, asserted, or identified by any reader are the sole responsibility of the author, whether resulting from the author's understanding (or lack thereof), characterization, or interpretation of the relevant *shari'a* principle or precept, and are in no way attributable to any of the *shari'a* scholars mentioned in footnote 1 of this essay.

[5] Bank for International Settlements 2003: sections 502 and 503. Securitization is to be distinguished from factoring (although the differences may be slight in sophisticated securitization transactions). In a factoring transaction, the factor purchases receivables from the originator at a discount and the factor thereafter

502. A *traditional securitization* is a structure where the cash flow from an underlying pool of exposures is used to service at least two different stratified risk positions or tranches reflecting different degrees of credit risk. Payments to the investors depend upon the performance of the specified underlying exposures, as opposed to being derived from an obligation of the entity originating those exposures. The stratified/tranched structures that characterize securitizations differ from ordinary senior/subordinated debt instruments in that junior securitization tranches can absorb losses without interrupting contractual payments to more senior tranches, whereas subordination in a senior/subordinated debt structure is a matter of priority of rights to the proceeds of a liquidation.

503. A *synthetic securitization* is a structure with at least two different stratified risk positions or tranches that reflect different degrees of credit risk where credit risk of an underlying pool of exposures is transferred, [in] whole or in part, through the use of funded (e.g. credit-linked notes) or unfunded (e.g. credit default swaps) credit derivatives or guarantees that serve to hedge the credit risk of the portfolio. Accordingly, the investors' potential risk is dependent upon the performance of the underlying pool.

As a general matter,[6] any securitization begins by identifying assets that can be used to raise funds. In the typical case, these assets are receivables that represent rights to payments at future dates. The types of receivables, and other cash flows, that have been and are being securitized is extensive and constantly expanding and includes residential mortgage loans, commercial mortgage loans, aircraft leases, rolling stock leases, automobile leases, other equipment leases, credit card receivables, patent

---

collects on the receivable. In a securitization transaction, a "Special Purpose Vehicle" is established and that Special Purpose Vehicle purchases the receivables and issues asset-backed securities based upon the receivables. The Special Purpose Vehicle relies upon the quality of the receivables (and the statistical construction of the pool of receivables, among other factors) to reduce risk, rather than on its ability to collect on those receivables.

[6] This essay provides only a general description of some of the more important and generic aspects of securitization. The securitization markets are now highly developed and sophisticated markets and there are a myriad of structures used for different types of securitizations. None of those more sophisticated structures is discussed in this essay. Similarly, this essay does not consider many of the essential features and considerations relating to even a relatively simple securitization, such as overcapitalization of the conduit special purpose entities, credit and liquidity enhancements, capitalization, or tax and accounting rules applicable to different types of single-seller conduit and multiple seller conduit securitizations. For an interesting comparison of the earliest securitizations with more recent securitization trends, compare *The Handbook of Mortgage-Backed Securities,* Frank J. Fabozzi, ed. (1985) (hereafter "Fabozzi 1985"), with the revised version of *The Handbook of Mortgage-Backed Securities*, Frank J. Fabozzi, ed. (2001).

payments, other intellectual property royalties, licensing fees and other payments, student loans, and virtually any other payment obligation.

In the securitization process, the owner of these rights to payments (the "Originator") transfers these assets to a newly-formed special purpose entity (for example, a corporation, trust, or other legal entity) (the "Special Purpose Vehicle"). This transfer must constitute a "true sale" under relevant bankruptcy laws, meaning that the sale is sufficient under those bankruptcy laws to remove the receivables from the bankruptcy estate of the Originator, and that the transaction does not constitute a secured loan from the Special Purpose Vehicle to the Originator.[7] This true sale has the important effect of separating the receivables, and the risks associated with payment on those receivables, from the risks associated with the Originator.

The Special Purpose Vehicle raises the funds to purchase the receivables by issuing securities (the "SPV Securities") in the capital markets. In transactions that are not compliant with the *shari'a*, these securities are usually debt or debt-like instruments, although some transactions involve equity instruments.[8] In the case of a *shari'a*-compliant transaction, there is issuance of a *sukuk* as a type of participation in the ownership of the assets that are the subject of the underlying *ijara* or other *shari'a*-compliant obligation.[9] The interest rate or payment rate on the SPV Securities is less than the cost of funds that would be applicable to securities issued by the Originator due to elimination from the transaction of risks associated with the Originator (including the risk of the bankruptcy of the Originator).[10] Payments in respect of the SPV Securities are made

[7] *See, e.g.*, 11 U.S.C. § 541 with respect to the bankruptcy laws of the United States of America.

[8] In contemporary sophisticated securitization transactions, the range of the different types of SPV Securities is broad and covers short-term, medium-term, and long-term instruments, including commercial paper and a broad range of different types of notes, as well as equity instruments.

[9] A *sukuk* has many similarities to a "pass through certificate" in the non-Islamic capital markets, although most pass through certificates do not represent interests in *shari'a*-compliant assets or receivables pertaining to *shari'a*-compliant assets. *See, e.g.*, Fabozzi 1985, pages 101-147 discussing mortgage pass through certificates in the early years of securitizations.

[10] Unless otherwise noted, this essay assumes (a) that the SPV Securities will not be "pass through certificates" or similar securities that are structured so that the holder of the SPV Securities owns a fractional undivided interest in the individual or pooled receivables and all of the payments in respect of the receivables are passed through to the holder of the SPV Securities, and (b) that the yield on the SPV Securities is established as a designated rate of interest or profit. The pass through structure, and variations on that structure, are akin to *sukuk* structures in which the holder of the *sukuk* owns a fractional undivided interest in the assets which have been leased to end users pursuant to different *ijara* arrangements that provide the receivable for payment of the *sukuk*.

exclusively from the cash flows of the receivables that are the subject of the transaction.[11]

The Special Purpose Vehicle must be structured to be "bankruptcy remote," particularly if the securities issued by the Special Purpose Vehicle are to be rated by any of the primary "rating agencies."[12] Bankruptcy remoteness in this context means that the Special Purpose Vehicle is unlikely to be adversely affected by a bankruptcy of the Originator. Bankruptcy remoteness is achieved by (a) strictly limiting the permitted business activities of the Special Purpose Vehicle, (b) isolating the management and operations of the Special Purpose Vehicle from those of other entities (particularly the Originator), (c) requiring the Special Purpose Vehicle to observe third party formalities with entities with whom it conducts business (particularly the Originator), and (d) otherwise maintaining operational and management independence. The foregoing types of provisions reduce the risk that the bankrupt Originator will cause the Special Purpose Vehicle to file for bankruptcy and the risk that a bankruptcy court, in the exercise of its equitable powers, will substantively consolidate the assets and liabilities of the Special Purpose Vehicle with those of the Originator.

THE SOUTH KOREAN SECURITIZATION CASE STUDY

Facts, Overall Transaction, Compulsory Considerations, Assumptions

The reason for considering the Securitized Acquisition Financing Transaction is that an investor (the "*Shari'a*-Compliant Investor") desires to participate in the Securitized Acquisition Financing Transaction and desires that its participation be compliant with the *shari'a*. It is assumed for purposes of this essay that the *Shari'a*-Compliant Investor desires to achieve a specific internal rate of return (the "Target IRR") on its investment and is willing to participate at a level of risk that is generally associated with equity capital investments. It is further assumed that the *Shari'a*-Compliant Investor is willing to forgo returns in excess of the Target IRR.[13]

---

[11] Note, however, that SPV Securities may bear credit enhancements, such as guarantees and insurance, and payments might then be made from the proceeds of the credit enhancement device.

[12] The most well-known "rating agencies" are Standard & Poor's Ratings Group, Moody's Investors Services, Inc., Duff and Phelps, and Fitch Investors Service, Inc.

[13] These assumptions regarding the Target IRR and returns in excess of the Target IRR are consistent with the position of the actual *Shari'a*-Compliant Investor in the transaction that forms the basis for the case study discussed in this essay. However,

The Securitized Acquisition Finance Transaction involves the acquisition by a South Korean special purpose entity (the "Project Owner")[14] of a commercial office property in South Korea, including a large tract of land and multiple office buildings (the "Project"). The acquisition occurs pursuant to a property sale and purchase agreement (the "Property Sale Agreement") between the Project Owner and the seller of the Project (the "Seller"). Pursuant to the Property Sale Agreement, the Seller conveys its fee interest in the Project to the Project Owner and the Project Owner pays the Seller the agreed price for the Project (the "Acquisition Price").

At the time of the acquisition of the Project, the Project is leased to a number of different commercial enterprises (the "End User Tenants"), which occupy the buildings pursuant to end user tenant leases of various terms, including long-term end user tenant leases (the "End User Leases"). A significant number of the End User Tenants do not conduct business in compliance with the *shari'a.* These include a conventional insurance company and a capital company that makes interest-bearing loans. The acquisition of the Project is made subject to the End User Leases. Periodic rents under the End User Leases (the "Rent") are payable by the End User Tenants to the Project Owner.

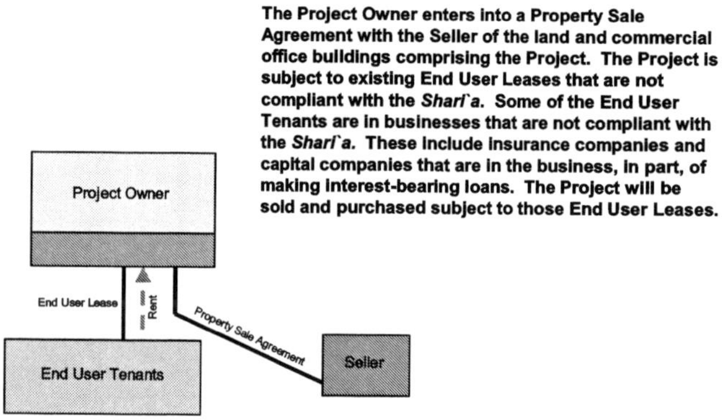

Figure 4. Purchase of the Project Subject to Non-Conforming End User Leases

---

that actual *Shari'a*-Compliant Investor was also willing to invest on a "pure equity" basis, with all attendant equity risks and rewards, including entitlement to returns in excess of the Target IRR. The structure that was developed for the transaction and that is discussed in this essay allowed for either type of participation by the *Shari'a*-Compliant Investor.

[14] The special purpose entity will have no assets other than the Project.

The primary source of financing for acquisition of the Project in the Securitized Acquisition Financing Transaction is (and must be) conventional interest-bearing debt in accordance with the South Korean securitization laws. In summary, the relevant provisions of the South Korean securitization laws require a bond financing structure comprised of two tranches of bonds: senior secured bonds and junior bonds. The senior secured bonds (the "Senior Bonds") are issued to the banks and other financial institutions providing interest-based acquisition financing for the transaction (collectively, the "Senior Bond Holder"). The Senior Bond Holder provides an amount of financing (say, 70 percent of the purchase price of the Project) as agreed between the Senior Bond Holder and the other parties on negotiated terms that are customary for a transaction of this type (the "Senior Bond Amount"). Those terms include a first mortgage on the Project to secure amounts payable under the Senior Bonds.[15] The Senior Bonds bear interest at either a fixed rate or a variable rate and are otherwise on customary terms for transactions of this type that are not compliant with the *shari'a*.

The second tranche of bonds that must be issued pursuant to the South Korean securitization laws are the junior bonds (the "Junior Bonds"), which are issued to the entity providing the junior financing amount (the "Residual Interest Purchaser"). The Junior Bonds issued to the Residual Interest Purchaser are "subordinated" bonds and are issued in an amount that is approximately equal to the excess of the purchase price of the Project over the Senior Bond Amount (the "Junior Bond Amount").[16] There is some flexibility as to the structuring of the payments on the Junior Bonds. Basically, however, the payments on the Junior Bonds are equal to all amounts of the Rent remaining after payment of operating costs in respect of the Project, funding of appropriate reserves (such as maintenance, capital improvement, working capital, tax, insurance, and debt service reserves),

---

[15] The mortgage and other security documents securing the Senior Bonds are not discussed in this essay and are not shown on the accompanying slides.

[16] The Junior Bond Amount will usually be greater than the amount of the excess of the Acquisition Price over the Senior Bond Amount so as to provide for other deposits, payments, and reserves. Such other deposits, payments, and reserves may include (a) payment of transaction costs, (b) provision of working capital, (c) initial funding of reserves (such as maintenance reserves, capital improvement reserves, tax reserves, insurance reserves, and debt service reserves), and (d) provision for certain other identifiable future payments. These deposits, payments, and reserves will be determined and negotiated on a case-by-case, transaction-by-transaction basis. In addition, the structuring of the transaction in accordance with applicable laws, particularly applicable tax laws in a number of different jurisdictions, may have the effect of reducing the Junior Bond Amount. *See* the section of this essay entitled "Economics and Pricing."

and payment of the Senior Bonds.[17] The "subordination" is such that failure to pay the Junior Bonds will not result in a default and the Junior Bonds will not have a liquidation preference for a specified sum. The Junior Bonds bear interest at a fixed rate or a variable rate, although payment of principal and interest on the Junior Bonds will be made only after payment of scheduled principal and interest on the Senior Bonds, and payments on the Junior Bonds will be made only out of free cash flow after other required payments, including payments on the Senior Bonds. The Junior Bonds may be secured by a subordinate mortgage on the Project.[18]

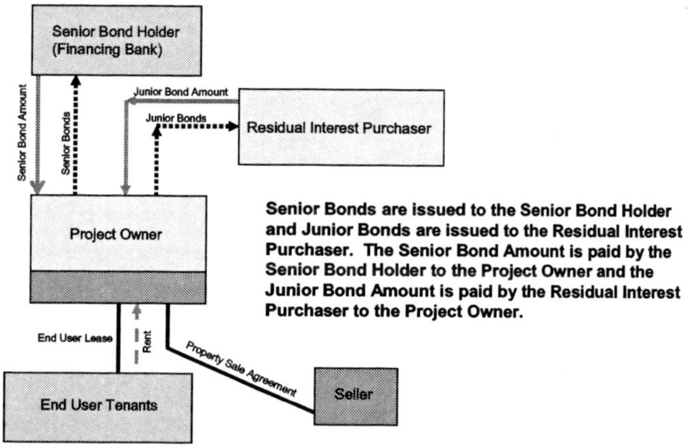

Figure 5. South Korean Securitization Requirements of Senior Bonds and Junior Bonds

The Senior Bond Holder pays the Senior Bond Amount to the Project Owner and receives the Senior Bonds from the Project Owner. The Residual Interest Purchaser pays the Junior Bond Amount to the Project Owner and receives the Junior Bonds from the Project Owner. The sum of

[17] As an example of a structural variation, there may be an equity entity, in addition to the Senior Bond Holder and the Residual Interest Purchaser, that receives pure equity payments after the making of all payments in respect of the Senior Bonds and the Junior Bonds. That variation is not presented in this essay. This essay assumes that the Residual Interest Purchaser, as the holder of the Junior Bonds, will receive all amounts remaining in the Project Owner after payment of the Senior Bonds (and after payment of operating costs and funding of reserves). Thus, the Junior Bonds effectively constitute pure equity for purposes of this transaction. These assumptions are in accordance with the structure of the actual transaction that forms the basis of this case study.

[18] The mortgage and other security documents securing the Junior Bonds are not discussed in this essay.

the Senior Bond Amount and the Junior Bond Amount[19] is paid by the Project Owner to the Seller as the Acquisition Price, and the ownership of the Project will be transferred by the Seller to the Project Owner.[20]

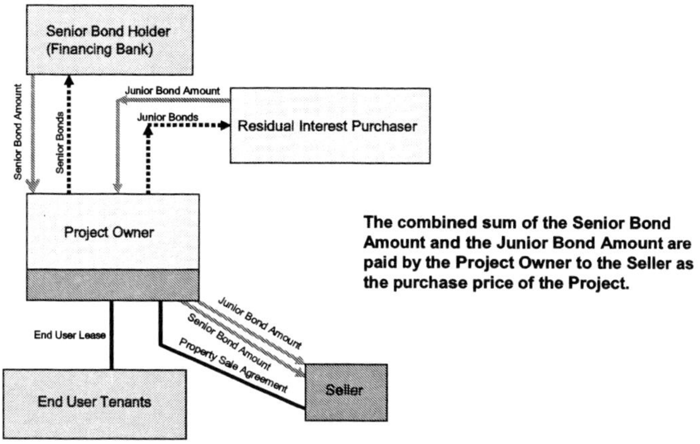

Figure 6. Payment of the Purchase Price for the Project

Upon receipt of the Rent, the Project Owner (a) pays operating expenses in respect of the Project, (b) funds appropriate reserves in respect of the Project, (c) makes periodic payments to the Senior Bond Holder in respect of the Senior Bonds, and (d) makes payments to the Residual Interest Purchaser in respect of the Junior Bonds. Customarily, payments are made in the order set forth in the preceding sentence. In all cases, payment in full of scheduled principal and interest is made on the Senior Bonds prior to the making of any payments in respect of the Junior Bonds.[21]

[19] Less the amounts referred to in footnotes 15 and 21.
[20] *But see* the section of this essay entitled "Economics and Pricing."
[21] The nature of the operating payments, deposits, and reserves, and the order in which each is made or funded, varies from transaction to transaction and is heavily negotiated in every transaction. For example, there may be maintenance reserves, capital improvement reserves, working capital reserves, tax reserves, insurance reserves, debt service reserves in respect of the Senior Bonds, and a wide range of other reserve accounts and categories. The parties will negotiate the amount and timing of deposits to each of the reserve accounts. Similarly, the parties will negotiate the order in which operating expense payments are made and the order, relative to all other deposits and payments, in which payments are made in respect of the Senior Bonds. These parameters, including the amounts and order of deposit and payment, will be set forth in the documents in a series of provisions (collectively often referred to as the "cashcade" or "waterfall") that may vary

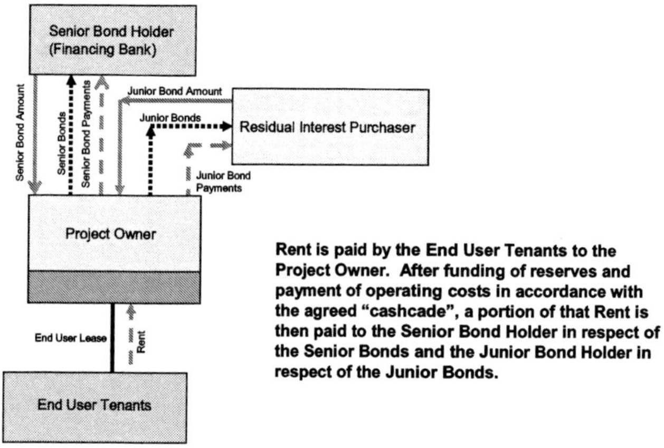

Figure 7. Payment of Senior Bonds and Junior Bonds

For purposes of this essay, except as otherwise noted, it is assumed that the equity in the Project Company is held by the Residual Interest Purchaser and that the equity in the Residual Interest Purchaser is held by a third party that is unrelated to the *Shari'a*-Compliant Investor (the "Ultimate Tax Owner").[22]

This essay also assumes that the End User Lease is a "true lease" and that the tax benefits of ownership of the Project flow through the ownership chain from the Project Company to the Residual Interest Purchaser to the Ultimate Tax Owner. Although the tax ownership and true lease laws and regulations vary from country to country, for convenience this essay assumes that true lease characterization is obtained based upon criteria that are applicable in the United States of America under Revenue Procedure 75-21 and related revenue rulings and revenue procedures[23] and that

---

depending upon the financial strength of the Project and the absence or existence of an event of default (as well as other factors).

[22] The Ultimate Tax Owner is not shown on the diagrams included in this essay. Although not discussed in this essay, the structure that was developed for the Securitized Acquisition Financing Transaction can also be used where this ownership assumption is not true and there is either joint ownership of the Project Company by another third party entity as well as the Residual Interest Purchaser or exclusive ownership by such a third party; in each such case there will be modifications to the economics and pricing of the Junior Bonds, the purchase of the residual interest, and the sale of the shares in the Investor Entity.

[23] Revenue Procedure 75-21 (1975), Internal Revenue Service of the United States of America Department of the Treasury ("Rev. Proc. 75-21"). *See also* Revenue Procedure 75-28, which elaborated on the guidelines set forth in Rev. Proc. 75-21

allowable depreciation is substantially the same as that permitted under applicable laws and regulations of the United States of America.[24] Thus, for example, it is assumed that (a) the Project Company, as the lessor, will maintain a 20 percent minimum at-risk equity investment throughout the lease term of the End User Lease, (b) the residual value of the Project (comprising the value of the residual interest) at the end of the term of the End User Lease will be at least equal to 20 percent of the original cost of the Project, without regard to inflation or deflation, and (c) the remaining useful life of the Project at the end of the term of the End User Lease will be at least 20 percent of the estimated useful life of the Project.[25] These assumptions, which are substantially in accord with the facts of the South Korean transaction, are critical to, and essential constraints upon, structuring the economics and pricing arrangements of, and contractual arrangements for, the structure that was developed to allow participation by a *Shari'a*-Compliant Investor.

---

and certain filing information requirements, Revenue Procedure 76-30 (1976), which addressed the definition of "limited use property," and Revenue Procedure 79-48, which addresses certain lessee-funded improvements to leased property. Revenue Ruling 55-540 (1955-2 Cumulative Bulletin 39), although superseded in substantial part by Rev. Proc. 75-21, is useful for an historical understanding of factors that may indicate that a transaction is a conditional sale rather than a true lease.

[24] For example, the essay assumes that, for depreciation purposes, the buildings constituting real property will be depreciable over 30 years on a straight-line basis and that certain other property constituting portions of the Project will be depreciable over other, sometimes much shorter, periods on different accelerated depreciation formulas. This essay assumes that a qualified consultant will determine the applicable depreciation class and methodology for each asset constituting a part of the Project, as is customarily done in transactions of this type.

[25] Rev. Proc. 75-21 and related Revenue Procedures address a number of other factors, of less importance to this essay, that relate to true lease characterization, including: (1) the definition of the term of the lease (here, the End User Lease) for purposes of determinations of true lease status; (2) fair market value lease renewal terms; (3) provision of the cost of the property by the lessee (the End User Tenant) and related parties; (4) prohibitions on the provision of debt financing by the lessee (the End User Tenant) and related parties to the lessor (the Project Company); (5) demonstrations of the likelihood of profit on the leasing transaction apart from tax benefits, including profits in respect of the residual interest or residual value of the property; (6) uneven rent considerations; (7) prohibitions on the inclusion of "limited use property" in true leases; (8) lessee financing of improvements; (9) residual interest or residual value sharing arrangements; and (9) the payment of transaction costs for true lease transactions.

Some Relevant Principles of Property, Property Interests, and Sales

Before considering the structure that will allow the *Shari'a*-Compliant Investor to make an investment in the Project in compliance with the *shari'a*, it is useful to examine a few secular and *shari'a* principles and precepts that underlie the structure that was developed for the Securitized Acquisition Financing Transaction and then to summarize the application of those principles to the facts of the Securitized Acquisition Financing Transaction. Consideration is given to some principles applicable to the nature of property generally and then to the types of property interests affecting the sale and purchase transaction that is the basis for the Securitized Acquisition Financing Transaction and, thereafter, to the primary principles applicable to sales of property interests.

1. Property interests

Property of any type consists of the assets comprising the property (here, the land and the buildings). But that is not the end of the matter. The interests in that property must also be considered. There are "current interests" in property (such as current title to the property, leasehold interests in the property, easement interests in the property, and license interests in the property), and there are "residual interests" in property, or interests in property that relate to the future (such as title interests in the residual value or residual interest in the property that arise after the expiration of current interests in the property).

For purposes of the Securitized Acquisition Financing Transaction and this essay, ownership of property commences with only a current interest in existence. However, property rights are divisible and differentiable. Thus, the property rights may be differentiated into a current interest and a residual interest. Upon any such differentiation and thereafter until the current interest and the residual interest are again merged, there are two current property ownership interests in the Project: the "current interest," which is defined by reference to a then-current point in time, and the "residual interest," which is defined by reference to either a set of conditions or a specified point in time. At any given time, one person or entity may own the current use, while another person or entity may own the residual interest, or a single person or entity may own both the current interest and the residual interest. At such time as the residual interest commences, the current interest and the residual interest are merged and there is again only a current interest until such time as the property interests are again differentiated.

Distinct from then-current ownership rights in the Project at any specific date are rights to use the Project at that date and at various future dates. These interests of use may also be variable, with respect to any one person or entity, in each of the current interest and the residual interest. Thus, for example, prior to commencement of the residual interest period the owner of the residual interest may have certain limited current use rights relating to the land. These may include, for example, rights to protect the residual interest, such as the right to enter upon the property and inspect the same, and correct waste by the current user during the current interest period. But these would not include any other rights in respect of the land and buildings until such time as the residual interest period shall commence (and thus be merged with the then-current current interest). Thus, for example, prior to commencement of the residual interest period, the owner of the residual interest would not be entitled to till the land, or build upon the land, or modify the improvements, or destroy the buildings on the land, all of which rights will be exercisable only by the owner of the current interest until commencement of the residual interest period, whereupon the owner of the current interest prior to such commencement will lose the ability to exercise any such rights with respect to the land without further act or deed and the owner of the residual interest will acquire the exclusive ability to exercise all such rights without further act or deed.

At any time after the disassociation of the property interests into the "current interest" and the "residual interest" but prior to the time when the current interest is merged with the residual interest (*i.e.*, prior to the satisfaction of the conditions that render the residual interest current and thus cause commencement of the residual interest term), both the "current interest" and the "residual interest" are existent interests in property that can be separately owned and sold. A person or entity can irrevocably own and sell a current property interest that relates only to the future (*i.e.*, the residual interest). The disassociation of the current interest and the residual interest is accomplished pursuant to contract.

2. Secular legal principles

Secular legal principles take cognizance of the differentiation of current interests from residual interests in a wide range of contexts. One of the most familiar examples pertains to the residual value or remainder interest in equipment upon termination of an equipment lease. Similar examples with respect to land and other property interests include the recognition by tax law and other laws of residual interests in land or other property and the recognition of "charitable remainder" and similar "remainder" trusts and conveyances, including those upon which educational and other charitable institutions focus and depend. Another example relates to expropriation and condemnation. If there is total condemnation of property after the disassociation of the current interest from the residual interest prior to the merger and reassociation of those interests, the owner of the current interest and the owner of the residual interest would each be entitled to a portion of the condemnation award based upon the relative values of their interests.

As another example, contracts are often fashioned to allow a present conveyance and transfer of the current ownership of a future use of a property to a third party, with current rights of ownership and use being retained in a different party (say, for the life of the conveying party or for a term of years). There can be a present irrevocable sale and delivery (transfer and conveyance) of current ownership of future rights and interests in that property.[26] That is, the seller and the purchaser are permitted to enter into a valid and binding contract that is presently effective for the sale and purchase of property (such as real property) whereby the purchaser will have a present ownership interest in and of the residual interest in the property, and certain attendant rights, but will not be entitled to exercise all rights in respect of use of the property until a future date. The applicable contract may or may not contain a wide range of terms and conditions pertaining to, for example, (1) the present possession and use of the subject property, (2) allocations of obligations and liabilities in respect of the subject property, particularly upon the occurrence of different specified events and conditions (for example, environmental liabilities arising prior to the transfer of possession to the residual owner), and (3) adjustments to the pricing or other terms and conditions of the sale and transfer upon the occurrence of specified events (for example, a partial or total condemnation or other taking by a governmental authority prior to such transfer of possession to the residual owner).

The object of a sale and purchase *(bay')* is to transfer ownership of the property being sold and purchased to the purchaser and to transfer ownership of the purchase price to the seller. And rights of use may be differentiated from rights of ownership. The critical considerations for purposes of this essay relate to (a) the transfer of ownership of the relevant property and property right (the residual interest in the Project) to the purchaser at the time of entering into the contract with the ability to exercise the right to use the Project not being exercisable by the purchaser until some future time, and (b) the payment of the purchase price on an installment basis.

---

[26] Any such sale, transfer, and conveyance must meet applicable legal requirements pertaining to the validity of the transaction and the applicable contract. Thus, for example, the transaction and related contract cannot be in violation of public policy and must comply with requisite formalities. It is assumed for purposes of this essay that all such requirements are met and that the transaction is legally permissible. A discussion of those requirements and formalities is beyond the scope of this essay.

3. Shari'a principles

A brief overview of some of the *shari'a* principles and precepts[27] applicable to sales of the types contemplated by this essay provides context for the discussion of the development of the structure for the Securitized Acquisition Financing Transaction. In order to have a valid sale and purchase under the *shari'a,* the property must be in existence, be capable of delivery *(taslim),* have specific value, be known to the purchaser, and be precisely described and defined.[28] Sales may be made subject to conditions, and those conditions may be established by the parties at the time of the making of the contract of sale.[29]

While the *Majelle* does not specifically address the sale of a residual interest (at least in those terms), it does express address the sale (and resale) of fractional undivided interests in real property[30] and it does address the sale of easements, rights of way and rights relating to the use of land and assets on or under real property (such as water).[31] In the case of the sale and purchase of real property, the purchaser can sell such real property to

---

[27] While it does not constitute definitive substantive law and does not take into account variations among the different schools of Islamic jurisprudence with respect to any specific principle or precept, for convenience this essay makes reference to the English language translation of the *Majallat Al-Akham Al-`Adliyya* made by Judge C. A. Hooper, *The Civil Law of Palestine and Trans-Jordan,* Volumes I & II (1933), reprinted in 4 *Arab Law Quarterly* (August 1986) (the "*Majelle*"), as illustrative of applicable *shari'a* principles and precepts. Reference is also made to Financial Transactions in Islamic Jurisprudence, Wahban Al-Zuhayli's Al-Fiqh Al-Islami wa 'Adillatuh (Islamic Jurisprudence and its Proofs), translated by Mahmoud A. El-Gammal (2003) ("*Al-Zuhayli –El-Gamal*"), which is a translation of Volume 5 of Al-*Fiqh* Al-'Islami wa 'Adillatuh, fourth edition (Damascus 1997) and appears in two volumes.

[28] *Mejelle,* Articles 197 – 200, 205, 209, 221 and 363; Al-Zuhayli – El-Gamal, Volume I, Chapters 1 – 4, pages 5–163. *See, also, Majelle,* Articles 230 – 236 in respect of appurtenances, fixtures, and items of property, including fruits of, or increases in, the property prior to delivery of the property.

[29] *Mejelle,* Articles 186 – 189.

[30] *Majelle,* Articles 214 and 215. Article 214 indicates that the "sale of an ascertained, jointly owned undivided share in a piece of real property owned in absolute ownership prior to division, ... is valid*."* Article 215 provides that a person "may sell his undivided jointly owned share to some other person without obtaining the permission of his partner," although various *shari'a* scholars, in discussions with the author, have indicated that contractual provisions may be used to introduce the concept of partner consent to this type of arrangement.

[31] *Majelle,* Article 216, which states: "The sale of a right of way, and the right of taking water and of a right of flow attached to land and of water attached to canals[,] is valid."

another person or entity before taking possession of such real property (although the same rule is not applicable to movable property).[32]

The price for the property to be sold and purchased must be established at the time of the making of the contract of sale and must be ascertained.[33] A valid sale may be concluded in which payment of the price is deferred and is made in installments and, in such a case, the period of installment payment must be definitely ascertained and fixed.[34] Unless the parties otherwise agree, and the parties may otherwise agree (as in an installment sale transaction), the purchaser must deliver the purchase price to the seller before the seller is obligated to deliver the property to the purchaser.[35] A seller of property has the right to dispose of the purchase price for such property prior to receiving the same, as where the purchase price is assigned to a creditor.[36] A concomitant, and broader, principle is that the taking of delivery of the purchased property is not an essential condition of sale.[37]

In many instances, the seller of property has a right of retention of the property until receipt of payment in full where the sale is structured to be for immediate payment in full.[38] There is no right of retention in the seller if the transaction is a sale on credit, in which case the property subject to the sale must be delivered immediately to the purchaser.[39] Notably, however, there is no right of the seller to withhold or retain where payment of the purchase price is agreed to be on an installment sale basis as the seller in such a transaction has voluntarily agreed otherwise, and the right to

---

32 *Majelle,* Article 253; Al-Zuhayli – El-Gamal, Volume 1, § 3.2.2, at pages 56 and 60-61 (noting also that not all *shari'a* scholars are in agreement that the real property may be sold by the purchaser before receipt).

33 *Majelle*, Articles 237 and 238.

34 *Majelle*, Articles 245 – 250; Al-Zuhayli – El-Gamal, Volume 1, § 3.2.1, at page 53, § 3.2.2, at page 63 (citing Al-Sarakhsi (1st edition) ((Hanafi), vol. 13, p. 192), Al-Kasani (Hanafi), vol. 5, p. 244, 'Ibn Al-Humam ((Hanafi), vol. 5, p. 109), and 'Ibn 'Abidin ((Hanafi), vol. 4, p. 43 onwards, and noting that the seller has voluntarily forfeited its right to withhold in an agreed installment sale transaction), and § 4.3.9, at pages 119-120 (noting that all four major schools of Islamic jurisprudence consider the installment sale a valid sale arrangement).

35 Al-Zuhayli – El-Gamal, Volume 1, § 3.2.2, at page 57.

36 *Majelle*, Article 252; Al-Zuhayli – El-Gamal, Volume 1, § 3.2.2, at pages 56 and 61-62.

37 *Majelle*, Article 262.

38 *Majelle*, Article 278, which states the rule for transactions of sale for immediate payment. The right of retention may be lost in various circumstances, including where the seller gives delivery without having received the purchase price or where the seller postpones payment of the price after having sold for immediate payment. *See, e.g., Majelle*, Articles 281 and 284, respectively. *See, also*, Al-Zuhayli – El-Gamal, Volume 1, § 3.2.2, at pages 64-66.

39 *Majelle*, Article 284; Al-Zuhayli – El-Gamal, Volume 1, § 3.2.2.

withhold or retain is voided by the deferral of the payment of the purchase price.[40]

Various types of options *(khiyarat)* are permitted under the *shari'a*, and these options may allow cancellation or ratification of the relevant contract and related transaction.[41] These include, among others, options in respect of: (1) misdescriptions,[42] (2) selection of property,[43] (3) inspection *(al-ru'ya)*,[44] (4) defects,[45] and (5) payment (including installment payments).[46]

Agreements in respect of sales for immediate payment are concluded by offer and acceptance in the same manner as other agreements for sales, and require that there be a statement as to a determinable quality and quantity.[47] An essential element to the validity of such a sale agreement is that there be immediate payment at the time of the making of such agreement.[48]

Delivery, for purposes of the *shari'a*, relates to the removal of obstacles by the seller between the purchaser and the object of the sale (the property), allowing the purchaser to take ownership and control of the object.[49] As a general matter, the purchaser must have full access to or possession of the property with the full permission of the seller under applicable Hanafi, Maliki, and Shafi'i rules, while the Hanbali school is of

---

[40] Al-Zuhayli – El-Gamal, Volume 1, § 3.2.2, at page 64, noting that the Hanbali school is of the position that the seller must deliver the property prior to receipt of the purchase price in all cases, including installment sale transactions.

[41] *Majelle*, Article 300; Al-Zuhayli – El-Gamal, Volume 1, chapter 5, at pages 165-231, which discusses the various types of options recognized by each of the four major schools of Islamic jurisprudence (seventeen by the Hanafis, two by the Malikis, sixteen by the Shafi'is, and eight by the Hanbalis). The options must be exercised within a defined time period. *See*, *Majelle*, Articles 301 – 309.

[42] *Majelle*, Articles 310 – 312. *See, also*, *Majelle*, Articles 356 – 360 in respect of misrepresentation and deceit.

[43] *Majelle*, Articles 316 – 317.

[44] *Majelle*, Articles 320 – 335.

[45] *Majelle*, Articles 336 – 355.

[46] *Majelle*, Articles 313 – 315.

[47] *Majelle*, Articles 380 – 387.

[48] *Majelle*, Article 387.

[49] Al-Zuhayli – El-Gamal, Volume 1, § 3.2.2, at pages 66-70. This discussion notes that "if a person purchases wheat in a house, and the seller gives him the key to the house saying: 'I have given you full access and permission to take the object of sale', then the buyer would have received the object of sale" (pages 66-67), and, in footnote 44, noting that giving full access and permission to the buyer is receipt by the buyer even if the buyer did not literally receive the property. This discussion notes a similar position by the Malikis and the Shafi'is with respect to access and permission, stating that delivery of the keys would constitute access and permission. The Hanbali position, as summarized in that same work, is that possession is determined by the nature of the property. With respect to the Hanbali position in the Kingdom of Saudi Arabia, see McMillen 2001.

the position that the taking of possession is determined in accordance with the nature of the property being sold and purchased.

Residual Interests and *Shari'a* Determinations in the Case Study

In the Securitized Acquisition Financing Transaction, the set of conditions, and time, at which the residual interest becomes the current interest is defined as (a) the payment in full of the Senior Bonds, (b) the payment in full of the Junior Bonds, and (c) the termination of the End User Lease (the date on which such occupational use may commence, the "Commencement of Residual Use").[50]

The deed of transfer is executed (and recorded) at the present, thus effecting the transfer at the present time, although use is delayed until a specified further time. In the South Korean transaction, as in most transactions, there is significant value to the residual interest: the land is located in a desirable prime location and the End User Lease will terminate in all cases prior to the last day of the useful life of the buildings (and certainly prior to the end of the useful life of the land).

Considering the relevant *shari'a* principles and precepts, the object of the sale (the Project, consisting of the land and buildings) is currently in existence and will be in existence at the Commencement of Residual Use, it has determinable value, it is known to the purchaser, and it otherwise meets the relevant *shari'a* requirements for a valid contract of sale and purchase.[51]

---

[50] The residual interest itself exists at the time the contract of purchase and sale is made and at the time of the transfer of the ownership of the residual interest; it has value at the time of the making of such contract and thereafter. Thus, at the time of "delivery" (see the further discussion in this section) of the residual interest to the purchaser (which is in the present, at the time of the making of the contract and the execution of the related deed) and thereafter, all benefits appertaining to the residual interest will be for the account of the purchaser.

[51] Absent a total condemnation and taking, which is addressed in the relevant contracts, the land will be in existence at the Commencement of Residual Use. The building may not be in existence, or may be in existence in modified form at the Commencement of Residual Use. If the relevant contract of sale and purchase is otherwise drafted in accordance with the *shari'a* (for example, with respect to maintenance requirements, delineation of property elements constituting the Project and allocation of price to each of such elements, and adjustments to be made to the purchase price in respect of loss, damage, and destruction depending upon causation, compensation, and other relevant factors), the purchase price in an installment sale would be appropriately adjusted in accordance with the assets in existence, and the condition of such assets, at the time of Commencement of Residual Use. The parties would agree on the relevant risk allocation provisions, consistent with the *shari'a*, in the contract of sale and purchase.

Shari'a scholars who were consulted in connection with the Securitized Acquisition Financing Transaction, and other *shari'a* scholars with whom the author has discussed this transaction and other transactions of this type, have indicated that *shari'a* principles applicable to undivided interests and divisible rights in real property would be applicable to the concept of a residual interest in real property and that the concept of a "residual interest" is valid under the *shari'a*. Those scholars have also indicated that *shari'a* principles and precepts applicable to sales generally would be applicable to permit a binding present sale of the entirety of the Project (land and buildings) with delivery of possession and use at a future date.

Delivery of the present residual interest in the Project occurs at the time of the execution of the contract of sale and purchase and the related deed. The purchaser will then have full possession and use of the residual interest, although the purchaser will not have the right to occupational use of the Project until Commencement of Residual Use. The purchaser will be entitled to all value appertaining to the residual interest, and benefits therefrom, and will have all discretionary rights and all burdens with respect to the residual interest from the time of execution of the contract of sale and purchase and the conveyance of the deed. Thus, for *shari'a* purposes (as well as secular purposes) the "key" to the residual interest in the Project will have been delivered at the time of conveyance of the deed even though occupational use will be delayed until Commencement of Residual Use. Thus, for example, if there were a permanent condemnation or taking of the Project after the date of the contract or sale and purchase but prior to the Commencement of Residual Use, the seller would be entitled to compensation for the value of the Project prior to the Commencement of Residual Use, and the purchaser would be entitled to compensation for the value of the Project on and after the Commencement of Residual Use. Similarly, by way of another example, absent contractual limitations the purchaser would be entitled to use the residual interest as collateral for a financing or other obligations and would be exclusively entitled to grant a *rahn* (mortgage or pledge) on the residual interest.

The price for the purchase and sale is established at the time of the execution of the contract for purchase and sale of the Project and is payable in periodic installments during the period from the making of the contract to and including the Commencement of Residual Use. The seller is entitled to use the purchase price payments in its discretion in accordance with the *shari'a*. The payment provisions are structured in accordance with the *shari'a*, including with respect to individualization of the descriptions of the assets comprising the Project, allocation of the purchase price to the various assets, and adjustments to the purchase price in respect of various types of loss, damage, and destruction to those assets. There are also terms with respect to use of the Project during the period prior to the Commencement of Residual Use, including maintenance provisions.

Purchase of the Residual Interest

Returning to a description of the Securitized Acquisition Financing Transaction, the *Shari'a*-Compliant Investor desires to make an investment in the Project. For purposes of the transaction, the *Shari'a*-Compliant Investor will establish a wholly-owned special purpose entity (the "Intermediate Investor Entity") which, in turn, will own all of the equity in another special purpose entity (the "Investor Entity").[52] Pursuant to a residual interest sale and purchase agreement and related agreements, documents, and instruments, including a deed (the "Residual Interest Purchase Agreement"), the Investor Entity acquires all of the residual interest in the Project (the "Residual Interest") from the Project Owner for an agreed purchase price (the "Residual Interest Purchase Price"). The Residual Interest Purchase Price will be established on the basis of the current value of the Residual Interest.[53]

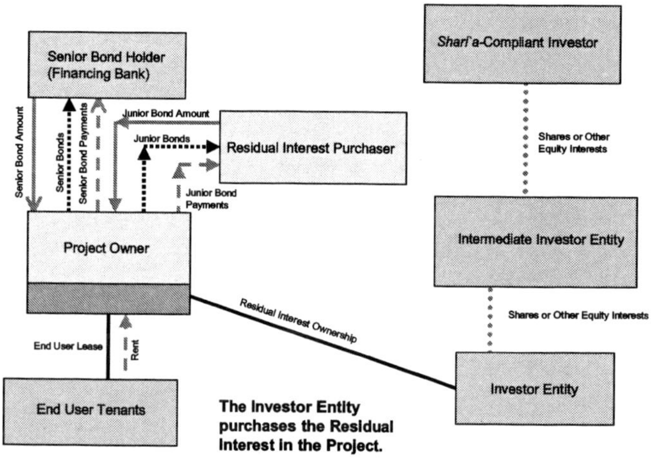

Figure 8. Purchase of the Residual Interest

---

[52] The use of both the Intermediate Investor Entity and the Investor Entity is frequently necessitated by applicable real estate laws (including laws pertaining to foreign ownership of real property in a given country), tax laws (including those pertaining to taxation of interests in real property, those pertaining to taxation of sales of stock, and those pertaining to the ability to make payments to offshore entities with the minimum amount of taxation), and other applicable laws.

[53] See the section of this essay entitled "Economics and Pricing."

Sale of Shares in the Investor Entity

After the Investor Entity has acquired the Residual Interest, the Intermediate Investor Entity enters into an equity interest sale and purchase agreement with the Residual Interest Purchaser (the "Equity Interest Sale Agreement"). Pursuant to the Equity Interest Sale Agreement, all of the shares *(hissas)* representing ownership in the Investor Entity are sold to the Residual Interest Purchaser on a deferred purchase basis. The purchase price for these shares (the "Hissa Purchase Price") is determined by reference to the anticipated value of the Residual Interest.[54]

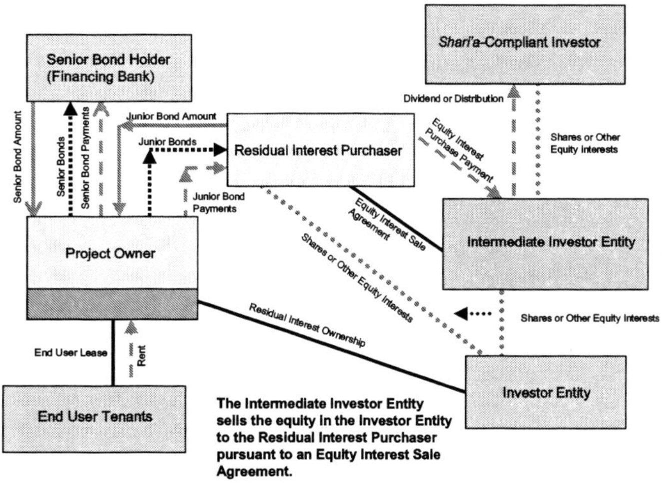

Figure 9. Sale of Residual Interest

Economics and Pricing

The foregoing structural elements allow the *Shari'a*-Compliant Investor to achieve participation in the Project by virtue of the purchase and sale of the residual interest. The exact manner in which the economics and pricing of the component transactions are achieved for the *Shari'a*-Compliant Investor will depend upon many factors and varies from jurisdiction to jurisdiction, and from transaction to transaction, and is subject to complicated economic and pricing determinations based upon the existing facts. Matters in respect of the primary component transactions that

[54] Ibid.

are subject to economic and pricing factors are: (a) establishing the absolute amount of the Junior Amount at the inception of the transaction; (b) establishing the structure, terms, and tenor of the Junior Bonds, including the interest rates payable on the Junior Bonds; (c) establishing the purchase price for the residual interest at the time the residual interest is purchased by the Investor Entity from the Project Company; and (d) establishing the purchase price of the shares in the Investor Entity at the time that those shares are sold by the Intermediate Investor Entity to the Residual Interest Purchaser.[55]

A few examples of the factors affecting the economics and pricing of the component transactions will illustrate the complexity of structuring a transaction of this type.

In certain jurisdictions as a matter of law, and in certain transactions as a matter of business and political considerations, real estate interests (such as the residual interest) can be owned and held only by local (here, South Korean) entities and not by foreign entities. In any such circumstance, both the Investor Entity and the Residual Interest Purchaser will have to be established as local entities. Similarly, securitization, tax, collateral security, and other laws may require that the holder of Junior Bonds must be a local entity rather than a foreign entity.

Tax laws will affect the structuring at various points. Taxation and recordation requirements pertaining to interests in real property (such as the residual interests in the Project), particularly where those interests are held by a local (South Korean) entity may have a greater or lesser burden on the economics of the transaction from the vantage of the *Shari'a*-Compliant Investor than sales of shares in a local entity (such as the Investor Entity), particularly where the sale of the shares is made offshore. Other legal, business, and political considerations may make it more palatable to sell shares in the Investor Entity offshore rather than attempting to have an offshore entity purchase real estate interests (the residual interests in the Project). Tax (and other) laws applicable to offshore share sales to an onshore entity must be compared with tax (and other) laws applicable to purchases of onshore real estate interests by offshore entities and to sales of onshore real estate interests by an offshore entity to an onshore entity.

One of the most difficult aspects of a transaction such as the South Korean case study involves the determinations of (a) the economic

---

[55] There are other similar matters in respect of the component transactions that relate to "closing out" the overall transaction (*e.g.*, the sale of the residual interest, the shares in the Investor Entity, or the shares of the Project Company after the Commencement of Residual Use). *See* "Closing Out the Transaction." However, the structure was designed to ensure flexibility at the time of Commencement of Residual Use so that determinations and allocations made at the commencement of the financing transaction would not unduly restrict available alternatives at the time of Commencement of Residual Use. Thus, this essay does not focus on the economics and pricing of these "closing out" transactions.

contributions to be made by the Residual Interest Purchaser in respect of the Junior Amount, (b) the pricing of the sale and purchase by the residual interest in the Project by the Investor Entity, and (c) the pricing and sale of the shares by the Intermediate Investor Entity to the Residual Interest Purchaser. The sum total of the Junior Amount and the purchase price of the residual interest in the Project (the "Investor Total Contribution") is the total investment by the *Shari'a*-Compliant Investor.[56]

If the Senior Amount is a specified percentage of the purchase price for the Project that is paid to the Seller (say, 70 percent), there is a mandatory requirement as to the minimum amount of the Investor Total Contribution at the inception of the Project (*i.e.*, 30 percent). The *Shari'a*-Compliant Investor will be resistant to payment of more than the required minimum amount of the Total Investor Contribution as it will not desire to have excess capital in the transaction and an attendant diminution in the efficiency of the deployment of its capital. On the other hand, the concept of, and requirements pertaining to, the Junior Bonds will exert pressure on the structure to maximize the portion of the Investor Total Contribution that is contributed to the transaction through the Residual Interest Purchaser as a portion of the Junior Amount.

In a jurisdiction where it is possible to structure the Junior Bonds as an equity equivalent (*i.e.*, the Junior Bond payments are truly the excess of rent over (a) operating costs, (b) reserve fundings, and (c) Senior Bond payments), the pressure to contribute through the Residual Interest Holder as part of the Junior Amount is considerably alleviated. Further alleviation of the pressure to contribute through the Residual Interest Purchaser as part of the Junior Amount results from the fact that the Ultimate Tax Owner is entitled to depreciation, certain available tax credits, and possibly other tax incentives (collectively, "Depreciation and Tax Benefits"). To the extent that the Ultimate Tax Owner realizes depreciation and tax benefits, particularly in the early periods of the overall transaction, there is a greater amount of cash available to the Residual Interest Purchaser for payments in respect of the Share Sale Price.

Each of these considerations, in turn, allows significantly greater flexibility in structuring the transaction (1) to increase the amount paid by the Investor Entity in respect of the Residual Interest and (2) to increase the

---

[56] The *Shari'a*-Compliant Investor will have to fund the Junior Amount by getting money, directly or indirectly, into the Residual Interest Purchaser. The *Shari'a*-Compliant Investor may not hold an equity interest in the Residual Interest Purchaser because the Junior Bonds will bear a rate of interest and because the Residual Interest Purchaser will hold an actual or constructive equity interest in the Project Owner (the Project Owner will have non-conforming obligations on the Senior Bonds as well as the Junior Bonds and the Project Owner will be a party to a non-compliant End User Lease with an End User Tenant in a non-conforming business). A *qard hassan*, non-interest-bearing loan, from the *Shari'a*-Compliant Investor or the Intermediate Investor Entity is one alternative solution to this issue.

amount of the Share Sale Price payable by the Residual Interest Purchaser to the Intermediate Investor Entity in respect of the sale and purchase of the Investor Entity Shares. That increased flexibility, in turn, allows the transaction to be structured more precisely in accordance with the most beneficial interpretation and use of tax laws (including differentials between tax laws applicable to real estate and share sales) and other applicable laws.

Closing Out the Transaction

As final steps in the overall transaction, the structure must consider how the transaction might proceed on and after the Commencement of Residual Use. At such time, by definition, the Senior Bonds will have been paid in full, the End User Leases with the non-conforming End User Tenants will have terminated, and, if the Junior Bonds are not pure equity for *shari'a* purposes, the Junior Bonds will have been paid in full. The structure of the Securitized Acquisition Financing Transaction allows for a number of alternatives on and after Commencement of Residual Use. First, the End User Leases can be structured as leases that conform with the *shari'a* and End User Tenants that operate in accordance with the *shari'a* can be obtained. This will allow for restructuring of the transaction to allow direct ownership of the Project Owner by or on behalf of the *Shari'a*-Compliant Investor. If the *Shari'a*-Compliant Investor desires to own and hold the Project, the Residual Interest can be sold directly to the *Shari'a*-Compliant Investor (directly or indirectly by sale to the Intermediate Investor Entity or the Investor Entity). Alternatively, various share ownership transfers are available for consideration, including a transfer of the shares in the Investor Entity to the *Shari'a*-Compliant Investor or one or more of its affiliates. The various possibilities can be structured into the relevant documentation at the beginning of the transaction, allowing the *Shari'a*-Compliant Investor, directly or indirectly, to choose that alternative or set of alternatives that is most advantageous (including in respect of taxation) at the time of effectuation of the various transfers.

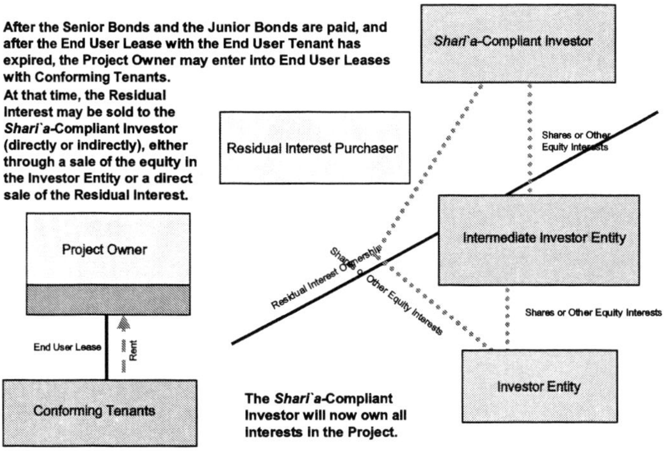

Figure 10. Conforming Tenant and Sale of the Project

STRUCTURING FROM FIRST PRINCIPLES

To the date of this essay, the application of securitization concepts in Islamic finance has been through the use of *sukuk* structures. As noted in this essay, the *sukuk* structures are akin to "pass through" asset-backed securities in the conventional markets in that they focus on fractional undivided ownership of assets and current cash flows relating to the use of those assets. That focus seems to preclude *shari'a*-compliant securitizations in transactions involving interest-based financing. The great bulk of financings in the world, be they of real estate, equipment, intellectual property, or other assets, involve interest-based financing. The result may be that the Islamic financing industry will not be able to participate in the great bulk of financings in the world. And that is the proper result if participation in those financings cannot be effected in compliance with the *shari'a*.

Developments in thinking of *shari'a*-compliant uses of the *sukuk* have been gratifying and highly creative, even as embodied in the initial and elementary structures used to date. These developments give a glimpse of a bright future. Further thinking about the use of the *sukuk* structure will undoubtedly result in greater refinements and sophistication, coverage of a wider range of assets, and significant advances in the range of *shari'a*-compliant products. The *sukuk* structure should be, and will be, a primary focus of efforts in the Islamic finance industry for years to come.

But is the *sukuk* structure the only structure to be considered for approaching the concept of securitization? This essay takes the position that the *sukuk* is not the only structure to be considered in thinking about securitization.

This essay takes the position that the Islamic finance industry should reconsider the entirety of Islamic jurisprudence and the *shari'a* in considering the development of an Islamic economy constituted by a truly diversified range of product offerings. It is important to note what the term "reconsider" does not mean, as well as what it means. Reconsideration does not reject the traditional learning or experience or seek to modify that learning or experience. It means consider again, examine again, and entails a return to the historical learning rather than a rejection of that learning. It means that examination should proceed from well-established traditional and conventional *shari'a* principles, precepts, and concepts. It means a return in order to achieve a thorough understanding in the context of present circumstances. The examination should be based upon first principles that have long been accepted in Islamic jurisprudence and scholarship. Creative structuring should be based upon a sound historical and jurisprudential base. The scholarship and wisdom of our forefathers should weigh heavily in the analysis and the creative efforts of the present.

In the context of *shari'a*-compliant securitizations, this essay focuses on one small aspect of the broad spectrum of principles, precepts, and concepts that should be reconsidered, namely the nature and components of "property" and "assets." It challenges the Islamic finance industry to start with the basic questions relating to the nature of property and assets: What is "property"? What is an "asset"? How can the essential elements of property be reconfigured in the context of a sophisticated modern financing? How can the nominated contracts be applied to these traditional concepts in new ways?

Further, this essay is intended to challenge the conventional wisdom that it is not possible to effect *shari'a*-compliant securitizations if interest-based financing is present somewhere in the transaction. Careful structuring of *shari'a*-compliant transactions in other contexts has demonstrated that the presence of interest-based financing is not itself preclusive of involvement of devout Muslim investors.[57] Careful structuring of transactions in the securitization realm should make the development of

---

[57] *See, for example,* the discussions of current transactions at Michael J. T. McMillen, "Shari'a-Compliant Finance Structures and the Development of an Islamic Economy," *The Proceedings of the Fifth Harvard University Forum on Islamic Finance: Islamic Finance: Dynamics and Development* (2003), 89–102; McMillen 2001; and Michael J. T. McMillen, "Islamic Shari'a-Compliant Project Finance: Collateral Security and Financing Structure Case Studies," *The Proceedings of the Third Harvard University Forum on Islamic Finance: Local Challenges, Global Opportunities* (2000), 111-131.

shari'a-compliant securitization structures equally tenable despite the presence of interest-based financing in the broader transaction.

This essay considers a case study, the Securitized Acquisition Financing Transaction, in which a structure was developed in the context of interest-based financing as required by secular South Korean securitization laws in a transaction in which the End User Leases were not compliant with the *shari'a* and the End User Tenants were in businesses that are not *shari'a*-compliant (non-mutual insurance and interest-based lending). The structure that was developed focuses on the essential nature of "property" under both the *shari'a* and secular law. The development of the structure began with basic concepts of property that are considered by first year law students and sought to make use of those concepts in a modern transactional context. The structure that was developed allows the cash flows from a single rent stream to be structured to service "at least two different stratified risk positions or tranches reflecting different degrees of risk" with payments to investors depending "upon the performance of the specified underlying exposures, as opposed to being derived from an obligation of the entity originating those exposures."[58] While the Securitized Acquisition Financing Transaction involved "securitization" of the cash flows from a single property and asset, the transaction was also considered and structured with cognizance of methods of pooling that are used to provide for risk diversification, and the transaction was structured so as to be compatible with pooling securitizations.

The particulars of the structure presented for the Securitized Acquisition Financing Transaction are not presented for their own sake, they are not presented to provide a roadmap for effecting a transaction, although it is the author's hope that the particulars are of assistance to practitioners in the Islamic financing industry in thinking about creative approaches to *shari'a*-compliant securitizations.

The case study is presented to illustrate the concept, and the importance, of reconsideration and application of first principles, to illustrate that the wisdom and experience of the past is pertinent to the present and the future, and to challenge the Islamic finance industry to study and understand the body of knowledge that is the inheritance of the entire industry. The Islamic finance industry continues to develop into new and more challenging areas. The product base of *shari'a*-compliant products continues to expand, and the products continue to deeper and more complex levels of sophistication. The pace of development is increasing. The form of the Islamic economy is evolving and achieving greater penetration in financial markets throughout the world. The industry must remain firmly rooted in its base even as it becomes more creative and the debate intensifies with respect to what is appropriate in any given transactional

[58] Basel II Accord, section 502.

context. Hopefully, this essay will contribute to the debate, even initiate further debate.

Part III

Debating the Ethical Issues

Social Dynamics of the Debate on Default in Payment and Sale of Debt

M. Nejatullah Siddiqi[1]

The current debate on regulatory issues in Islamic finance reflects a variety of approaches. Most experts in Islamic law, *the fuqaha'*, employ analogical reasoning and use past rulings as a guide to a rule for today. Most economists, on the other hand, argue in terms of socio-economic consequences and seek rules that shape a desired state of the world. Jurists are trained to arrive at new rules governing a wholly or partly novel situation mostly by analogical and deductive reasoning. Social philosophers are concerned with certain values such as justice and fairness, even promotion of the common welfare. They evaluate new rules based on these criteria, often concluding that the new rules are insufficient. As long as there is a strong case for improvement, the jurists are obliged to have a second look by invoking methods that are more accommodative of the very values that concern the social scientists.

In the Islamic tradition we often come across rules arrived at by analogical reasoning *(qiyas)* that are abandoned in favor of rules designed to protect/promote the benefit *(maslaha)* desired. In economic literature there has been a debate between those who would maximize production (thereby creating as much new wealth as could be created) and those concerned primarily with social justice and ensuring dignity and security for every human being. Law is concerned primarily with fairness, whereas social good (including economic good) is conceived in terms of provisions that depend, ultimately, on production. Fairness is necessary to ensure dignity, whereas wealth is needed to guarantee security.

This brief paper proposes to demonstrate that a similar tension is discernable in the current debate on legal and regulatory issues in Islamic finance. It focuses on two issues that are attracting considerable attention: (1) how to deal with delays in payment of debts resulting from sales on

---

[1] Independent researcher. The author is thankful to M. Anas Zarqa and M. Umer Chapra for their comments on an earlier draft of this paper.

credit, mostly in *murabaha* deals, and (2) the permissibility of securitization and sale of debts resulting from *murabaha* and other credit transactions.

Widely different positions have been taken on these issues. The paper will propose that these differences may be rooted in the priorities of the position taker. Those placing greater importance on production and the creation of wealth value efficiency. They seek to ensure the flow of credit, economize on the use of cash, etc. By contrast, those more concerned with fair dealings and social justice seek to avoid any involvement with *riba*/interest, whose prohibition is the first threshold in deterring injustice and unfair practices. For them, characterizing any procedure as involving *riba*/interest amounts to declaring it to be unfair and unjust.

Islamic economics as a discipline is concerned about justice and fairness as well as efficiency. It acknowledges that in a balanced realization, the two complement each other. This does not, however, preclude the possibility that scholars of different backgrounds may differ in their priorities. Economists tend to care more about efficiency, or at least seem to give it higher priority. The more that is produced, the fairer one can be in distribution. The less that one has, the greater the temptation to be self-serving. Therefore, economists always seek to maximize efficiency. Law, by contrast, focuses on fairness in a given situation. As the debate on current legal and regulatory issues in Islamic finance involves scholars drawn from various disciplines, tensions develop that have the fortunate potential of leading to resolutions that a narrower approach would fail to achieve.

THE DEBATE ON DELAY IN PAYMENT

The debate on *mumathala*, or delay in payment of a debt incurred in a credit purchase, predates the debate on the sale of debt *(bay' al-dayn)*. It began in earnest late in the last century. The practice of *murabaha*, the chief source of debts under discussion, had been spreading, bringing this issue to the forefront. The possibility of delay in payment raised the questions of how and when to penalize the defaulter, whether to compensate the creditor, and if so, how? The principle of penalizing a defaulter who is capable of payment is universally accepted, but neither the need to compensate the creditor nor the method of doing it so as to prevent *riba* is agreed upon.[2]

The debate was conducted in various forums, including *shari'a* advisory boards, seminars and conferences, and academic journals. This paper will focus on the last, particularly the journal published by the Center for Research in Islamic Economics at the King Abdulaziz University in

[2] Saleh 2002: 92-93.

Jedda.[3] A good summary of the debate is provided by a paper jointly authored by Mohammad Anas Zarqa and Mohammad Ali Elgari (henceforth referred to as Zarqa and Elgari).[4]

The issue, restated, is how we are to deal with one who buys on the promise to pay within a certain date but delays payment, thereby inflicting harm on the seller/creditor? Zarqa and Elgari rightly begin their paper by highlighting the importance of this issue in a system that does not charge interest. They also note the importance of credit in an economy that thrives on the division of labor and exchange. Islamic finance needs a mechanism capable of eradicating the phenomenon of delay in payment by those capable of timely payment, a phenomenon characterized as delinquency.

How can we deter the delinquent? Do we compensate the creditor? If yes, why, how, and when? The answers to these questions vary. Some propose deterrence by punishment through incarceration, or even corporal punishment for the debtor. Blacklisting delinquents and exposing them to the public has also been suggested. All these proposals, however, involve courts of law, and litigation requires time. This is rightly seen as a disadvantage that decreases the efficiency of the Islamic financial system. Efficiency calls for a mechanism that is triggered automatically. One mechanism can be a financial penalty. Such a fine can be proportional to the sum of money involved. It can also be related to the actual length of delay. This approach, however, would be similar to *riba*/interest in form if not in spirit. Some also claim that it may not be an effective deterrent, insofar as the market rate of interest at any particular time may be higher than the rate at which the fine is imposed. In such a case, the delinquent debtor can pay the fine and "roll over" the debt, much to the chagrin of the creditor.

Proposals on deterring the delinquent can be classified into two categories. A monetary penalty automatically triggered ensures efficiency. It should be noted, however, that proponents of a fine nevertheless opine that only a court of law can fix its quantity. It cannot form part of the contract and come into effect automatically. On the other hand, the obligation to avoid interest prompts some scholars to reject the fine option altogether, irrespective of who levies it. Out of the eight opinions listed by Zarqa and Elgari, one scholar (Nazeeh Hammad) insists that only punishment by a court of law can deter a delinquent.[5] Two scholars (Shaikh Mustafa Zarqa and Zakiuddin Sha'ban) opt for a fine that must be decreed by a court.[6] Two other scholars agree to a predetermined fine that, according to one (Ali al-Saloos, who combines incarceration with a fine),

[3] Because the same scholars have been involved in all these forums, hopefully no substantial issues will be overlooked.
[4] Zarqa and Elgari 1991: 25-57.
[5] Hammad 1985: 104, 106.
[6] Zarqa 1985: 96.

goes to a charity.[7] Another suggestion is to send the fine to a special fund under the aegis of the state (Siddiqi). The remaining scholars (Siddiq al-Dareer and Zaki Abdul Barr) agree on a fine that would serve as a deterrent, but insist that it should not exceed the actual harm suffered by the creditor/Islamic bank.[8] Al-Dareer regards the average rate of profit earned by the bank in the relevant period as a good measure of its loss.

With respect to compensation, one opinion (Nazeeh Hammad) rejects the idea, arguing that it is only the original sum owed that a creditor may collect. One can say that the possibility of delay must have been factored into the mark-up, the increase over and above the cash price. Sheikh Dareer would compensate only to the extent of actual profit lost, which he then equates with the average profit earned by the creditor (Islamic bank, for example).[9] In effect, this is what the creditor would get according to the formula approved by Shaikh Zarqa. But Zaki Abdul Barr is not comfortable with this formula; he would rather have it analyzed by a court and have compensation given in exceptional cases only.[10] Siddiqi would make the affected creditor seek compensation from the special fund under the auspices of the state to which all fines go.[11]

Mention ought also to be made of the proposal of the authors themselves, Zarqa and Elgari. In their view, the delinquent debtor is to be obliged, by a court of law, to make a counter-loan (interest free) to the creditor in the amount owed and for a period equal to the period of delay. The idea is to compensate for a lost opportunity by providing a similar opportunity, and no more. This proposal, however, has received no endorsements. One commentator described it as neither efficient nor fair.[12] The marginal efficiency of money to the creditor was not necessarily the same at the two points of time involved. The different timings of the two opportunities, the one lost due to delay and the one being provided as compensation, could not be treated as equal. Also, the counter loan provided as part of the contract made it similar to *riba*/interest, insofar as the extra time was matched by a "benefit."

Zarqa and Elgari, together with Siddiqi, visited the issue again in "Banking Law—A Suggested Model for Organizing the Islamic Banking Sector."[13] Appendix 9 to that text details what is provided briefly in clause 4 of the model law. All fines for delay are to go to a public fund supervised by the central bank. The fund serves society in various ways, but the lender does not benefit from it by any means.

---

[7] Zarqa and Elgari 1991: 37-38.
[8] al-Dareer 1985: 112, and Abdul Barr 1991: 61.
[9] al-Dareer 1985: 112.
[10] Abdul Barr 1991: 62.
[11] Zarqa and Elgari 1991: 37. Also in Elgari et al. 1993: 93 (Arabic section), clauses 4 and 5 of Appendix 9.
[12] al-Roobi 1992.
[13] Elgari et al. 1993.

In the year 2000, the Islamic *Fiqh* Academy, a subsidiary of the Organization of the Islamic Conference headquartered in Jedda, passed a resolution on this issue. That resolution went further than an earlier resolution in 1990 which stated: "If the buyer/debtor delays the payment of installments after the specified date it is not permissible to charge any amount in addition to its principal liability, whether it is made a precondition in the contract or it is claimed without a previous agreement, because it is *riba*, hence prohibited in *shari'a*."[14] The new resolution reaffirmed the above, but added: "It is permissible to include a Penalty Provision in all financial contracts except when the original commitment is a debt. Imposing a Penalty Provision in debt contract is usury in the strict sense." It also laid down that: "The loss that may be compensated includes actual financial loss incurred by the partner, any other material loss and the certainly obtainable gain that he misses as a result of his partner's default or delay. It does not include moral loss."[15] These resolutions provide some relief only to those affected by delays in fulfillment of *salam/istisna'* obligations. The amounts owed in installment sales and *murabaha* sales that have become debts remain outside their purview. In other words, little attention is paid to the efficiency-based pleas of the scholars reported above and the verdict focuses solely on the ethical aspect as surrogated by *riba*/interest.

The issue of delay in payment is taken up in Chapra and Khan (2000). Concerned with the efficiency of the Islamic financial system, they observe: "If the late payment does not lead to any penalty, there is a danger that the default may tend to become a widespread phenomenon through the long run operation of self-enforcing mechanisms. This may lead to a breakdown of the payment system if the amounts involved are significantly large."[16]

They proceed to suggest an index of "loss given a default" (LGD) "to determine the compensation in a way that reduces subjectivity as well as the possibility of injustice to either the defaulting or the aggrieved party."[17] This comes, however with the proviso that "the concept of compensation for loss becomes accepted by the *fuqaha'*."[18] The authors report, without comment, the "conservative view" that "prohibits the imposition of any compensation to the aggrieved party for fear that this may become equivalent to interest."[19]

The latest response to this issue seeks a balance. It makes a penalty for default/delay automatic, but the proceeds of the penalty go to charity. With

---

[14] Islamic *Fiqh* Academy 2000: 104.
[15] Ibid., 252.
[16] Chapra and Khan 2000: 72.
[17] Ibid., 73.
[18] Ibid., 73.
[19] Ibid., 72.

respect to compensation for harm done, the issue is left to courts of law. In its guidelines relating to *murabaha*, the State Bank of Pakistan states:

> It can be stipulated while entering into the agreement that in case of late payment or default by the client he shall be liable to pay penalty calculated at percent per day or per annum that will go to the charity fund constituted by the bank. The amount of penalty cannot be taken to be a source of further return to the bank (the seller of the goods) but shall be used for charitable purposes. . . . The bank can also approach competent courts for award of solatium which shall be determined by the courts at their discretion, on the basis of direct and indirect costs incurred, other than opportunity cost.[20]

One of the peculiarities of a market economy is the press for efficiency. This is achieved largely through competition. Unfortunately, the market has no similar mechanism to ensure justice and fairness. That is left, in the first instance, to the conscience of the players, the economic agents, and then the regulatory authorities. In other words, the market works for the private interests of the participants whereas the public interest (which includes the interests of non-participants) is the responsibility of the state, the guardian of public interest. Islam works on the conscience of the economic agents through moral orientation. Also, social authority is empowered to take the steps necessary to protect public interest, a principle enshrined in the traditional Islamic institution of *hisba*. Because the prohibition of *riba*/interest is directed at ensuring justice, the jurists rightly insist that no provision should involve *riba*/interest. But can they stop there? If they do (as they seem to have done until now) can the market stop pressing for an efficient solution to the problem under scrutiny?

SALE AND SECURITIZATION OF DEBT

The second issue we analyze is the sale of debt, *bay' al-dayn*. Prohibition of interest almost eliminates the direct lending of money for business. There is no bond market in an Islamic economy whose liquidity is at issue. Direct lending of money is replaced by *murabaha* and similar credit transactions, effectively tying the expansion of credit with the growth of the economy. In place of conventional treasury bonds, Islamic financial markets have bonds based on *ijara* (leasing), *salam* (prepaid orders), or *istisna'* (manufacturing orders on a pay as you get basis). But there is also a huge debt created by installment sales and *murabaha*. To some, waiting until maturity implies waste. This waste occurs at two levels. Firstly, those holding IOUs will need credit to command real resources to continue producing, having presumably exhausted their own resources in producing what they already

[20] State Bank of Pakistan 2004: 3.

sold on credit. This means that society will always carry a large amount of non-liquid assets, the IOUs. This may secondly force sellers/producers to refuse to sell on credit and to instead demand cash. A society in which all IOUs must await redemption by the original debtor cannot economize on the use of cash.

It may rightly be noted that one must await the maturity of debts incurred in the process of acquiring command over real resources on credit. As Keynes pointed out in commenting on the "liquidity fetish," not everybody can be liquid all the time. It is, however, more efficient to provide opportunities for exchange between those who are willing to wait and share the risks involved (given that the Islamic framework does not reward pure waiting) and those who seek liquidity. One way to do so is to allow IOUs as collaterals for fresh credit—a practice already in vogue in the Islamic financial market. It is also permissible to exchange these IOUs for goods and services. But some believe more should be offered.

The juristic objection to the sale of debts resulting from *murabaha* is the same as in the case of selling a debt created by a money loan. If I buy for 90 an IOU worth 100 after a year, I am doing so in order to earn 10 as interest. Jurists see no reason to distinguish between IOUs created by *murabaha* and IOUs created by lending money. This is what seems to underlie the latest Islamic *Fiqh* Academy resolution on the subject, which states:

> It is not permissible to sell a deferred debt by the non-debtor for a prompt cash, from its type or otherwise, because this results in *riba* (usury). Likewise it is not permissible to sell it for a deferred cash, from its type or otherwise, because it is similar to a sale of debt for debt which is prohibited in Islam. There is no difference whether the debt is the result of a loan or whether it is deferred sale.[21]

However, the view equating money loans with debts resulting from credit has been challenged. There are reasons to treat the two differently, say Chapra and Khan:

> The debt is created by the *murabaha* mode of financing permitted by the *shari'a* and the price, according to the *fuqaha'* themselves, includes the profit on the transaction and not interest. Therefore, when the bank sells such a debt instrument at a discount, what it is relinquishing, or what the buyer is getting, is not interest but rather a share in profit.[22]

In other words, a debt resulting from *murabaha* has an element absent from a debt arising from borrowing money—the mark-up on spot price. The sale

---

[21] Islamic *Fiqh* Academy 2000: 234.
[22] Chapra and Khan 2000: 78.

and purchase of *murabaha*-based debt would take place on this extra profit margin.

There is a problem with this proposition. That which was a profit margin for the seller of goods and services (on a *murabaha* basis) may not necessarily remain so when the same seller "sells" the IOU arising from that transaction. Some of the factors involved in the determination of the mark-up on spot price in *murabaha* may be different from those involved in the sale of the resulting IOU at a discount. Furthermore, the extra profits earned in *murabaha* sale, over and above those that can be earned in selling for cash, are still made against the sale of goods and services. But the portion that goes to the buyer of the *murabaha*-based IOU (according to the above rationale) has no goods and services corresponding to it. It is money for money with only a difference of dates.

Chapra and Khan proceed to argue that there is hardly any *gharar* involved in the sale of debt-instruments under discussion, a point we will not address given the limited scope of this paper. What is more noteworthy is their plea that the *fuqaha'* reconsider the case of asset-based debt instruments and allow their sale, as it would lead "to the accelerated development of an Islamic money market."[23] They proceed to emphasize the need for such a market by pointing out that Islamic banks may face a liquidity crunch in its absence, thereby paralyzing the whole system. They also believe "it is difficult for banks to play effectively their role of financial intermediation, without being able to securitize their receivables."[24] After discussing alternative avenues of raising large funds required by client companies through banks, they conclude that "it would be preferable to allow banks to rely on the sale of their own assets to raise liquidity."[25]

So it is efficiency that is at stake, in an environment where the inefficient may not long survive. Again, the same story unfolds, that of jurists bent on ensuring justice by avoiding anything similar to *riba*/interest, while the economists are keen to maintain efficient markets. Do they understand each other's concerns? Is the rationale *(hikma)* of prohibiting *riba* also applicable to the sale of debts resulting from *murabaha* so that it must be blocked in order to ensure justice? What about a trade-off between the twin objectives of *shari'a*, justice and wealth creation? Is such a trade-off acceptable under certain circumstances? Is it sometimes unavoidable? Can we agree on a formula that ensures a reasonable degree of fairness with a reasonable level of efficiency? These questions have yet to be examined thoroughly. Those arguing in favor of legitimizing the sale of debt must demonstrate that no alternative methods of ensuring liquidity are available. They must also address the objection that once the sale of debt is allowed

---

[23] Ibid., 79

[24] Ibid.

[25] Ibid., 80.

insofar as asset-based IOUs are concerned, prohibiting the sale of IOUs based on money lending will be difficult, if not impossible, to sustain.

Bay'al-dayn is approved by Malaysian *shari'a* scholars.[26] It has a place in Islamic banking as practiced in Southeast Asia. *Shari'a* scholars in that region follow the Shafi'i school of Islamic law. They base their opinion on certain rulings with which scholars in the heartland of Islamic finance, who follow other schools, generally do not agree.[27] Bank Islam Malaysia is marketing Negotiable Islamic Deposit Certificates (NIDC) backed by *murabaha*-based assets.[28] According to al-Amine, "In Malaysia the Islamic benchmark bond was introduced in 1990 and is believed to be based on the *murabaha* concept. They are the most popular form of Islamic financing method used in Malaysia."[29] Al-Amine goes on to note, however, that controversy continues to surround the *shari'a* legitimacy of these bonds.[30] Many Islamic debt instruments on sale in the Malaysian market are criticized on the ground that they involve *bay' al-dayn* and *bay' al-'ina.*[31] But some scholars refer to certain Hanbali and Maliki jurists (e.g., Ibn Qayyim and Dasuqi, respectively) who "are of the opinion that selling *dayn* to a third party is not against syarak (*shar'*)."[32] It is noted that there is a difference between the debtor being asked by the creditor to pay more than the price agreed upon in a credit sale in lieu of delay in payment, and selling the IOU arising from that credit sale to a third party. In the latter case the seller on credit, who holds the IOU, is no longer dealing with the debtor. He is dealing with a third party to whom he sells the IOU. The deal between this third party, which now holds the IOU, and the debtor, is free of the constraints attending upon the deal between the seller on credit and the one who buys on credit. According to Ishak, *bay' al-dayn* to a third party, however, is distinguishable because a third party does not ask for an increase in price from the debtor. The debtor will just pay according to the initial contract. As *dayn* has been sold to a third party, the initial creditor will no longer make a claim but the third party will.[33] Ishak proceeds to argue:

> Can *haqq al-dayn* (be) sold at a lower price? The answer is yes, because it is not a currency and the attributes transferred when bought consist of *haqq mall* not currency. . . . Based on the above, if the initial seller is willing to reduce his right and give the third party the full right, it is not at all against syriah (shari'a) principles. The same with share certificates traded, it is an ownership

[26] Securities Commission 2002.
[27] Usmani 2000a.
[28] Archer and Karim 2002: 132.
[29] al-Amine 2001: 3.
[30] Ibid., 4.
[31] Rosley and Sanusi 1999.
[32] Ishak 1997: 6.
[33] Ibid., 7

> right in a company and when sold in the secondary market the price is essentially different from the initial price.[34]

This argument is unconvincing, as a shareholder does not hold a claim to a definite sum of money to be paid in the future. But there is no need for me to evaluate these arguments in analogical terms. What matters is their focus on distancing the sale of debt from *riba*/interest and trying to present it as a fair trade, free of the injustice symbolized by *riba*/interest. Hence, the claim that asset-based securities are like share certificates and necessary for the well being of people. This is evidenced by Ishak's appeal to the *shari'a* principles of *ra'fa* and *takhfif* in his conclusion.[35] In other words, it is being asserted that allowing the sale of debt arising from credit sales is neither unjust nor unfair as it does not involve *riba*/interest. It is also emphasized that it should be permitted in order to make life easy and prosperous. Perhaps it would have been more beneficial if, instead of analogizing between a certificate of ownership in a company and an IOU, Ishak had pursued the *maslaha*-based arguments on which he bases his conclusions.

It would be far better to conduct the debate openly in the framework of ease versus hardship, efficiency versus fairness, and growth versus distribution. The trade-offs could then be openly examined, even measured. At the macroeconomic level, we need to know why liquidity cannot be guaranteed without legitimizing the sale of debt. It must be discussed how giving debt-financing a greater role is likely to change the nature of the Islamic economy, which emphasizes risk sharing and participatory finance. Unfortunately, this is not how legal issues are handled, especially in an industry in a hurry (as the Islamic financial industry currently seems to be) under pressure from its more "efficient" competitors. While the *shari'a* scholar sitting on an Islamic bank's advisory board may not have the time necessary to consult relevant texts as to whether a particular type of analogical reasoning is acceptable, the task of the social scientists and moral philosophers is more contemplative and time consuming. An appeal to *maqasid al-shari'a* (objectives of *shari'a*) is not as easy as it may initially seem to the uninitiated. It involves an understanding of Islam as a way of life, a process of social reconstruction, and a mission with humanity—an understanding far deeper than what one would normally expect from a contemporary legal expert. Islamic finance should consider all of these objectives, many of which are difficult to realize through analogical reasoning, and even financial engineering.

---

[34] Ibid.

[35] Ibid., 8.

Limits and Dangers of *Shari'a* Arbitrage

Mahmoud A. El-Gamal[1]

INTRODUCTION: THE MARKET FOR *SHARI'A* ARBITRAGE

> "Islamic banking and other Islamic financial institutions are rapidly approaching a crossroads," Sheikh Ahmad bin Mohammad Al Khalifa told the opening session of a conference on Islamic Banking and Finance in Manama [in late February, 2004]. "Islamic banks have grown primarily by providing services to a captive market, people who will only deal with a financial institution that strictly adheres to Islamic principles."[2]

Islamic finance is fundamentally a prohibition-driven industry. Its beginnings can be traced to mid-twentieth-century literature on Islamic economics, which emphasized the presumed equity and stability consequences of adhering to Islamic legal and economic principles. However, the nature of this industry is best exemplified in the titles of some of the earliest and most influential writings on Islamic banking, for instance:

---

[1] Professor of Economics and Statistics at Rice University, where the author holds the endowed Chair in Islamic Economics, Finance and Management. Address: Dept. of Economics – MS 22, Rice University, Houston, TX 77005, elgamal@rice.edu.

[2] Opening speech by the governor of the Bahrain Monetary Agency, as reported in *Monday Morning*, February 25, 2004, cf. www.zawya.com/story.cfm?id=ZAWYA20040225134523. The issue of strict adherence to Islamic principles is normally reduced to approval by *shari'a* boards. Indeed, recent Islamic banking laws in a number of countries and jurisdictions explicitly list the need for appointment of a three-member *shari'a* board that is required to write periodic reports on adherence to the *shari'a*, which reports must be included in Islamic financial institutions' annual reports. See, for instance, the Islamic banking Law no. 30 of 2003, published (with corrections) by the official Kuwaiti government newspaper *Al-Kuwait Al-Yawm* (*Kuwait Today*) on June 8, 2003 (issue 619, 49th year), Article 93.

- Baqir al-Sadr, *The Riba-Based Bank in Islam: A treatise on replacement of Riba, and a study of the various activities of banks in light of Islamic Jurisprudence (fiqh).*[3]
- Sami Humud, *Evolution of Banking Operations in a Manner that Agrees with Islamic Law (Shari`a).*[4]

Most other writings on the subject started from a fundamental assumption that banking interest is the forbidden *riba*, and proceeded to propose means of operating "banks without interest."[5] Despite repeated questions regarding distinctions between interest and *riba*, jurists affiliated with or supportive of the Islamic financial industry have maintained that there is an irrefutable consensus as to what is forbidden and how to avoid it.[6]

While most Islamic economics writings suggested the evolution of a distinctive financial system under Islamic law,[7] the titles of the two books by al-Sadr and Humud were better predictors of the Islamic finance industry to ensue. Both titles suggested that the starting point for Islamic finance is conventional financial practice. The authors reasoned that to the extent that standard banking operations were based on *riba*, that *riba* should be removed from the system. Otherwise, the goal and agenda was simple: find the closest approximation to conventional financial practice that can be deemed to avoid forbidden elements.[8] Often, this approximation is form-based rather than substance-based.

Ever since the introduction of Western-style finance to the Islamic world in the late nineteenth century, large numbers of Muslims have felt uneasy about the new transactions, which they either believed or suspected to be forbidden under classical Islamic jurisprudence. In response, the twentieth century witnessed a vast literature on Islamic economics and

---

3 Al-Sadr 1969.

4 Humud 1976.

5 For instance, M. Uzair, *An Outline of Interestless Banking* (Karachi: Idaratul Ma`arif, 1955), and M. N. Siddiqi, *Banking without Interest* (Leicester, UK: The Islamic Foundation, 1983).

6 For a discussion of a recent heated debate, see M. El-Gamal, "Interest and the Paradox of Contemporary Islamic Law and Finance," *Fordham International Law Review* (December 2003), 108-149.

7 For instance, see M. S. Khan and A. Mirakhor (eds.), *Theoretical Studies in Islamic Banking and Finance* (Houston: The Institute for Research and Islamic Studies, 1988).

8 Initially, the focus was on the prohibition of *riba*. More recently, avoiding forbidden *gharar* has also been important to the development of *takaful* as an alternative to conventional insurance, as well as the ongoing attempts to synthesize Islamic derivative securities to replace conventional options. For an economic explanation of the roots of this "closest permissible alternative" approach, see M. El-Gamal, "The Economics of 21st Century Islamic Financial Jurisprudence," *Proceedings of the Fourth Harvard University Forum on Islamic Finance* (Cambridge: Center for Middle Eastern Studies, Harvard University, 2002), 7-12.

finance starting in mid-century, followed by the evolution of an Islamic finance industry later in the century. Many early practitioners of Islamic finance lamented the large gap between Islamic economic and finance rhetoric, which focused on the substance and spirit of Islamic jurisprudence, and the practice of Islamic finance, which focused on its medieval forms.[9] However, the captive market, of which the governor of the BMA spoke in the opening quotation of this section, had already been established as follows: (1) conventional financial practice is certainly forbidden, (2) at least in theory, an Islamic financial alternative is available, and (3) even if the industry seems excessively to adhere to forms of Islamic jurisprudence rather than substance, it is now impermissible to use conventional finance based on the law of necessity.[10]

THE NATURE OF *SHARI'A* ARBITRAGE

Arbitrage opportunities occur when discrepancies exist between prices of the same product in different markets. Hence, the arbitrageur can buy the product in the market within which it is sold cheaply and sell it in the other, provided that the price difference exceeds transaction costs. A related type of arbitrage opportunity is called regulatory arbitrage, wherein the arbitrageur attempts to generate a profit based on certain financial practices being disallowed (at any price) within the legal system of one country or region (say, country A) but allowed in others (including, say, country B). In this case, financial professionals and lawyers cooperate to manufacture an analog of the financial product for country A. Often this is accomplished using the product in country B as a building block, and heavily relying on offshore special purpose entities to structure transactions in a manner

[9] Al-Najjar 1993. See also, Sheikh Saleh Kamel's acceptance speech for the Islamic Development Bank's prize in Islamic finance in 1996 (quoted in El-Gamal, "Interest and the Paradox").

[10] This focus on form rather than substance defies a famous Islamic juristic dictum: "What matters in contracts is substance (lit. meaning), and not wording and form" c.f. ibn Qayyim al-Jawziyyah, *I`lam al-Muwaqqi`in `an Rabb al-`Alamin* (Bayrut, Dar al-Kutub al-`Ilmiyyah, 1996), vol.3, pp.78-80. However, as distasteful as it may sound, surprisingly many Islamic finance practitioners defend legalistic formalism with the example of marriage contracts, wherein the contract form can distinguish between one of the best permissible practices (valid marriage), and one of the worst sins (adultery). Since this example has been repeated frequently, it is worthwhile to note that its tastelessness is surpassed only by its jurisprudential incoherence. A fundamental difference between this example and the case of financial transactions (which renders the analogy flagrantly invalid) is the default ruling of prohibition of sexual relations unless legalized through a marriage contract, as opposed to the default ruling of permissibility of all financial transactions, except for those including a prohibiting factor (e.g., *riba* or *gharar*).

acceptable to country A. This type of regulatory arbitrage played a pivotal role in giving rise to and sustaining the securitization industry in the 1980s and 1990s.

Shari'a arbitrage is a particular form of regulatory arbitrage, wherein a captive market of pious Muslims voluntarily chooses not to use certain financial products. Lawyers, in partnership with bankers and jurists, strive to provide them a reengineered version of those products. Conventional financial products are used as building blocks for the reengineered Islamic products approved by jurists. For instance, a special purpose vehicle may be created by a conventional bank. The SPV may receive a credit line from the mother bank (whether or not it is a wholly owned subsidiary thereof), but deal with its "Islamic finance" customers in terms of reengineered nominate contracts (e.g., under the name of *murabaha*-financing). Thus, the Islamic customer is separated from the interest-bearing loan by the SPV and juristic focus on the contract in which the customer is a party. This approach will become obvious in light of the example of HSBC's auto-financing *shari'a* board pronouncements cited in the following section.

Murabaha (cost-plus) financing is one of the oldest and most commonly used means of Islamic finance. The full technical name of this contract is "a credit sale with mark-up to one who ordered the initial purchase" *(al-murabaha lil-amir b-il-shira' ma'a bay'bi-thaman 'ajil).* Sami Humud envisioned one of the earliest manifestations of this transaction as a substitute for bank loans in his above-cited book (which was based on his Ph.D. dissertation). Over the years, a number of additional alterations have been added to make the contract as close to an interest-based loan as possible. For instance, a customer's promise to buy the property from the bank at the mark-up credit price was made binding by jurists, once the bank buys the property to finance its ultimate purchase by the customer.[11] Further pronouncements allowed the bank to appoint the customer as its buying agent – to negotiate the price and purchase the property on its behalf, and then as its selling agent – to sell the property to himself:

> If in cases of genuine need, the financier appoints the client his agent to purchase the commodity on his behalf, his different capacities (i.e. as agent and as ultimate purchaser) should be clearly distinguished. As an agent, he is a trustee. . . .
>
> After he purchases the commodity in his capacity as agent, he must inform the financier that, in fulfilling his obligation as his agent, he has taken delivery of the purchased commodity and now he extends his offer to purchase it from him. When, in response to this offer, the financier conveys his acceptance to

[11] *See* al-Qaradawi 1987. The binding promise *fatwa* was based on the opinion of the Maliki jurist ibn Shubruma, and adopted in the first international conference of Islamic banks in Dubai, 1978.

> this offer, the sale will be deemed to be complete, and the risk of the property will be passed on to the client as purchaser. At this point he will become a debtor. . . .[12]

In the eyes of M. Taqi Usmani, a highly respected jurist who is frequently retained by Islamic financial institutions worldwide, the formalistic invocation of the buying agent's possessions of trust *(amana)*, which keeps liability *(daman)* with the bank until the final sale, justifies the distinction between the bank's legitimate return on *murabaha* financing and the forbidden interest the bank would earn on a conventional secured lending operation. This distinction between possessions of trust and guarantee is indeed central to the formative classical jurisprudence. However, that classical distinction becomes obsolete in light of the contemporary conventional financial practice of secured lending, wherein the bank puts a lien on the financed property. Indeed, when the Office of the Comptroller of the Currency was asked to write an approving letter of understanding regarding *murabaha* financing in the United States, it reasoned as follows:

> [OCC #867, 1999:] . . . lending takes many forms . . . *murabaha* financing proposals are functionally equivalent to, or a logical outgrowth of secured real estate lending and inventory and equipment financing, activities that are part of the business of banking.[13]

Thus, the task of *shari'a* arbitrage is accomplished: a conventional bank (in this case the United Bank of Kuwait, which later stopped its Manzil USA program but continued its similar Manzil UK program), can use its regular funds to finance the purchase of a home in an "Islamic" manner, through *murabaha* (or *ijara*) financing. Regulators are successfully convinced that this is an acceptable form of secured lending, while customers are convinced that it is done Islamically. Indeed, the *shari'a* boards of various Islamic home finance providers in the United States explicitly warn customers that due to state and federal regulations, their mortgage documents may include the terms "mortgage," "loan," "interest," "borrower," "note," etc. However, they are assured that such language is used only because regulators require it. Moreover, customers are told that they will receive form 1098 (mortgage interest statement), which they can use to deduct the "markup" or "rent" component that was listed as interest. As a consequence, most potential customers ignore the industry and –

---

[12] Usmani 2002: 67.

[13] Available on the OCC website at www.occ.treas.gov/interp/nov99/int867.pdf. Similar language was used earlier for lease financing (under the Arabic term *ijara*), essentially accepting UBK's argument that "the economic substance" of *ijara* financing makes the transaction equivalent to secured lending, which is part of conventional banking practice; see www.occ.treas.gov/interp/dec97/int806.pdf.

depending on their initial preference and conviction – either continue to use conventional finance, or continue to avoid all forms of organized finance (of which they see Islamic finance as a thinly disguised variety). However, two groups of clients allow the industry to continue its *modus operandi*: (1) a critical mass of captive clients who attach sacred authority to the pronouncements of Islamic banks' *shari'a* boards, and (2) a group of clients who participate in the market hoping that it will eventually outgrow its current (*shari'a* arbitrage) mode of operation.

MECHANICS OF *SHARI'A* ARBITRAGE

Shari'a arbitrage relies on two main tools to achieve its objective: (1) dual characterization of a financial dealing, one for jurists and one for regulators, as discussed in the previous section, and (2) the addition of one or more degrees of separation between Islamic finance clients and the underlying conventional financial products. The latter is often achieved by inspecting each part of a complex transaction in isolation, rather than studying the entire transaction. The one degree of separation principle was – perhaps unwittingly – best described by HSBC when it launched its home finance program in the UAE. The following are excerpts from the Frequently Asked Questions (FAQ) circular that was published in the Islamic finance section of www.zawya.com on February 3, 2003:

> *Question:* How can a conventional (interest-based) bank offer a *shari'a* compliant financial service?
>
> *Answer:* Islamic law *(shari'a)* does not require that the seller of a product be Muslim, or that its other services be *shari'a* compliant as well. This is the considered opinion of our *Shari'a* Supervisory Committee. Conventional banks charge and pay interest, and the HSBC Group, of which we are a part, is a conventional bank. But we are also a customer-driven institution, and we provide *shari'a* compliant products to serve a genuine financial need among Muslims. Of course, our *shari'a* compliant products are available for Muslims and non-Muslims alike.
>
> *Question:* Since HSBC is an interest-based bank, what would be an acceptable source of funding for HSBC MEFCO? Are you going to mix conventional and *shari'a* compliant funds?
>
> *Answer:* The *shari'a* (Islamic law) does not require that the seller of a product be Muslim or that his/her own income be *halal* (permitted). We will therefore, initially use funds from conventional sources to finance Amana Vehicle Finance. Muslims may be understandably concerned about mixing conventional funds with *shari'a* compliant funds. It is important, however, to understand where the two can and cannot meet according to Islamic law

> *(shari'a)*. To open an account or invest money, funds must be segregated from interest-based funds so that returns are *halal* (permitted). To buy something or obtain financing, however, funds do not have to be from a *halal* source. The relationship with the seller must be in line with the *shari'a*—the seller's relationship with other parties, however, is not the purchaser's responsibility. This is the opinion of HSBC's *Shari'a* Supervisory Committee.
>
> *Question:* How do you calculate the price of Amana Vehicle Finance? Are the payments similar to a conventional vehicle loan? If so, is this acceptable under the *shari'a* (Islamic law)?
>
> *Answer:* HSBC MEFCO determines the rates on Amana Vehicle Finance using a fixed payment scheme that is competitive with conventional vehicle loans. According to the *shari'a*, the profit rate in a *Murabaha* transaction can be set at any value agreed between the buyer and seller. Also under *Murabaha* financing, HSBC MEFCO is acting as a vehicle seller and not a moneylender. There is no particular reason why a vehicle financed Islamically should be any more or less expensive than a vehicle financed using a conventional vehicle loan. The criterion for acceptability by the *shari'a* is that the transaction be compliant with *shari'a*, regardless of the price of the good or how that price is determined.

The idea of making an impermissible transaction permissible through degrees of separation is not new. In fact, it underlies many of the juristic stratagems *(hiyal)* for circumventing prohibitions. Consider for instance the progression of juristic opinions on various lending practices:

- A lends B $100 today, with B to repay $105 in one year. All jurists are unanimous that this practice is a form of the forbidden *riba*.

- B sells a stapler to A, for the cash price of $100. A turns around and sells the stapler to B for a credit price of $105 payable in one year. This practice is called "same item sale-resale" *(bay'al-'ina)*. Some jurists (e.g., the Hanbalis) forbade it based on prophetic traditions, while others (e.g., the Malikis) forbade it based on the principle of "prevention of stratagems to achieve illegal ends through legal means" *(sadd al-dhara'i)*. However, some others (e.g., the Hanafi jurist Abu Yusuf and al-Shafi'i) allowed the contract, ruling on each of the two separate valid sales separately. Provided that the second sale is not stipulated in the first, they reasoned, one cannot forbid the practice based on speculation about the contracting parties' unobservable intentions.[14]

---

[14] For a comprehensive list of opinions and texts upon which they were based, see W. al-Zuhayli, *Financial Transactions in Islamic Jurisprudence* (trans. M. El-Gamal), (Damascus: Dar al-Fikr, 2003), 1:214-216.

- C sells a stapler to A, for the cash price of $100. A sells the stapler to B for the credit price of $105 payable in one year. B sells the stapler to C for the cash price of $100. This practice is called *tawarruq* (literally, monetization – of the stapler in this example). Abu Hanifa contemplated this contract as a variation on the previous one, with a third party serving as an intermediary to avoid the prohibition *(muhallil).* While he forbade the simple *'ina* (without a third party), he was more accommodative of *tawarruq*. Most jurists considered *tawarruq* invalid, defective, or reprehensible. However, there were two reports on ibn Hanbal's opinion on this contract,[15] thus allowing a faction of the Hanbali school to approve the contract, which is quickly replacing *murabaha* as the favorite mode of financing in GCC countries.

- C sells a stapler to A, for the cash price of $100. A sells the stapler to B for the credit price of $105 payable in one year. B sells the stapler to D for the cash price of $100. D sells the stapler to C for the cash price of $100. Now, we have added two intermediary entities (C and D) between lender (A, in all examples) and borrower (B). Contracts with larger numbers of intermediaries do not have explicit names in classical jurisprudence, and were not discussed in their writings.

It is easy to see how we can keep adding degrees of separation until eventually it would become impossible for any jurists, however strict, to prohibit the practice as merely a trick to subvert the substance of Islamic law (avoidance of interest-bearing loans from A to B) while adhering to its medieval juristic forms. When bankers wish to practice their standard lending practices, but cater to the captive clientele of Islamic finance, they need at least one degree of separation. Since multiple degrees of separation typically add transactional costs (legal fees, sales taxes, etc.), bankers prefer to keep the number of degrees of separation to a bare minimum. Often, one degree of separation is sufficient.

In this regard, it is worthwhile to examine the degrees of separation most recently utilized in Islamic finance:

- For issuances of bond-alternatives (usually called *sukuk*, which is an Arabic word for bonds or certificates, albeit different from the more conventional term for bonds, *sanadat*), governments and corporations have recently opted for a variation on *'ina*, which also incorporates lease-financing in a manner very reminiscent of the decade-old leveraged buy-out methodologies of conventional finance:

---

[15] Ibid., 217.

- A special purpose vehicle (SPV) is created for the sole purpose of issuing the *sukuk.*
- SVP sells certificates/bonds *(sukuk)* and receives proceeds.
- SPV uses the proceeds to buy land, equipment, etc., from the government or a corporation wishing to issue bond-alternatives.
- SPV leases land, equipment, etc., back to the government or corporation, collecting interest-only or principal plus interest in the form of rent, which is passed through to *sukuk* holders.
- At lease-end, SPV sells the land, equipment, etc., back to the government (or as in one variation for Qatar *sukuk*, gives it back as gift, if the principal was fully paid along with interest as part of rental payments).

In this practice, there is one intermediary entity (SPV) and one intermediary property (land, equipment, etc.) to distinguish the *sukuk* from conventional bonds. The actual legal difference (e.g., how much real ownership *sukuk*-holders have through the SPV) may not be revealed until we observe the first round of lawsuits associated with those *sukuk* issuances. In the meantime, the "benchmark" argument discussed above is commonly invoked, to list the "rate of return" *sukuk* pay in terms of market interest rates (e.g., LIBOR) plus the appropriate risk spread (e.g., 45 basis points above LIBOR for the June 2004 issuance of $250 million Bahrain *sukuk* rated A- by Standard and Poors).[16]

- For retail financing, GCC banks are increasingly moving toward *tawarruq* financing, which also employs one intermediary entity (C in our previous example) as well as some product (usually an easily tradeable commodity such as metals or grains) as degrees of separation for the interest-bearing loan.

DYNAMICS OF *SHARI'A* ARBITRAGE

It is interesting to note that many Islamic financial institutions could and may have in fact easily practiced *tawarruq* under the guise of *murabaha.* This is easy to understand: in the four cases considered in the previous section, it is easy to obtain *shari'a* board approval of part of the *tawarruq*

[16] See *Bahrain Times*, July 13, 2004: "Bahrain: $250 million BMA *Sukuk* listed on BSE."

transaction as a *murabaha* one: "Islamic financial institution will buy commodity from C and sell it to A on credit and at a markup," ignoring the fact that A will turn around and sell the commodity back to C for its cash price (less transaction fees). In fact, for the *shari'a* board regulating Islamic financial institution B, one may argue that the first two steps of *tawarruq* constitute the only part of the transaction that matters, since it is the only part in which B is involved (the third leg of the *tawarruq* transaction is between A and C).

Thus, since the preponderance of *murabaha* financing made it easy to gain *shari'a* board acceptability, and since *tawarruq* is not as widely accepted outside of a subset of the Hanbali school, it was easier for bankers to structure transactions (including ones with the intent of providing liquidity rather than actual trade financing) as *murabaha*s. As more competition joined the market, including multinational financial behemoths such as Citibank, HSBC, etc., profit margins became narrower, and further innovations were introduced in *murabaha* practice to minimize costs (e.g. appointing the customer as agent, etc.). Finally, it became clear that *murabaha* transactions are more costly than *tawarruq*, especially if the customer's intent was not in fact to purchase an automobile or a house, but merely to get liquidity for whatever purpose. In fact, it is sometimes cheaper to use *tawarruq* (in trading a commodity such as metals), even if the customer in fact wanted liquidity to finance the purchase of property such as real estate (given that the bank's initial purchase of that property may result in additional sales taxes, registration fees, etc.).[17]

However, practicing *tawarruq* under the guise of *murabaha*, by keeping the three legs of the transaction separate, results in additional costs relative to treating the entire operation as a single transaction, especially one wherein the bank can serve as agent for the other two parties. Thus, as competition drove profit margins down, banks had to resort to *tawarruq* (despite its less than universal acceptability) for two economic reasons: (1) to gain better access to borrowers who simply need cash, student loans, etc., that do not easily lend themselves to *murabaha*, and (2) to provide more efficient credit facilities through *tawarruq* to others who would have previously obtained them through *murabaha*s, the objects of which they would immediately sell for cash.

This illustrates a general feature of *shari'a* arbitrage. The existence of a captive market initially makes it possible to implement even the most inefficient replications of conventional financial products through degrees

---

[17] At least one banker operating in the United States indicated to me that he would prefer financing auto purchases through *tawarruq*, since the transactions costs associated with *murabaha* (which requires two sales of the car) and *ijara* (which requires additional costs for title, insurance, etc.) are simply too high. In his view, *tawarruq* gives him a tool to offer auto loans at more competitive rates, using a method that is approved by the relevant jurists.

of separation. Profit margins in the early stages of *shari'a* arbitrage are sufficiently large to cover legal and jurist costs, as well as other transaction costs associated with the less efficient product. However, as competition increases, industry participants need to seek new markets and market segments, and also to enhance efficiency by cutting transactions costs wherever possible. In this manner, an industry built on *shari'a* arbitrage sows the seeds of its own downfall.

DANGERS OF *SHARI'A* ARBITRAGE

The dynamics of *shari'a* arbitrage, as analyzed in the previous section, identify two main dangers that are inherent in an industry built on that mode of operation. One of those dangers is religious, and the other is secular. The religious danger lies in the fact that the industry thus configured is destined to move away, rather than toward, strict adherence to Islamic jurisprudence.

Capitalization on arbitrage opportunities necessarily requires the payment of various transactions costs. In Islamic finance, those transactions costs are incurred due to conducting otherwise unnecessary transactions (e.g., in *tawarruq,* lending through three sales), as well as the additional legal and jurist fees required to structure a product and certify it. Although it is perhaps not sufficient, the profitability of *shari'a* arbitrage is certainly necessary to get bankers and lawyers involved in Islamic finance.

To the extent that classical Islamic jurisprudence is generally understood by contemporary jurists to forbid conventional financial practice, movement toward strict adherence to Islamic principles requires movement away from conventional finance. To the extent that profitability is tied to efficiency of the Islamized analogues of conventional financial practices, the profit motive dictates movement toward conventional financial practice, and thus away from strict adherence to Islamic principles as understood by contemporary jurists who are active in this industry.

Indeed, this is precisely the root of frustrations for early players in Islamic banking such as those cited in footnote 9. In the industry's earlier stages, minimal compromises (e.g., in making promises binding in *murabaha* financing) were deemed harmless temporary requirements until the industry matures. One could still make the distinction at this point between "asset-based" Islamic financing on the one hand, and conventional finance that operates based on "renting money" or "selling money for money." Of course, as competition in this sector increased, *murabaha*s begat *tawarruq*, where the underlying asset may for all practical purposes be fictional, just like fiat money used in conventional finance.

If one believes (as I do) that much of conventional finance in fact does not clash with Islamic law *(shari'a)* and classical jurisprudence *(fiqh),* one may think that this profit-driven trend toward closer approximations of conventional finance is a good thing. However, if one also believes (as I do) that some aspects of conventional finance do in fact contradict the substance of Islamic law, as well as the forms studied in classical jurisprudence, then one can see an impending danger of subversion of Islamic law. Indeed, by approving and eventually codifying (through AAOIFI, IFSB, OIC *Fiqh* Academy, etc.) legal stratagems to replicate conventional financial practices, jurists and bankers eventually drown the substance of Islamic law in their contemporary reconstructions of medieval forms of classical jurisprudence.[18] Indeed, through Islamic financing, an individual can get excessively indebted (e.g., becoming "house poor," as many Americans do by spending substantial portions of their incomes on their home mortgages, now "Islamized"), take excessive risks (e.g., by investing in shorting-based hedge funds that have recently surfaced), etc. By focusing on medieval juristic forms rather than eternal legal principles of Islam, the industry may in fact violate those principles and become less Islamic than prudent utilization of conventional financial products.

There is also a frightening worldly danger associated with current practices of *shari'a*-arbitrage-based Islamic finance. The three stages of development of an Islamic financial product bear a striking resemblance to methods used by money launderers and terrorist financiers. The degrees of separation often required for *shari'a*-arbitrage-based Islamic finance, as discussed in "Mechanics of *Shari`a* Arbitrage," are often structured along the lines developed in the 1980s and 1990s for asset protection and minimization of tax burdens (a legal form of tax evasion). Separation is accomplished through the establishment of bankruptcy-remote special purpose vehicles (SPVs) or entities (SPEs), usually incorporated at offshore financial centers that act as tax havens for investments of high-net-worth individuals.

Some degrees of separation are introduced in Islamic financial products by virtue of being part of the conventional product being mimicked, while others are introduced merely to separate the conventional part of a financial transaction from its Islamic part. For instance, protected capital mutual funds marketed in Saudi Arabia tend to rely on non-Islamic partners or advisers to receive an option-like payment as management or advisory fees (e.g., by capping investor returns at some percentage, and giving the partner/adviser all excess returns above that level as fees, i.e., paying with a call option). Of course, those partners or advisers, European and American investment banks, can turn around and hedge that risk by trading in options markets. Thus, Islamic product providers can offer the payoff structures generated by derivative securities without themselves trading in those securities.

Degrees of separation help isolate sources of funds or financial products from their destinations. The multiple-case example described

[18] Please see M. N. Siddiqi's paper in this book, which discusses the issues of legal objectives *(maqasid al-shari'a)* much more extensively, and eloquently, than I do.

earlier showed how by going from a loan, to *'ina*, to *tawarruq*, and then adding more intermediaries, the degree of jurist acceptability increases with the number of intermediaries. Unfortunately, this is the same methodology used by money launderers and criminal financiers to separate the sources of funds from their destinations. In that criminal context, the process is called layering, and it is the pivotal middle-step in a three-step process. The other two steps are placement of the funds into the legitimate financial system, and integration which allows the funds to reach their final destination through that legitimate system. In the case of Islamic finance, the parallel to placement is identification of a captive clientele, organizing them into a market, and marketing the Islamized product therein. The analog of integration is the stage at which conventional financial providers finally collect their profits, interest payments, etc., that were generated from that captive market.

The similarity of methodologies is not coincidental, since *shari'a*-arbitrage Islamic financial practice strives to separate "Islamic" parts of a transaction from its conventional parts, whereas criminal financial activities aim to separate sources of funds from their destinations. In this regard, the highly celebrated "asset-based" or "trade-based" nature of Islamic finance is a liability rather than an asset. One of the classical criminal financing tricks is to convert money into a commodity (diamonds, gold, Swiss watches, etc.), which can be taken through a number of layers, and finally – through over-invoicing or under-invoicing – a sum of money is cleansed or transferred to its intended party. To the extent that *shari'a*-arbitrage Islamic financial practice utilizes the same tools as criminal finance, the industry may be vulnerable to abuse. For instance, if someone wished to get a large sum of money from one country to another, it would be difficult to do that through a loan with exorbitant interest. However, if the loan is structured as *tawarruq* through *murabaha*, diamonds may be bought in one place with under-invoicing, and sold elsewhere at a very large profit (equal to the desired transfer).

To the extent that everything carrying the "Islamic" label (e.g., charities, etc.) is particularly suspect in the aftermath of September 11, 2001, the effects of abuse of Islamic financial practice – even on a very limited scale – can be catastrophic for the industry. Indeed, much smaller events such as the failure of Islamic finance "fund mobilization companies" in Egypt, accused by the government and many analysts of running pyramid schemes,[19] has made it virtually impossible for Islamic finance to flourish in Egypt, which could otherwise be a primary market. Of course, in light of this perceived danger, Islamic financial providers tend to exercise extreme care in "knowing their customers" and in using more reputable offshore financial centers, etc. However, as competition continues to drive profit margins down, the temptation to cut costs along those dimensions can be

[19] Abdel-Fadil 1989.

expected to drive some market participants to take unnecessary risks. All industries suffer occasional scandalous collapses (e.g., Barings Bank, Enron, LTCM, BCCI) due to careless risk taking, driven by greed. However, an industry as young as Islamic finance, not to mention one that exists purely based on its "Islamic" brand-name which is (unjustifiably, but understandably) suspect at this time, cannot survive such a scandal. The current modus-operandi of *shari'a*-arbitrage Islamic financing is too dangerous.

CONCLUDING REMARKS

I opened this paper with a partial quotation of remarks by the BMA governor at a conference. The remainder of the governor's remarks read as follows:

> If the Islamic sector is to continue to grow and to become a powerful force in international financial markets, it must also be able to attract the business of those persons who might prefer to use Islamic banks, but are also prepared to deal with conventional banks and other financial institutions. Islamic banking must do this without in any way compromising its Islamic principles.[20]

The real question is whether "Islamic principles" should continue to be judged purely on juristic grounds. If they are, then any contracts approved by jurists on Islamic financial institutions' payrolls will continue to be deemed "Islamic." This reading of the governor's remarks implies that Islamic finance will simply continue along its current *shari'a*-arbitrage trend.

Alternatively, Islamic finance could strive to adhere to Islamic principles by considering the true spirit of Islamic law. That would require examining the evolution of classical Islamic jurisprudence by the standards of its own time, legal limitations, and economic understanding. If that is accomplished, perhaps the industry can transcend the governor's vision of serving those who would prefer to use Islamic finance, but only if it is competitive. This group also constitutes a captive market, albeit not as captive as the group who refuse to deal with conventional financial providers. In that regard, while the governor's vision is ambitious relative to the current industry's mode of operation, it is quite timid compared to the industry's true potential.

If we take the universal message of Islam seriously, we must believe that enshrined in the *shari'a* (divine law, as opposed to the human understanding – *fiqh* – of a given time and place), then we must believe that Islamic finance will be better finance. In fact, it should be so good as to

[20] *Monday Morning*, February 25, 2004.

attract those who are indifferent as to whether or not it is called Islamic, and whether or not professional financial jurists approve its contracts. It is popularly said that a cobbler complained to Martin Luther that he was just a cobbler, and wondered how he could act as a good Christian within his trade. Luther, the popular story says, instructed him: "make a good shoe and sell it at a fair price."[21] When Islamic finance is truly Islamic, rather than profit-driven *shari'a* arbitrage, it should be good finance at a fair price. At that point, the industry can proudly abandon the "Islamic" brand-name, to everyone's benefit.

---

[21] This popular saying (cited by everyone from evangelical preachers, to music bands, see, respectively, www.covchurch.org/cov/news/item3369.html and www.ocweekly.com/ink/02/47/music-kane.php) is likely an elaboration (possibly apocryphal, but illustrative nonetheless) on a passage in Luther's "Address to the Nobility of the German Nation" in 1520, wherein he said: "A cobbler, a smith, a peasant, every man, has the office and function of his calling, and yet all alike are consecrated priests and bishops, and every man should by his office or function be useful and beneficial to the rest, so that various kinds of work may all be united for the furtherance of body and soul, just as the members of the body all serve one another," c.f. Fordham University's Modern History Sourcebook at www.fordham.edu/halsall/mod/luther-nobility.html. Banking, like all other professions, can be beneficial to society when practiced in an ethical and professional manner. In that regard, an Islamic banker does not need to market his craft as "Islamic banking," just as religious practitioners of other trades do not need to use religious brand-names.

*Fatwa*s and the Fate of Islamic Finance: A Critique of the Practice of *Fatwa* in Contemporary Islamic Financial Markets

Walid Hegazy[1]

INTRODUCTION

Since the emergence of contemporary Islamic financial markets a few decades ago, the institution of *fatwa* (a legal opinion issued by a qualified *mufti*, jurisconsult) has been one of its key features. Islamic financial institutions (IFIs) increasingly rely on *fatwa*s as a source of regulation for the *shari'a* aspects of their practice. This paper argues that there are inherent risks in relying on a *fatwa*-based regulatory system in today's Islamic financial markets. Following a brief review of the influential role that the institution of *fatwa* plays in current Islamic financial markets, the paper addresses certain concerns regarding the practice of *fatwa* in contemporary Islamic finance and offers some suggestions to ameliorate the *shari'a* regulation of Islamic financial markets.

First, a major and easily detected problem of Islamic finance *fatwa*s are the conflicts of interest inherent in the relationship between Islamic financial institutions (IFIs) and IFI *muftis* (*muftis* serving as IFI *shari'a* board members or providing IFIs with ad hoc consulting services).[2] This IFI-*mufti* relationship raises concerns about the independence of such *muftis* and the conflicts of interest arising from the *mufti*'s dual role as IFI *shari'a* auditor and consultant. Such concerns will be examined from both Islamic and conventional perspectives.

Second, unlike a public legislative or regulatory authority, *muftis* are neither equipped nor required to take into account public policy concerns or the needs of different societal interest groups. Rather, *muftis* have a very

---

[1] International Consultant, Fulbright & Jaworski (Houston, Texas).

[2] A relatively small percentage of contemporary Islamic finance *fatwas* are issued by scholars who do not hold any employment or advisory positions at IFIs, such as the *fatwas* issued by the Grand Sheikh of al-Azhar University in Cairo, government-appointed *muftis,* and members of other *fiqh* research institutions or committees.

limited mandate to produce *fatwa*s that respond to specific questions regarding the permissibility of certain acts. To that extent, *muftis* are more concerned with the question of whether a certain act is *halal* (permissible) or *haram* (prohibited) than the question of whether such an act is consistent with the legislative intent *(maqasid al-shari'a)*, the relevant legal principles *(qawa'id)*, or the public policy objectives *(maslaha)* of their society.

Third, *fatwa*s are susceptible to various forms of abusive practices. Being the primary *mustaftis* (sing. *mustafti*, the persons seeking *fatwa*s) in Islamic financial markets and, therefore, the primary source of the *fatwa* questions, IFIs can influence, or even manipulate, the *shari'a* regulation of such markets. IFIs can achieve such manipulation by being able to select important elements of the *fatwa,* including its subject matter and its issuer. Another important source of *fatwa* abuses is the *muftis*' tendency to use circumventive methodologies such as *hila* (juristic stratagem) and *talfiq* (biased amalgamation of previous opinions to circumvent a prohibition) to reach a judgment of permissibility despite a violation of established Islamic principles.

THE INFLUENTIAL ROLE OF ISLAMIC FINANCE *FATWA*S

In its classical and medieval settings, the institution of *fatwa* had a predominant role in the development of the Islamic jurisprudence of both *ibadat* (acts of worship) and *mu'amalat* (worldly affairs such as personal status and commercial affairs). In contemporary Muslim societies, *fatwa* remains an important source of law in the areas of ritual and personal status matters. In the area of commercial law, however, it was not until the emergence of the Islamic finance movement a few decades ago that *fatwa* gained a significant status. With such emergence, many aspects of Muslim countries' secular commercial laws, such as the provisions dealing with questions of interest and damages, were declared by the theorists of the Islamic finance movement to be non-Islamic and to be replaced by *shari'a* compliant rules. This declaration created a legal vacuum in newly emerging Islamic financial markets, which so far has been filled by *fatwa*s issued mainly by the IFIs' *shari'a* boards.

As IFIs continue to grow, Islamic finance *fatwa*s have increasingly gained wide recognition across the Islamic world and beyond. While some *fatwa*s gain such recognition from the reputation of the Islamic scholar or institution issuing them, others gain their recognition because of the lenient interpretations they adopt. In recent years, many such *fatwa*s have become general standards adopted by most IFIs, particularly those *fatwa*s that permit transactions that were once perceived as unacceptable forms of trade according to Islamic principles.

Examples of such *fatwa*s are those that approved the contracts of *tawarruq* (a double sale transaction by which a person, in need of cash, buys an item on credit and immediately sells it for cash to a third party) and *murabaha li-amir bi-al-shira'* (mark-up sale upon the instructions of the potential purchaser). Despite many controversies surrounding the *fiqh* methodologies used to reach such *fatwa*s, most IFIs continue to depend on them in order to practice such contracts.

INDEPENDENCE OF ISLAMIC FINANCE *MUFTIS*

Any successful financial system requires independent and objective regulators. In the current practice of Islamic finance, IFI *muftis* are the *de facto* regulatory authority of the *shari'a* aspects of IFIs' activities. The independence of such *muftis* and the objectivity of their *fatwa*s are challenged by severe conflicts of interest inherent in the relationship between the *muftis* and IFIs. This section will examine such conflicts from both Islamic and conventional perspectives in order to assess to what extent the *fatwa* can successfully function as an independent and objective source of regulation. Before proceeding, however, it is important to mention that the subject of the professional independence of *muftis* is by no means new to Islamic literature. Classical Islamic literature contains extensive discussions about the legal and economic independence of such *muftis*. Such academic discussions were never perceived as attacks on the personal integrity of *muftis*. By raising legitimate and objective questions concerning the IFI-*mufti* relationship, this part of the paper hopes to continue on the path of those academic discussions.

The *fiqh* literature contains voluminous pages of scholarly advice to *muftis* instructing them to maintain a strict code of ethics and warning them against biased and abusive practices. This code of ethics appears to hold *muftis* to a higher standard of professional independence than that required of similar professions in the conventional world. For example, while it is acceptable under conventional auditing standards that external auditors receive compensation from the companies they audit, the same cannot be said about *muftis'* compensation. The issue of whether or not a *mufti* is allowed to receive any *ajr* (stipend) in compensation for producing his *fatwa*s has been controversial, to say the least. This is particularly true with regard to compensation when paid by the *mustafti*.

Islamic Position on *Muftis'* Compensation

A great number of juristic opinions have accumulated against paying the *mufti* an *ajr* for his *fatwa.* In fact, the number of opinions that do not favor the practice of employing *muftis* is so great that the famous scholar Abu Bakr al-Mazari has reported that a juristic consensus had been reached on its prohibition. Other jurists, such as Nawawi, Khanib, and Baghdadi, have remained in favor of appointing jurists as gainfully employed *muftis*, if their stipend is paid from a public treasury (one can see that the last stipulation is meant to ensure the independence of such *muftis*). Those jurists who approved the remuneration of *muftis* have cited the practice of the second Caliph, Umar ibn al-Khattab, as an authoritative precedent. Umar is reported to have allotted an annual stipend of one hundred *dinars* to those who dedicated their time to working on *ifta'*.[3]

There is only one exception found in classical literature to this general rule of prohibiting *muftis* from receiving any type of financial reward from their *mustaftis*. Classical Islamic scholars have allowed *muftis* to receive reimbursement from *mustaftis* for the paper and ink used in writing the *fatwa*. In today's world, this exception can be extended to similar expenses such as airline tickets and hotel bills.

In debating the permissibility of compensating the *mufti* for his *ifta'*, classical scholars discussed two main concerns. On the one hand, a compensation paid by the *mustafti* may impose pressure or influence over the *mufti*. This may undermine *muftis'* assumed objectivity in issuing their *fatwa*s. On the other hand classical scholars were aware of the *mufti*'s need to have a source of income if he is to be completely dedicated to the study of Islamic jurisprudence and other Arabic and Islamic sciences.

The two concerns raised by classical scholars are equally valid and relevant to our time. However, the question of whether a *mufti* should be allowed to receive a stipend for his work of *ifta'* (the study of Islamic jurisprudence for the purpose of issuing *fatwa*s) is only relevant to the case of professional *muftis* who have no other source of income besides their *fatwa* work. When *muftis* are not fully dedicated to the work of *ifta'* or hold other income-earning positions, such as university professorships (whether this was in thirteenth century Baghdad's al-Mustansiriyya or at a modern university), their need for a salary from their work as *muftis* belongs to the area of additional needs *(hajat)* rather than necessities or basic needs *(darurat)*. Scholars determined such *muftis* are not eligible for receiving financial reward for issuing *fatwa*s, whether from their *mustaftis* or an independent entity such as the public treasury.

In the context of Islamic finance, IFIs hire *shari'a* scholars to serve as members of IFIs' *shari'a* supervisory boards (SSB). In general, an IFI pays its SBB members a financial reward for their services in the form of a fixed

---

[3] Riyaa 1996: 325-329.

annual salary, usually determined by a general shareholders assembly based on recommendation of its board of directors. In some instances, SSB members receive a percentage of the IFI's net profit. For example, according to article 42 of the bylaws of Faisal Islamic Bank of Egypt (FIBE), members of the SSB receive 5 to 10 percent of the bank's net profit in the form of rewards and allowances.[4]

Therefore, there is at least a theoretical ground to suggest that SSB members' interest in increasing their income (by increasing the number of approved transactions) may interfere with their *shari'a* auditing task. Even in the case where SSB members receive fixed salaries only, there is still the potential for conflicts of interest because of a lack of independence. SSB members have an incentive, at least in theory, to issue *fatwa*s permitting their employers to carry out the transactions proposed by the IFI executives and staff. As long as some IFI *muftis* are willing to approve a certain transaction, other *muftis* will likely be under pressure to follow such approval.

Aware of these potential conflicts of interest, the majority of classical and medieval Muslim jurists disapproved the payment of salaries to *muftis*, except from independent sources such as the public treasury. However, despite the strict Islamic position regarding *muftis'* remuneration, the different types of financial reward paid by IFIs to their SSB members has not triggered any serious discussion in contemporary Islamic finance literature.

The Independence of IFI *Muftis* under Conventional Professional Standards

Under conventional professional rules, a conflict of interest exists whenever a professional's duty to provide independent opinion or to report accurate information about a client conflicts with that professional's own private interest. As one author puts it, a "[c]onflict of interest is generally thought of as any situation involving hidden 'self-dealing,' 'related-party transactions,' 'non-arms length relationships,' or 'serving two masters' that results in gain to one party at the expense of another."[5] Potential conflicts of interest are very much embedded in the practice of many modern professions such as accounting and financial and legal consultancy.

As is the case in the conventional auditing world, the functions of IFI *shari'a* boards include conflicting consulting and auditing duties. Their consulting duties include reviewing financial contracts and transactions from a *shari'a* perspective and providing *shari'a* opinions in response to

---

[4] al-Ba'li 1991: 247, 248.
[5] Simmons 1997.

fiqh questions posed by IFIs' employees. As IFI *shari'a* auditors, SSB members issue an annual statement indicating to what degree the activities of the IFI, on whose *shari'a* board they serve, do or do not comply with the *shari'a*. Article 40 of the bylaws of Faisal Islamic Bank of Egypt states that "the function of the *Shari'a* Board is to provide counseling and auditing services in connection with the [bank's] application of the rules of *shari'a*. In this regard, the *Shari'a* Board shall have the same powers and authority as those given to the [bank's] accounting auditors."[6] A more detailed description of SSB functions can be found in the bylaws of the Faisal Islamic Bank of Sudan. The bylaws state that the SSB's duties include, among other things, assisting bank officials in creating contract templates used as a basis for the bank's transactions, providing *shari'a* opinions in response to questions submitted by the bank's board of directors, auditing the bank's transactions to ensure its compliance with the *shari'a*, and submitting an annual report to the bank's general assembly in which the SSB opines on the bank's general compliance with the *shari'a*.[7]

The above examples of the SSB's duties raise the same type of conflicts of interest as those existing in a conventional public auditor's activities. IFI *muftis* have two main conflicting duties: First, as IFI *shari'a* counsels, they provide *shari'a* opinions in response to questions submitted to them by IFI officials; second, as *shari'a* auditors, they report to IFI shareholders, customers, and the general public on the extent to which their employer's activities conform to the *shari'a*.

Although there are some similarities between the professional duties of *muftis* and those of lawyers, IFI *muftis* are more comparable to public auditors. In many aspects, the *mufti*'s task of providing *fatwa*s is similar to that of a lawyer providing legal opinions to his clients. Lawyers and *muftis* both have a public duty to safeguard the law and assist judges in establishing societal justice. Lawyers search for legal solutions that protect the interest of their clients without violating the minimum requirements of the law, even if this means resorting to the use of legal loopholes. Similarly, *muftis* have traditionally exerted their legal talents to find a legal basis for legitimizing an act or objective, even if that caused them to use exceptional rules, weak or minority views, or *makharij al-shar'iyya* (lawful devices used by jurists to find alternative bases for permitting certain acts that appear to violate *shari'a* rules), provided that such devices do not circumvent *maqasid al-shari'a* (the legislative intent). However, there is also evidence in the classical *fiqh* literature that *muftis* have frequently used *hiyal* (sing. *hila*, a juristic trick that aims at circumventing the legislative intent behind a certain rule).

---

[6] al-Ba'li 1991: 247.
[7] Ibid., 252-253.

However, there is an important difference between lawyers and *muftis*. While lawyers "make representations of [both] fact and law to judges,"[8] *muftis* make only representations of law to the public, leaving the representations of the facts to the person seeking the *fatwa*. In addition, the lawyer's public duty as an officer of the court does not preclude him from receiving legal fees from his clients, to whom he owes a duty of confidentiality. In that sense, lawyers do not claim to be independent from their clients. *Muftis*, on the other hand, are supposed to be independent from those seeking their advice.

In addition to the *muftis'* traditional task as providers of *shari'a* advice, contemporary IFI *muftis* take on another responsibility as IFI *shari'a* auditors. In this capacity, IFI *muftis* report to IFI shareholders, clients, and the public at large any IFI violations of *shari'a*. In this regard, IFI *muftis* are different from lawyers who don't have such a public auditing responsibility. Quite to the contrary, a lawyer's duty of client confidentiality prohibits disclosure of any information provided to them by the latter, except if either imminent death or serious bodily injury is feared.

In this regard, IFI *muftis* are more comparable to public accountants who in some countries are allowed to offer to the same client both consulting and auditing services. However, following the Enron – Arthur Anderson scandal in the United States and the severe conflicts of interest it revealed, many financial markets have witnessed legislative changes aiming at separating accountants' consultancy services from their function as public auditors. In the United States, for example, the new Sarbanes-Oxley rules prevent public accountants from auditing companies to which they offer consultancy services. No similar actions have been proposed by Islamic finance regulators or scholars despite the striking similarity between the conflicts of interest resulting from combining accountants' consulting and auditing services and those arising from IFI *muftis'* corresponding dual roles.

In fact, there is a more pressing need for separating the consultancy services of IFI *muftis* from their auditing duties. As *shari'a* experts, IFI *muftis* are not just entrusted with applying the law, as is the case with public accountants and auditors. They are also entrusted with interpreting the law and, in this capacity, hardly subject to any regulatory review. As *mujtahids* (jurists who exert their legal talents to find the proper interpretation of the law), *muftis* enjoy a spectacular latitude of freedom in reaching their opinions. Such freedom is not enjoyed by public accountants.

---

[8] Fox 2000: 1103.

PROBLEMS ASSOCIATED WITH *FATWAS'* FOCUS ON PERMISSIBILITY

*Fatwa*s have traditionally been concerned with the question of permissibility, whether an act is *halal* (permissible) or *haram* (forbidden). This concern with permissibility causes *muftis* to overlook important implications of their *fatwa*s, such as conformity with the general principles of Islamic law *(qawa'id)* or the public policy objectives of the society.

Since the default judgment regarding human actions is permissiveness *(al-asl fi al-umur al-ibaha)*, to reach a judgment of permissibility, a jurist needs nothing more than to refute the evidence that supports a prohibition. Thus, such a judgment can be produced by weakening the arguments that attempt to establish prohibition. This can be achieved through the use of *rukhas* (sing. *rukhsa*, exemptions),[9] which are exceptional legal rules permitting a more relaxed application of the law because of the existence of necessity.

In his *Muwafaqat,* Shanibi defines *rukhsa* as "that which is permitted by the *shari'a* as an exception to the general rule . . . of prohibition limited to the case of necessity required [by the *shari'a*] for it."[10] A liberal use of exceptional rules may be legitimate for *muftis* who are concerned with finding answers to individual questions in particular circumstances. What would be perplexing, however, is to grant a *rukhsa*-based *fatwa* recognition as the rule of law under normal circumstances or to relax the conditions required to establish a case of necessity in order to justify the application of such *fatwa*s to other cases. To do so would result in a system defined by anomalies and exceptions and render unreasonable the claim that such a system is Islamic, as it would not reflect well-established Islamic principles *(qawa'id).*

Some of the problems associated with the wide application of permissibility *fatwa*s are reflected in the contemporary practice of Islamic finance. Islamic finance *muftis* tend to focus on whether a particular transaction is valid from a pure juristic perspective without considering whether the application of such a transaction in Islamic markets,

---

9 This is based on a classical distinction in *usul al-fiqh* (principles of legal reasoning) literature between *azima* (the *hukm* under normal circumstance) and *rukhsa* (*hukm* under exceptional circumstances or case of necessity). *Usuli* scholars divide *rukhas* into three different levels: (1) *rukhas wajiba* (mandatory exceptional dispensations), which must be followed upon the occurrence of its specified circumstance or conditions, e.g., the *rukhsa* given to a starving person with no access to food to eat *mayta* (meat of non-ritually slaughtered animals), otherwise prohibited under *shari'a;* (2) *rukhas manduba* (recommended exceptional dispensations), e.g., the permission to shorten the daily prayers during travel time; and (3) *rukhas mubaha* (dispensations that are neither recommended nor reprehensible), e.g., *salam* (forward sale contract). See Qasim 1988: 235.

10 al-Shanibi 2000, 1: 213.

particularly at an institutional level, will be appropriate from a public interest perspective. While it is true that a *mufti* can address public policy questions if posed to him by government or similar institutions, contemporary Islamic finance *fatwa*s usually address individual cases where the task of the *mufti,* usually an IFI *shari'a* board member, is to find a judgment of permissibility.

The main exceptions to this general practice are the *fatwa*s and professional rules issued by the OIC *Fiqh* Academy, the Accounting and Auditing Organization for Islamic Financial Institutions (AAOIFI), and other similar Islamic banking organizations where public interest concerns can sometimes be detected. However, the *fatwa*s issued by the latter organizations do not yet play a significant role toward establishing a *shari'a* regulatory system for Islamic banking. Unlike the OIC *Fiqh* Academy, which addresses a very broad scope of *fiqh* issues, AAOIFI has emerged as a specialized organization serving the Islamic finance and banking industry. Although the main objectives of AAOIFI address IFI accounting standards, the young organization also has *shari'a* related objectives. One such objective is:

> achieving conformity or similarity—to the extent possible—in concepts and applications among the *shari'a* supervisory boards to avoid contradiction and inconsistency between the *fatwa*s and the applications by these institutions, with a view to activate the role of the *shari'a* supervisory boards of Islamic financial institutions and central banks through the preparation, issuance and interpretations of *shari'a* standards and *shari'a* rules for investment, financing and insurance.[11]

It is also encouraging that the AAOIFI's Accounting and Auditing Standards Board represents varying viewpoints, including those of accountants, bankers, *shari'a* scholars, and academics. However, once again, to ensure the board's objectivity, its *shari'a*-related members should be independent scholars who do not simultaneously hold any IFI position, including ad hoc consulting positions. In addition, in order to enhance the regulatory role of the above organizations, the interests of other important participant groups, such as IFI shareholders and clients, central bankers, and other relevant government agencies, must be directly represented.

POTENTIAL *FATWA* ABUSES IN THE PRACTICE OF ISLAMIC FINANCE

*Fatwa*s are nothing more than legal answers to questions posed voluntarily by individuals or institutions interested in finding out whether a certain act

[11] AAOIFI 2004.

is permissible. Consequently, the nature of the *fatwa* questions posed to the *muftis* at one end (the input) determines to a great extent the nature of the *fatwa* answers produced at the output. The fact that the questioner *(mustafti)* decides which question he should ask, and which he should not, gives the questioner the leading role in determining "the output" of the *fatwa*. Also, a *mustafti* has the opportunity to formulate the *fatwa* question in a way that serves his purpose. In addition to selecting the *fatwa* question, a *mustafti* also selects his *mufti*. Therefore, a *mustafti* may be able to influence the outcome of the *fatwa* even further by selecting a *mufti* who is likely, based on his previous opinions, for example, to give the *mustafti* the desired answer.

Classical Islamic scholars have repeatedly advised *muftis* to be cautious in issuing their *fatwas*, warning them that while some questioners may be asking questions with good intentions, others may attempt to abuse the *fatwas* to circumvent the law. One scholar who dealt at length with the Islamic ethics of *ifta'* (issuing *fatwas*) was medieval scholar Ibn Qayyim. In a recommendation *(fa'ida)*, among a long list of recommendations regarding this subject in his "I'lam al-Muwaqqi'in," Ibn Qayyim warns *muftis* from turning their *fatwas* into legal tools in the hands of those who aim to circumvent the law:

> When a query is stated with dishonesty *(tahayul)* aiming at avoiding an obligation or neutralizing a prohibition, it is forbidden for a *mufti* to aid the questioner in achieving his goal or answer him based on his wording [as if the *mufti* has not been aware of the questioner's objectives]. Rather, the *mufti* must be on the lookout for people's deceptions and their dispositions [to benefit themselves]. The *mufti* should not blindly trust his questioners, but rather be cautious and shrewd, to be a scholar *(faqih)* who applies his subtle understanding to the reality, assisted by his subtle understanding of the law *(fiqh)*. Otherwise, he will have both [gone] astray and caused others to go astray *(zagha wa 'azagha)*. How many an issue appear to be good but are, in essence, deception, dishonesty, and sham.[12]

In the context of Islamic finance, *fatwas* resolve questions posed by Islamic finance practitioners, usually indicating that a particular transaction is *halal* (permissible) or *haram* (prohibited).[13] Because these practitioners usually come with conventional financial training and expectations, their questions tend to focus on the permissibility of either a conventional financial practice or a traditional practice that has been reengineered by bankers and lawyers to fit into the conventional banking model.

---

[12] Ibn Qayyim 1998: 4:229.

[13] There are five possible qualifications to any act under *shari'a*: *wajib* (obligatory), *mandub* (recommended), *mubah* (indifferent), *makruh* (reprehensible), and *haram* (forbidden).

Furthermore, some *muftis* employ circumventing *fiqh* methodologies to arrive at a judgment of the permissibility of an act that stands in contradiction with the general principles of Islamic law or the legislative intent. This happens when a *hila* (stratagem) or *talfiq* (amalgamation) is used.

In its lexical definition, *hila* is used to indicate a trick. In the context of *shari'a*, the term *hila* (stratagem, device) is used by Muslim jurists to refer to the attempt by a person (usually with the help of jurists) to circumvent and avoid legal responsibility. This is achieved by changing one or more of the components of the legal judgment or rule *(hukm)* or the conditions under which a given judgment applies, such as the time, place, or the qualifications of the person to whom the judgment applies *(mukallaf)*.

Based on the objective desired, a *hila* takes one of two forms:[14] (1) a *hila* whose objective is lawful, such as establishing rights and resisting wrongdoing, and (2) a *hila* that leads to an unlawful objective. The unlawfulness of the objective to be achieved by the *hila* makes it prohibited. Depending on the means used in achieving the lawful objective intended for it by the *shari'a*, the first type of *hila* may employ either: (1) unlawful means as in the case of using false testimony before a court to establish a legitimate right; (2) lawful means intended specifically for achieving such a lawful objective, as in the case of a stipulation put in a marriage contract providing the wife with the right of divorce in the event her husband marries a second woman; or (3) lawful but not intended, at least primarily, for an objective intended for it by the *shari'a,* as in the case of marrying a woman in order to benefit from her wealth or prestige (as scholars consider the primary purposes of marriage are for seeking company in life, raising children, and non-promiscuity). While the first form of this category of *hila* is unlawful due to its illegitimate means, both the second and third forms of *hila* are permissible, as both their objectives and means are lawful under *shari'a.*

Muslim jurists differ as to the legitimacy of *hiyal*. While the Malikis and Hanbalis condemn the use of all *hiyal* as an illegitimate circumvention of the law, Hanafis and Shafi'is tend to be more lenient toward such use. Other jurists as renowned as the medieval scholar Ibn Qayyim have rigorously argued against the use of *hila*. In his "I'lam al-Muwaqq'in," Ibn Qayyim explains that:

> Allah has prohibited *riba* and *zina* (usury and adultery) as well as derivatives thereof and means thereto because of [their evil effects] and permitted *bay'* (trade) and *nikah* (marriage) and their derivatives for the pure benefits they have. There must be a real difference between *halal* and *haram* or else *bay'* would be treated like *riba* and *nikah* like *zina*. It is well known that the difference in the form without the substance is not meant by Allah, the

[14] Buhayri 1974: 24-27.

> Prophet and the *fitra* (instinct) of His servants for only the intentions and meanings are what is considered or counted in any act or speech. Therefore, words (or actions) of different forms but one meaning (or *maqsad* – legislative intent) have the same *hukm* (rule) and words that have different meanings (or objectives) have different *ahkam* (rules).[15]

Notwithstanding the scholarly debate about the legitimacy of different types of *hila*, most Muslim scholars frown upon uses of certain famous *hiyal,* such as (1) declaring apostasy in order to void *(faskh)* a marriage contract, (2) bidding a high price in order to deceive a potential buyer, (3) a debtor's circumventing his obligation to pay his due debts by giving his property as a gift *(hiba)* to his wife or son in order to become a *mu'sir* (insolvent) and thus qualifying for a grace period allowed by the *shari'a* in such a case, or (4) transferring ownership of property subject to *zakat al-mal* (an obligatory tax levied on property) to one's wife before the time the *zakat* is due. *Zakat al-mal* is due upon completion of *al-hawl* (one lunar year during which a taxable property remained in one's possession). In all of these examples, the focus of the jurist who uses a stratagem in his reasoning is the desirable outcome (rather than consistency or commitment to principles). The way his goal is achieved is through the deconstruction of the components of the legal judgment in order to neutralize one or more of such components to ultimately avoid legal responsibility.

The use of *hila* to avoid the prohibition of *riba*, in particular, and other Islamic legal principles, in general, is by no means a new phenomenon. Throughout Islamic history, there were many episodes where *hila* was used to circumvent the prohibition of *riba,* and Islamic scholars have always been critical of such *hiyal.* The *fiqh* literature provides countless examples of scholars declaring their objections to the expansive spread of *riba*-related *hiyal* in their respective times. Al-Lubudi, a fifteenth-century Muslim scholar, stated that "there is no doubt that every mindful person knows that most debt transactions in this time are *riba* even though people trade in silk or cloth to circumvent such prohibition. [Indeed] the Lord of all lords is aware of what is inside the hearts (He knows the secret and beyond).[16,17] In one further bit of advice, Ibn Qayyim warns *muftis* against falling into the trap of *hila* but encourages them to employ the *makharij al-shar'iyya* (legal tools aimed at finding legitimate alternatives for a prohibited act):

> It is not permissible for a *mufti* to develop a habit of deliberately using stratagems *(hiyal)* whether prohibited *(haram)* or reprehensible *(makruh).*[18]

---

[15] Ibn Qayyim 1998: 3:163-164.

[16] Qur'an 20:7.

[17] al-Shaybani 1997: 159.

[18] There is a distinction between stratagems that are used to turn a prohibited act into a permissible one (prohibited stratagems) and stratagems that are used to turn a reprehensible act into a permissible one (reprehensible stratagems). Allowable

> Nor is it permissible for him to constantly deliver extenuated judgments *(rukhas)* to questioners whom he wishes to benefit and help. Such [an act] would be a grave sin *(fisq)*, and it would be impermissible to query a *mufti* [whose habit it is to do such things]. [However], if a well-intended *mufti* makes use of an allowable stratagem *(hila ja'iza)* that has no dubious affinity with illegal acts and involves no harm *(mafsada)* in order to rid the questioner of a hardship, this would be acceptable or even commendable. God has guided his apostle Job to avoid having to breach his oath [to hit his wife a hundred times] by [pointing that Job could] use a tree-branch that has a hundred twigs and hit his wife with it only once. [Furthermore], the Prophet has guided Bilal [Ibn al-Arith al-Muzani] to sell the dates Bilal bought for *dirhams* and use these to buy [the other kind] of dates [which he wanted to exchange for the dates he initially had] in order to avoid falling into usurious trading.[19] [In fact], legal devices are at their best when used to avoid incurring sins, and stratagems are at their worst when they cause the falling into a prohibition or neutralize a duty, which God or the Prophet has prescribed.[20]

In the contemporary practice of Islamic finance, the use of *hila* varies in degree from one country to another and even from one IFI to another within one country. The most commonly used *hila* in Islamic financial markets is that of *bay' al-'ina,* which is a double sale that takes place between a lender and borrower with the sole purpose of producing an interest-based loan. The practice of *'ina* is common in Pakistan.[21] Another *hila* technique that is used by IFIs throughout the world is the infamous *bay' al-wafa'*, which is a sale with the right of redemption. In this *hila,* a borrower agrees to sell a property to a lender for a cash price but reserves the right to repurchase such a property at its original price after leasing it from that lender for a certain period of time. During the lease period, the borrower pays rent equaling interest. "Despite condemnation by the OIC Fiqh Academy, bay` al-wafa' has reportedly seen use even in the Gulf."[22]

A third example of Islamic finance *hiyal* is the contract *of tawarruq* under which a person in need of cash purchases a property from his lender

---

stratagems *(makharij shar'iyya)* are legal techniques that ease the legal requirements in a given case without turning a prohibited or a reprehensible act into an allowable one.

[19] This story is known in both Bukhari and Muslim's collections of Prophetic reports and establishes the prohibition of the exchange of good dates for bad dates without the mediation of currency (here *dirham*). This report, coupled with others that extend the prohibition to other goods (often six, despite the difference in determining them), is the main source of prohibiting what is known as *riba al-faal* (*riba* of excess; an excess in the exchange of certain goods that are considered *ribawi* items, susceptible to *riba*) under *shari'a.* Discussions among Hanafi and Shafi'i jurists about the rationale behind this prohibition are particularly heated. See al-Zanjani and Ialih 1987.

[20] Ibn Qayyim 1998: 4:222.

[21] Vogel and Hayes 1998: 40.

[22] Ibid., 40.

on installment and immediately resells it to a third party at a cash discounted price. The *tawarruq* arrangement has been used openly and extensively in the Gulf and other Muslim regions. In fact, many IFIs such as HSBC and Emirates Bank advertise their *tawarruq* product on the Internet. Offering contemporary *tawarruq* products is not limited to the cases of necessity. Many IFIs offer *tawarruq* for financing luxury consumer products, such as cars and vacations. Under all major Sunni Schools, except the Hanbali, *tawarruq* is classified as a type of *'ina* sale that is prohibited from being an alternative *hila* to circumvent the *riba* prohibition. Even under the Hanbali School, *tawarruq* is *makruh* (reprehensible) according to Ahmad ibn Hanbal.[23] However, the *Fiqh* Council of the Muslim World League, for example, issued a decision approving *tawarruq* as a valid sale transaction that does not involve *riba*.[24]

IFIs abused this decision and have been extensively using a distorted form of *tawarruq* under which the IFI sells a product to a client at a deferred price and immediately resells it on behalf of that client to a third party for cash price. The fact that IFI is the seller in the two transactions, once as principal and once as agent of the *mustawriq* (the client seeking *tawarruq*) turns this form of *tawarruq* into a practical equivalent of *'ina* which is considered impermissible according to the majority of *fiqh* views. IFIs' abusive practice of *tawarruq* led the Islamic *Fiqh* Council to issue a new fatwa disapproving such practices.[25] Despite the Council's disapproval, IFIs continue to practice the distorted form of *tawarruq* under the excuse of the necessity to compete with conventional banks.

A different method used by Islamic finance jurists to reach a compromise between the requirements of *shari'a* and modern banking is that of *talfiq,* which, as pointed out earlier, is a process of patching or combining views carefully selected from the different schools to obtain a new opinion desired by the *mulaffiq* (the jurist practicing *talfiq*) and not allowed under any of the early views used in the *talfiq* process. However, a jurist may circumvent the accusation of resorting to *talfiq* by acknowledging the use of opinions of previous jurists but still insisting that it was the soundness of their arguments that caused the jurist to do so. However, this does not change the fact that this selective reliance on early juristic views to produce totally new ones puts at risk the very consistency to which these early jurists were committed and thus leads us to expect that the producer of a *talfiq* opinion will have very powerful arguments of his own independent of the authority of those whom he cites.

---

[23] Ibn Taymiyya 1987: 3:363.

[24] Decision issued by the Council's fifteenth session held in Mecca on October 31, 1998.

[25] Decision issued by the Council's seventeenth session held in Mecca on December 13-17, 2003; cited in "*al-Tawarruq ka-ma Tujrih ba'd al-Masarif fi al-Waqt al-Hadir*" by 'Abdul Allah ibn Muhammad Zuqayl, available at http://saaid.net/Doat/Zugail/298.htm (visited November 6, 2004).

Some scholars consider the *fatwa* that approved the commonly practiced contract of *murabaha li-amir bi-al-shira'* as an example of contemporary *talfiq*. *Murabaha li-amir bi-al-shira'* was first introduced in contemporary Islamic finance in the mid 1970s by Sami Hummud, a well-known Jordanian economist and banker, based on a *fatwa* by Sheikh Faraj al-Sanhuri.[26] Hummud was searching for an Islamically-acceptable financial instrument capable of competing with conventional consumer-finance products.[27] IFIs welcomed this new addition from *fiqh* that allowed them to replace a significant part of their practice of high-risk *amana* financing, such as *mudaraba* and *musharaka*. However, in its initial stages, the practice of *murabaha li-amir bi-al-shira'* revealed some risks that IFIs were not prepared to deal with. The non-binding nature of the potential purchaser's promise (the first legal instrument) entitled the potential purchaser (the client) to revoke his promise at any time before concluding the *murabaha* contract (the second legal instrument).

In searching for a solution to such a problem, IFIs began to inquire about possible legal arguments under which the potential purchaser's promise can be legally binding. Citing the late Islamic scholar Mustafa al-Zarqa, Hummud suggested a promise may be legally binding under a popular view within the Maliki school, provided that the promisee has entered into another binding relationship relying on such a promise.[28] The question was then put to IFI *muftis* working as members of the *shari'a* supervisory boards of IFIs. IFI *muftis* started surveying the *fiqh* literature looking for a basis for the required *fatwa*.

A second *fatwa* (second *murabaha fatwa*) was issued by the first conference on Islamic banks, which took place in Dubai in 1978, based upon the approval and recommendation of many Islamic finance *muftis*. Quoting the opinion of Ibn Shubruma, a Maliki scholar from the second Islamic century, this *fatwa* pronounced the permissibility of the previously discussed contract of the *murabaha li-amir bi-al-shira'*.[29] As many scholars noted, the new *fatwa* is contrary to a long-standing traditional view of the majority of all Islamic schools that considers the *wa'd* legally non-binding and revocable by either party.[30] This second *murabaha fatwa* was confirmed by an opinion issued by the OIC *Fiqh* Academy extending a binding nature to *wa'd al-amir bi-al-shira'*. In its fifth conference held in the City of Kuwait in 1988, the OIC *Fiqh* Academy declared that *wa'd*, though ethically binding on the promisor, is not legally binding on such promisor

---

[26] Hummud 1976: 497.

[27] Ibid., 476-481.

[28] Ibid., 306, 307.

[29] For more detail on this contract, see al-Ashqar 1995: 13-48, and 'Aniyyah 1986: 114.

[30] See the opinion of Sheikh 'Abdul 'Aziz Bin Baz, the late grand mufti and head of the Council of Senior Religious Scholars in Saudi Arabia, cited in al-Ashqar 1995: 54-55; Misri 2001: 250-253; Ashqar 1995: 12-48.

"unless it is made conditional upon the fulfillment of an obligation, and the promisee has incurred expenses on the basis of such a promise."[31] According to this *Fiqh* Academy Resolution, the effect of this binding *wa'd* is that the promisor must fulfill it or pay compensation for damages caused due to its unjustifiable non-fulfillment.[32]

Therefore, the contract of *murabaha li-amir bi-al-shira'*, which represents over 70 percent of Islamic financial transactions entered into by IFIs, is the outcome of two *fatwa*s. The first *fatwa,* of Sheikh Faraj al-Sanhuri, which was based on a minority view in the *fiqh*, allowed the *murabaha li-amir bi-al-shira'* contract, but placed restrictions on its practice. The second *fatwa* then removed all such restrictions.

Some authors have questioned both the content of the second *murabaha fatwa* and the imprudent procedures that surrounded its issuance, and have suggested that this *fatwa* has opened the door for IFIs to circumvent the prohibition of interest-based lending. According to one critic, "the participants of the conference did not have sufficient time to access any research or consult their own resources [which] may have caused them to commit a historical error, only God knows its ramifications. [Based on this *fatwa*], the *riba,* which banks around the world are made to practice, has become purely Islamic by only changing its name!"[33] Other scholars saw in a *fatwa* like the second *murabaha fatwa* a means for IFIs to offer conventional banking services, but at a higher price.

The controversy over this second *murabaha fatwa* led scholars to question the very rationale of contemporary Islamic finance, calling for the abandonment of Islamic finance and the resort to the secular system. Interestingly, one of the main skeptics of contemporary Islamic finance is Sheikh Sayyid Eannawi, the Grand Sheikh of al-Azhar, who went so far as to claim that conventional (secular) banks are more Islamic than the IFIs themselves.

As a result of the harsh critiques against the binding *murabaha li-amir bi-al-shira'*, some of its proponents revised their positions and qualified their approval of such transactions.[34] Abdul Sattar Abu Ghudda, who previously approved the binding nature of the *wa'd* in the *murabaha li-amir bi-al-shira'*, announced his reservations on the practice of this form of *murabaha*. He suggested that "in order to avoid the *shubha* (doubt and uncertainty about the permissibility of an act under Islamic law) [of the *murabaha li-amir bi-al-shira'*], it should be opined [by Muslim scholars] that the *wa'd* [of *al-amir bi-al-shira'*] is not binding." Despite such

[31] Islamic *Fiqh* Academy 2000: 86.
[32] Ibid.
[33] Ashqar 1995: 30-31.
[34] See Misri 2001: 50.

critiques, many IFIs continue to include the binding promise of the customer in their *murabaha li-amir bi-al-shira'* transactions.[35]

CONCLUSION

The use of *fatwa*s as the main *shari'a* regulatory instrument in contemporary Islamic financial markets has developed a system that increasingly converges with the conventional system, loses touch with its theological origin, and misses the mark on the original purpose of Islamic finance.

The modern trend permitting the *mufti*'s employment by IFIs ignores well-established legal traditions regarding compensation of the *mufti*, raises conflicts of interest, violates both Islamic and conventional standards of professional ethics, and undermines *muftis'* independence and objectivity.

The *mufti*'s principal task is to determine whether an act is permissible without considerations concerning public policy, the consistency of his opinion with other *muftis'* opinions, the general principles of Islamic law *(qawa'id)*, or the legislative intent *(maqasid al-shari'a)*. A general application of piecemeal *fatwa*s lacking the above considerations will eventually result in a system riddled with anomalies, exceptions, and uncertainty.

In addition, the process of producing a *fatwa* is vulnerable to many abuses. It can be influenced by a *mustafti* who in addition to determining the subject of the *fatwa* is able to select the *mufti* who issues the *fatwa*. Another form of *fatwa* abuse is the *mufti*'s ability to use circumventive *fiqh* methodologies, like *hila* and *talfiq*, to arrive at a judgment of permissibility. An excessive and systematic use of such methodologies will produce a body of irregular *fatwa* opinions which, again, departs from traditional principles and weakens the internal structure of the legal system.

[35] Fayyaa 1999: 27; Ashqar 1995: 87.

Part IV

Meeting the Challenges

The Impact of Basel II on the Future of Islamic Banking

Mansoor Shakil[1]

INTRODUCTION TO THE BASEL ACCORD

The international standards on capital adequacy grew out of the work of the Basel Committee. They were prompted by concerns about the deteriorating capital levels of international banks as a result of increasing competition and about the sovereign debt crisis of the mid-1980s in lesser developed countries (LDCs) that eventually evolved into a global debt crisis. This led the international community, as represented in the Basel Committee, to strengthen systemic defenses to credit risk through the issuance of risk-based capital adequacy standards in the 1988 Basel Accord.[2]

While the original Basel Accord of 1988 was revolutionary when it was introduced, it soon became apparent that it seriously lacked adaptability to the profiles of different banks. The one-size-fits-all approach was too crude, and new institutional structures and evolving market practices greatly reduced its effectiveness. The original Basel Accord dealt with credit risk and later, through a 1996 amendment, addressed market risk too. It came short of dealing with other risks, however, as it presumed that other risks would be covered under credit and market risk.

In view of the deficiencies of the existing accord, the Basel Committee on Banking Supervision (BCBS) embarked upon drawing up a new accord, called Basel II. BCBS issued its revised framework in June 2004 on the New Basel Accord after three consultative papers and three quantitative impact studies (QIS). BCBS aims to have a revised framework available for implementation by the end of 2006.[3]

---

[1] Manager, *Shari'a* Compliance, HSBC Financial Services (Middle East) Limited (Dubai, UAE).

[2] The Basel Committee comprises the G-10 countries plus Luxembourg and Switzerland.

[3] For an official summary of the New Basel Accord, *see* Basel Committee on Banking Supervision (BCBS) 2004.

Basel II is designed to align regulatory capital with underlying risks in order to enhance the capacity of banks to manage risk. The essence of Basel II is in its focus on risk differentiation and the need for enhanced approaches to assessing credit risk.[4]

Basel II is founded on three fundamental pillars:

1. Minimum Capital Requirements
2. Supervisory Review of Capital Adequacy
3. Public Disclosure

The focus of this paper is on Pillar 1 of Basel II: Minimum Capital Requirements. The paper will first summarize the approach adopted by BCBS to determine capital for credit risk in Basel II. Thereafter, it will analyze the impact of Basel II on the Islamic banking and finance industry (IBFI). The analysis carries a critique of Basel II from the perspective of Islamic banks.

The paper intends to demonstrate that while Islamic banks are in as much need of regulation and supervision as their conventional counterparts, a regulatory and supervisory setup more adaptive and responsive to their unique characteristics will not only better fit their needs but also address the underlying concern of BCBS, i.e., the stability of the global banking system.

PILLAR 1: MINIMUM CAPITAL REQUIREMENTS

The capital ratio is calculated using a definition of regulatory capital and risk-weighted assets. The total capital ratio must not be lower than 8 percent. Significant change occurs in the definition of risk-weighted assets used to measure the risk faced by the banks. There are two primary reasons for this change:

1. Substantive changes to the treatment of credit risk relative to the current accord
2. The introduction of an explicit treatment of operational risk such that a measure of operational risk is included in the denominator of a bank's capital ratio

One of the major changes brought by Basel II is the link created between the capital charge for credit risk to explicit indicators of credit quality, either measured externally (the standardized approach) or internally

[4] Saidenberg and Schuermann 2003.

(the internal ratings based approach (IRB)).[5] This stands in contrast to the current accord's one-size-fits-all approach. It also provides for three distinct approaches for the calculation of operational risk.

TABLE 1.

Credit Risk		Operational Risk	
1.	Standardized Approach	1.	Basic Indicator Approach
2.	Foundation IRB Approach	2.	Standardized Approach
3.	Advanced IRB Approach	3.	Advanced Measurement Approach

Credit Risk: Standardized Approach

The standardized approach is somewhat similar to the current accord in that it slots the borrowers in different categories for credit risk purposes based on readily observable credit risk. BCBS proposes to use the ratings mechanism to determine the credit risk of each borrower. The risk weights for sovereign, inter-bank, and corporate exposures are differentiated based on external credit assessments. If no ratings are available then the standardized approach, in most cases, mandates that a risk weighting of 100 percent be applied.

Credit Risk: Internal Ratings Based Approaches

The IRB approach has two versions: Foundation IRB Approach, and Advanced IRB (A-IRB) Approach. Compared to the current accord, the IRB approach is fundamentally different in concept, design, and implementation.[6] In the IRB approach, the banks' internal assessment of key risk drivers serve as primary inputs to the capital calculation. Since the approach is based on the banks' own internal assessment of the risk, the banks will be able to have a more risk sensitive capital requirement. "The IRB approach does not allow banks themselves to determine all of the elements needed to calculate their own capital requirements. Instead, the risk weights and thus capital charges are determined through the combination of quantitative inputs provided by banks and formulas specified by the Committee."[7]

---

[5] Hayes et al. 2002.
[6] *See* Saidenberg and Schuermann 2003: 8.
[7] *See* BCBS 2004.

Operational Risk

Operational risk is not considered explicitly in the current accord. At present, banks employ different approaches toward the calculation of operational risk. However, banks are a long way from developing operational risk calculation techniques comparable to the approaches available for credit risk. One of the major reasons for inclusion of operational risk as a measure for calculation of capital adequacy was to provide banks with an incentive to develop the techniques for the calculation of operational risk.

Basel II has two simpler approaches for the calculation of operational risk: the basic indicator approach, and the standardized approach. The basic indicator and the standardized approaches are less risk sensitive as they simply require banks to multiply the average annual gross income over the previous three years with a factor of 0.15 set by the bank to reach the capital requirement. Additionally, in the standardized approach, the banks will need such calculations for each business line.

While the banks have a natural incentive to move to the Advanced Measurement Approach (AMA) in that it is more risk sensitive, BCBS has also provided the banks with an added incentive to shift to AMA. This is by allowing banks that use AMA to recognize insurance as a risk mitigating factor, and by denying it to banks that use the basic indicator and the standardized approach.

Advantages of Pillar 1 of Basel II for the Islamic Banking Industry

There can be no doubt that the Islamic banking industry does need regulation and supervision. Islamic banks take deposits and essentially play the role of financial intermediaries in the same way as their conventional counterparts, albeit using different techniques. Their soundness and stability is as important as that of the conventional banks, and due to the risk sharing nature of Islamic banks, they need an even more effective system of regulation and supervision.

The A-IRB approach of Basel II provides a number of advantages to Islamic banks. Khan and Ahmad point out a number of benefits that the A-IRB approach will have for Islamic banks.[8] The products of Islamic banks are diverse and in many cases Islamic banks tailor-make a hybrid product for the specific demands of the customer. Since the A-IRB approach allows mapping the risk profile of each asset individually, it suits the Islamic banks better than the standardized approach. Secondly, the risks faced by Islamic

[8] *See* Khan and Ahmad 2001.

banks can be very different from the risks faced by conventional banks and vary in correlation with the diversity of products that they offer. The A-IRB approach also suits Islamic banks because it aligns the actual risk exposure of banks with their capital requirements. Thirdly, most of the Islamic banks are located in developing countries, where existing national regulatory and enforcement structures are weak, and where a great deal of work is required to improve the risk management culture for financial stability and efficiency. It is expected that the A-IRB approach will encourage Islamic banks to enhance their risk management mechanisms. Fourthly, it is hoped that the A-IRB approach will help generate reliable data and information, thereby enhancing transparency and market discipline. Fifthly, the A-IRB approach will use external credit assessment as a benchmark along with internal credit assessment and hence will combine the information access of an internal credit assessment with the objectivity of an external credit assessment, thereby playing an instrumental role in controlling moral hazard and capital arbitrage.[9]

Disadvantages of Pillar 1 of Basel II for the Islamic Banking Industry

While the approach in Basel II may prove to be in the long-term interest of Islamic banks, there may be subtle disadvantages that the Islamic banks may face in the implementation of Basel II.

1. First critique—Systemic risk as a mitigating factor in Islamic banks

Saidenberg argues that there are two sets of reasons for capital regulation.[10] One is the protection of the consumer and the other is the prevention of systemic risk. Banks pose a high level of systemic risk because of the central role that they play in the payment systems and the allocation of resources, coupled with the fact that they are highly leveraged.[11]

Islamic banks are well equipped to handle the systemic risk problem, since neither the profit nor the principal amount in the investment deposits of Islamic banks is guaranteed. Any loss on the asset side, in principle, can be passed on to the liability side within the investment deposits. This two-way transmission of risk from demand to investment deposits and vice versa

---

[9] Ibid.

[10] *See* Saidenberg and Schuermann 2003: 1.

[11] Ibid.

poses potential systemic risk for Islamic banks[12] and neutralizes their enhanced risk absorption capacity. The risk of loss in case of a run on the banks is a risk that is faced by all conventional banks. As far as the unavailability of deposit insurance and lender of last resort is concerned, these are not issues of inherent risk within the structure of an Islamic bank. These are issues that can and will be remedied as Islamic banking gains more and more mainstream acceptability. Islamic banks may therefore be better equipped to deal with systemic risk as compared to conventional banks.

Systemic risk has been a concern to BCBS. While there are no hard numbers to suggest the extent to which it is taken into consideration in the calculation of capital adequacy, if we can quantify the systemic risk reduction element of the Islamic banks we may be able to offset some of the added credit, operational, and market risk capital allocation within Islamic banks.

2. Second critique—Retail banks or investment banks?

Islamic banks enter into a profit and loss sharing partnership with their investment depositors. Investment depositors participate in the risk of the business of the bank in the same way as shareholders of a corporation take the risk of price movement of the share price of the stock. Therefore, Islamic banks could be treated like corporations and hence could be subject to a similar regulatory regime rather than the stringent regulation of the banking sector.

To assess the validity of this argument we need to analyze why a different and much more stringent regulatory regime is required for the banks. The reason that banks are regulated is that they are at the heart of the payment system, are highly leveraged, and their failure can cause systemic risk.[13] Islamic banks carry all these risks. They take deposits, are linked with the payment system, are leveraged, and can cause systemic risk. Therefore, the fact that Islamic banks perform some functions that resemble those performed by corporations does not derogate from the fact that they still require a banking regulatory regime based on the risks that their failure might cause. We may further note that the investment depositors in Islamic banks do not enjoy the same rights as equity investors in conventional

[12] In case of a run on the bank it is highly unlikely that the Islamic banks would be in a position to repay demand deposits. This effectively transfers the business risk from the investment deposits to demand deposits. Conversely the demand deposits increase the leverage of Islamic banks and as a result their financial risk and overall stability.

[13] *See* Saidenberg and Schuermann 2003: 1.

investment companies, but do share the same risks. Their protection further requires a higher level of supervision.

3. *Third critique—Banks from developing countries*

A third critique of Pillar 1 of Basel II is that it is disadvantageous to banks in developing countries. Most of the Islamic banks are based in the Middle East, Pakistan, Malaysia, Sudan, Iran, and Indonesia. The following table shows a distribution of Islamic financial institutions by region with respect to their numbers and funds managed by them.

TABLE 2.

Islamic Financial Institutions by Region (% Numbers)		Funds Managed by Islamic Financial Institutions by Regions (%)	
Europe & America	9.4%	Europe & America	8.2%
Africa	10.6%	Africa	1.2%
Other M.E.	15.3%	Other M.E.	19.7%
G.C.C	22.4%	G.C.C	64.7%
Asia	42.2%	Asia	8.2%

Clearly, Islamic financial institutions are concentrated in developing countries and hence are subject to the peculiar disadvantages faced by banks in developing countries from the implementation of Basel II.

Griffith-Jones, Segaviano, and Spratt argue that the adoption of the IRB approach by internationally active banks would result in a decline in lending to developing countries as it will be more expensive to lend money to developing countries than to developed countries.[14] While such an outcome may be a simple realization of the existing risk, Griffith-Jones, Segaviano, and Spratt counter that Basel II does not take into account international loan portfolio diversification and hence the risk calculation is not accurate. They base their argument on two hypotheses. First, they say that the "degree of correlation between the real and financial sectors of developed economies is greater than that which exists between developed and developing economies."[15] Their second hypothesis is that "An international loan portfolio which is diversified across the developed, emerging and developing regions enjoys a more efficient risk/return trade-off—and therefore lower overall portfolio level risk as measured by

[14] Griffith-Jones et al. 2002.
[15] Ibid.

unexpected losses—than one focused exclusively on developed markets."[16] They thus conclude that taking international loan diversification into account as a risk mitigating factor would allow internationally active banks to lend to developing countries.

BCBS has yet to take into account the potent argument for including the issue of international portfolio diversification. Decreased lending to developing countries would lead to increased difficulties for banks in such countries (including Islamic banks) to secure international financing. Additionally, the reduced lending by internationally active banks to developing countries will reduce competition for domestic banks from developing countries and this will actually lead to a growth of the banking sector in the developing countries. However, the cost of lending/financing for domestic banks would likely be higher, offsetting some or all of the benefit that the lack of international competition may bring.

4. Fourth critique—Pillar 1 of Basel II is disadvantageous to small banks

Islamic banks are generally smaller than their conventional counterparts in their respective jurisdictions and certainly with respect to international standards. While Islamic banking has enormous growth prospects, some of which are beginning to be realized, there remains a gulf between the magnitude of business they conduct and that of internationally active conventional banks. Recently, plans have been finalized to launch a new Islamic bank with a paid-up capital of US$1.5 billion and authorized capital of US$3 billion during the current year.

Table 1.3 below illustrates that Islamic banks in terms of both assets and capital will fall within the category of small banks.

[16] Ibid.

TABLE 3.

Islamic Banks and Financial Institutions by Size of Assets		Islamic Banks and Financial Institutions by Size of Capital	
Assets (US$ Millions)	*Frequency* Distribution	*Size of Capital* (US$ Millions)	*Frequency* Distribution
0-50	39	0-25	55
51-100	13	26-50	10
101-200	4	51-75	6
201-300	3	76-100	2
301-400	8	101-150	2
401-500	1	151-200	2
501-1000	3	201-300	2
> 1000	7	Total	79
Total	78		

[17]Source: *Directory of Islamic Banks and Financial Institutions* (Jedda: IAIB, 1996).

The cost of implementation, the requisite technology, and the expertise required to implement the A-IRB and/or AMA approach suggests that only the large banks have the resource wherewithal to take up these approaches. This suggests that only the larger banks will be able to lower their capital requirements by efficient calculation of risk. This will place the already disadvantaged small and medium-sized banks into further competitive disadvantage. The following is data from Quantitative Impact Study 3 (QIS3) about how A-IRB methods changed capital requirements compared to the current rules for twenty large U.S. banks.[18]

TABLE 4.

Corporate Loans	26% Reduction
Small to Medium-sized Enterprise Loans	39% Reduction
Residential Mortgages	56% Reduction
Credit Card Receivables	16% Reduction
Other Customer Loans	25% Reduction

Table 4 suggests that banks following the A-IRB approach will have significant advantages over other banks.

---

[17] The statistics are old but it is difficult to get hold of the most current statistics. Euromoney is working on a project to develop a detailed databank, but its project is still in the making.

[18] Zions Bancorporation 2003.

The competitive disadvantage for small banks would be reflected in the stock market. The Capital Asset Pricing Model has two drivers for valuing a stock: expected return on equity, and expected growth rate. Both of these would be hampered as a result of requiring small and medium-sized banks to hold more capital. This will lead to consolidation within the banking industry, which at one level may be acceptable but at another level may create banking "giants," which are "too big to fail" and will therefore pose a severe threat to systemic stability.[19] In the context of Islamic banking, this will also mean that bigger conventional international players entering the Islamic banking market will be a severe threat to small, indigenous Islamic banks.

5. Fifth critique—Penalizes lending to small and medium-sized enterprises (SMEs)

BCBS has made significant progress in the treatment of loans to SMEs. Under the third consultative document the treatment of loan exposure to SMEs of up to one million euros as retail exposure is a welcome improvement. However, there are still issues of concern. The granularity criterion, for instance, which was proposed in the standardized approach in the QIS 3 Technical Guidance that no aggregate exposure to one counterpart could exceed 0.2 percent of the overall regulatory retail portfolio, would discriminate against SME-retail customers of smaller banks.[20] Furthermore, under the standardized approach supervisors may determine higher risk weights for retail exposures. A lot of discretion has been left in this case to the supervisors and while they may increase the risk weights, no similar provision has been included for reduction of risk weights in light of the changed circumstances.

Most of the Islamic bank's customer base is within the SMEs. Under Basel II they will discover that lending to SMEs in some cases is not preferable. This will discourage lending to SMEs and will affect both the Islamic banks and the economy of the country—particularly given the crucial role of SMEs in the economy of any country in general and the economies with a significant Islamic banking presence in particular.[21]

---

[19] Ibid.

[20] For a detailed discussion on the issue *see* Basel Committee 2003.

[21] Ibid.

6. Sixth critique—Treatment of operational risk

Sundararajan and Errico argue that operational risk is a very crucial risk in Islamic banking operations.[22] They maintain that the peculiar nature of Islamic banks contributes to the operational risk that they face. The investment nature of Islamic banks require stringent internal control mechanisms to monitor compliance of the investment with the objectives of Islamic banks and proper accounting for their operations.[23]

In view of the fact that there is no developed mechanism for the analysis of operational risk, nor are there any recognized standards for translating operational risk components into capital standards, and that the nature of operational risk in Islamic banks is such that there is almost no data or model available to follow, it will be appropriate if operational risk is moved to Pillar 2 until such time when the tools for calculating operational risk are made available and refined.

PILLAR 2: SUPERVISORY REVIEW OF CAPITAL ADEQUACY

Under Pillar 2, supervisors are to ensure that each bank holds sufficient capital in view of its risk profile.[24] "[It] is inevitable that a capital adequacy framework, even the more forward looking Basel II, will lag to some extent behind the changing risk profiles of complex banking organizations, particularly as they take advantage of newly available business opportunities. Accordingly, this heightens the importance of, and attention supervisors must pay to pillar two."[25]

One of the aspects that the Islamic banks have been missing is a thorough supervisory review and support in accordance with their specialized operations. It can be hoped that they will receive more attention under Basel II. However, there are areas of concern. Under Basel II the burden on the regulators will increase tremendously. They will also be under pressure because of the *modus operandi* of the calculation of operational risk. The capacity and resources of regulators in the GCC countries vary significantly, as they do in other countries with a significant Islamic banking presence. It is feared that under Basel II the inconsistency between the regulatory regimes in place may increase tremendously. This will hurt the very basic objective of Basel II of "creating a level playing

---

22 *See* Sundararajan and Errico 2002: 4-5.
23 Ibid.
24 Comment by America's Community Bankers, November 3, 2003, to FDIC on the New Basel Accord.
25 BCBS 2004.

field"; in addition, it will also hurt those Islamic banks that may as a result be subjected to a more rigorous regulatory regime compared to banks under regimes that may have rather relaxed rules.[26]

PILLAR 3: PUBLIC DISCLOSURE

Pillar 3 complements Pillar 1 and Pillar 2. The Committee has developed a minimum set of disclosure rules that will allow market participants to assess key information about a bank's risk profile and level of capitalization.

Pillar 3 will help strengthen confidence in Islamic banks by requiring them to disclose information at an industry standard. This information disclosure is in addition to other avenues for disclosure of information that the banks may have. The minimum disclosure requirements may also help in bolstering further confidence in the two-tier *murabaha* model where the information asymmetry places the investor at a disadvantage in monitoring the performance of the bank.

CONCLUSION

In view of what has been discussed above, it is clear that Islamic banks are in as much need of regulation and supervision as their conventional counterparts. However, in view of their distinct characteristics, a regulatory and supervisory setup more sensitive to their unique characteristics and more adaptive and responsive to their emergence will more strongly address the underlying concern of BCBS, i.e., the stability of the banking system.

Khan and Ahmad argue that demand deposits and investment deposits of Islamic banks should be completely segregated. This will prevent the two-way transmission of systemic risk between demand and investment deposits. They propose separate capital adequacy standards for the demand and investment accounts and argue that this will "serve the firewalls and safety net requirements of major regulatory and supervisory jurisdictions around the world."[27] They suggest two alternatives to the existing setup. The first alternative would be to keep demand deposits in the banking book and investment deposits in the trading book, with separate capital adequacy requirements for the two books. This will prevent the two-way transmission of systemic risk between demand and investment deposits and hence enhance the stability of the overall banking system.

---

[26] *The Basel II Capital Accord: Where Do Arab Banks Stand?* (The Report of the Union of Arab Banks, September 2003). On file with the author.
[27] *See* Khan and Ahmad 2001.

The second alternative would be to pool the investment deposits of an Islamic bank into a securities subsidiary of the bank with independent capital adequacy standards and consolidated supervision.[28]

A third alternative is based on the idea of setting up two tiers of Islamic banks.[29] The first tier of banks would be responsible for the payment system of the country while the second tier would comprise a number of specialized *mudaraba* banks in different sectors of the economy. The diversification would make the second tier banks shock-proof as a whole in case of an economic downturn. On the other hand, the complete separation between the two tiers of banks would ensure that any shock in the *mudaraba* banks is not transmitted to the banks responsible for the payment system, thus eliminating or at least substantially reducing systemic risk, the major cause for banking regulation.

The proposed alternatives are more in line with the characteristics of Islamic banks and would bring more stability to the Islamic banking system. At the same time it is hoped that they would help enhance the credibility and acceptance of Islamic banks to the different regulatory regimes. Ishrat Hussain, governor of the State Bank of Pakistan, said at a recent conference that the objective of Islamic banking regulators is "to nurture a competitive dynamic, sustainable Islamic Financial Service Industry as an integral part of [the] Global Financial System."[30] It is hoped that the proposed alternatives will help achieve this objective and will result in the further growth of Islamic finance.

---

[28] Ibid.

[29] This alternative, an offspring of Narrow Banking, is being argued by Iqbal Kahn, CEO of HSBC Amanah, as the future course for Islamic banks.

[30] Presentation made at the Annual General Assembly Meeting of IFSB held at Nusua Dua, Indonesia, on March 31, 2004.

Islamic Banking and the Politics of International Financial Harmonization[1]

Kristin Smith[2]

INTRODUCTION

In the mid-1970s, the Arab Gulf made a dramatic entrance onto world financial markets. In one year, oil prices quadrupled, precipitating the fastest transfer of wealth in the twentieth century. Many Gulfis who previously had no dealings with financial institutions had their first introduction to banking. It quickly became apparent, however, that there was a tension between the institutions and norms underlying Western finance and the prevailing belief among many Gulfis that earning interest is forbidden by Islam. Throughout the Gulf, and particularly in Saudi Arabia, religiously observant individuals chose to leave their money in non-interest-bearing accounts rather than contravene Islamic law.

This cultural difference opened up the space for entrepreneurs to mediate between the global system and local beliefs and customs. The result was the creation of Islamic banks: financial intermediaries that offer services similar to those of conventional banks, but through financial instruments legally structured to comply with Islamic religious law *(shari'a)*. The entrepreneurs behind this institutional innovation have been able to create a profitable niche for themselves among the religiously conservative populations of the Gulf. Beyond their marketing advantage, they have likewise used demands for parity with conventional banks to receive government contracts, and the desire of foreign investors to present a "local" face on their business to market themselves for joint ventures. Their advantages are not strictly economic, however, as my research into the Islamic finance industry in Kuwait, Bahrain, and the UAE has shown.[3]

---

[1] This paper is based on field research made possible by the Fulbright Commission and the Social Science Research Council.
[2] *Qatar Postdoctoral Fellow*, Center for Contemporary Arab Studies, Georgetown University, Washington, D.C.
[3] See Smith 2004: 168-190.

Politically, the banks have been instrumental in creating synergistic relationships between Islamist businessmen, Islamist political candidates, and the Islamist political movements more generally. And socioculturally, the Islamic movements have been adept at using the public position of the banks within the economy to demonstrate the applicability of Islamic law to modern life, and to proselytize for Islamic values and lifestyle.

All of these advantages certainly make the cultural and structural difference of Islamic finance worth defending. This is not always easy, however, especially as the Islamic banks operate within a broader global economy completely oriented toward interest banking. In this setting "difference" can also be a liability, especially since the Asian financial crisis, as harmonization of business practices and regulations has been placed at the top of the agenda of international financial institutions (IFIs) and global policymakers. With the emphasis on standards and global norms, a premium is set on uniformity, putting Islamic banks at a disadvantage.

Clearly then there exists a tension for Islamic banks between their commitment to keeping their distinctive character and their desire to expand business through deeper integration into global markets. Their response has been to attempt an Islamic integration into the international financial system, which entails working with the existing international financial institutions to improve internal practices and to upgrade supervision of Islamic banks while simultaneously insisting on the distinctive nature of Islamic finance and therefore its need for separate regulation. To accomplish this, Islamic banks have adopted the surprising strategy of lobbying over the heads of their own state regulators, appealing directly to those international financial institutions that set the agenda for standardization and regulation, in the hope of winning their support in persuading their own central banks of the need for distinct regulations for Islamic finance. This has resulted in the realization of new transnational Islamic institutions for accounting standards, financial prudentials, the rating of individual banks and products, and the management of liquidity that mirror conventional ones and are meant to regulate and facilitate the functioning of Islamic finance internationally.

This outcome is remarkable. It runs counter to a decade-long trend of the growing irrelevance of regional standard-setting bodies that have come under intense pressure from IFIs and global businesses, which increasingly demand the adoption of uniform international standards as the cost of doing business. More surprising is the fact that these same IFIs appear to be granting their support and imprimatur to these Islamic standard-setting bodies, giving an enormous boost to Islamic finance in its search for international recognition and legitimacy.

Furthermore, the challenge of achieving international recognition on their own terms has pushed Islamic banks to greater levels of self-awareness and organization. The individual Islamic banks were forced to confront substantial obstacles to collective action and interest representation in order to pull together as an industry to create transnational institutions able to defend and speak for Islamic finance internationally. The outcome is nothing short of a new global market for Islamic finance, underpinned by distinct regulation and expanded through improved industry-government cooperation in the creation of new products.

In this paper I will recount this bold act of market creation and examine its impact. How did the new institutions of the Islamic market come about in the face of resistance from world policymakers and hostility from the majority of the Islamic countries' central banks? Now that a separate institutional framework for Islamic finance exists on a global level, what will be its relationship to the existing international financial architecture? Do these institutions simply facilitate the integration of Islamic finance into global finance, or can they be instrumentalized economically and politically to (1) negotiate favorable concessions in regulations, (2) promote regional markets and divert capital flows from the West toward Muslim countries, and (3) nurture Islamic unity and promote an Islamic worldview?

My underlying argument is that Islamic banks have sought to use their difference strategically to negotiate to their advantage while working *within* the global economic system. Yet at the same time, in constructing their difference institutionally on the global level, Islamic finance has now created a separate financial architecture distinct from conventional finance. Thus far the focus of Islamic financial institutions on the global stage has been on expanding commercial opportunities through international integration. However, there exists the potential that in the increasingly polarized political environment of the war on terrorism, these institutions may become instruments of those waving the banner of Islam in an attempt to mobilize political loyalities with the intent of shifting business patterns away from the West. I will examine this possibility in the conclusion of this paper.

THE NATURE OF INTERNATIONAL INTEGRATION

In the past two decades world financial markets have undergone dramatic changes. A wave of deregulation in the 1980s allowed for an unprecedented autonomization and internationalization of markets. Capital flows increased dramatically, as did the global reach of these financial markets, leaving few regions of the world untouched. This expansion of world capital markets has worked to the advantage of Islamic finance, allowing the industry to broaden its sights beyond domestic markets to Islamic communities throughout the Islamic world and in the West. Some leading institutions have grasped the potential of this expansion and are working to create transnational enterprises capable of providing a full range of Islamic banking and investment services globally.[4]

While the greater openness of international finance is favorable to the industry, some of its new regulatory expressions pose particular challenges. In response to a series of financial crises that sent shockwaves through the global financial system, the United States in coordination with IFIs has been leading a campaign to strengthen the infrastructure of the global financial architecture. This has involved a new wave of global regulatory initiatives aimed at harmonizing financial practices and enforcing global standards on issues such as capital adequacy and accounting and auditing standards. Thus Islamic financial institutions have found themselves under pressure to comply with these regulations and standards that are inattentive to their special characteristics and often detrimental to their interests. In this section, I examine their strategic options in approaching the challenge of preserving difference in the face of international financial standardization.

When faced with the obligation to comply with increased regulation, the economic literature suggests that firms—especially smaller ones—may choose to avoid the extra costs of regulation and retreat into the informal sector.[5] At first glance, informality may seem to be an attractive option for Islamic finance. Many of the Gulf Islamic banks have special status within their national regulatory environments which gives them some leeway in negotiating compliance with national banking laws. Also, Islamic firms already have considerable resources for self-regulation—specifically, a shared set of norms to guide them and internal supervisory committees (in the form of *shari'a* boards) to ensure that these norms are adhered to. Also, interviews conducted in the Gulf suggest that Islamic understandings of contracts already form a basis of understanding for many informal business arrangements carried out between small importers and traders.[6]

Despite these assets, informality has not been an option for most Islamic banks. Although Islamic banks are often small by global standards, they are usually too large to escape the notice of domestic regulators. Even

---

[4] The original transnational Islamic banks were the Saudi-owned Al-Baraka and Faisal Islamic Bank, but other domestically-oriented banks are now expanding. For example, Kuwait Finance House is now established in Turkey and Bahrain, has been granted a license to establish a bank in Malaysia, and has applied for one in Lebanon.

[5] For a discussion of the potential costs of implementing international standards, especially by small firms in the developing world, see the *2001-2 World Development Report* (WDR), "Institutions for Markets," the World Bank, section 1.71-1.75.

[6] Interview with Paul Kennedy, author of *Doing Business with Kuwait* (London: Kogan Page Ltd, 1997), December 1999. An example of a traditional Islamic transaction used in informal trade in Saudi Arabia is the "10-14," where a suq merchant could get an Islamically acceptable loan by paying 14 riyals on a old bag of rice worth only 10 riyals.

more importantly, Islamic banks are highly dependent on the financial markets of the West—although rather unusually for emerging markets, Gulf banks depend on global capital markets more as investment outlets, not as sources of capital. For example, a recent survey of Islamic mutual funds found that 70 percent of their holdings were directed toward the North American and European markets. The restricted size of stock markets in Muslim countries and the higher level of country risk both limit investment opportunities in the Islamic world.[7] Islamic banks also rely on partnerships with Western financial institutions for their financial expertise and international reach, and to manage their short-term liquidity. Thus, most Islamic financial institutions are globally integrated *in fact*, and must deal head-on with the reality of global harmonization and standard setting. In short, while the smaller, more autarkic banks may wish to "go it alone" through a combination of self-regulation and negotiation with national governments, this is simply not an option for the larger, more globally integrated Islamic banks. These banks depend on international partnerships to grow, and thus require the legitimacy conferred by regulatory approval to function in the global marketplace.

Given this need for international legitimacy, and more immediately the obligation to comply with state regulators, Islamic banks appeared to be left with no alternative but to apply the international standards set for conventional banks; indeed, most Islamic banks report to their central banks using the templates laid down by international bodies such as the International Accounting Board (IAB) and the Basel Committee of the Bank for International Settlements (BIS). But this arrangement has problems as well. As the framework used by conventional banking regulators is not specifically tailored to Islamic finance, there is considerable leeway in how Islamic banks choose to report their balance sheets. This "cherry-picking" in the application of international standards has led to the non-comparability of balance sheets among Islamic banks—a situation that is troubling even to international regulators. Furthermore, although individual Islamic banks may profit from the resulting loopholes, the industry as a whole feels disadvantaged by the inattention to the differences inherent in Islamic banking, especially as regulators and rating agencies appear to emphasize the risks of Islamic finance, without fully appreciating the mechanisms for alleviating those risks.

This has prompted the largest, most globally present Islamic banks to negotiate a "third way" between rejection and full integration by attempting an Islamic integration into global markets. This entails a vigorous defense of the need for distinctive standards for Islamic finance, while conceding the need for harmonization and improved governance and transparency within the Islamic banking industry. To carry out both tasks—the formation

[7] Wilson 2002. In December 2001 there existed 105 Islamic mutual funds, and only twelve of them were directed at emerging markets.

of new standards for Islamic banks, and the promotion of their adoption—an interlocking set of new transnational institutions is taking shape. The key institution leading this charge has been AAOIFI, the Accounting and Auditing Organization for Islamic Financial Institutions. In the next section, I will look at the creation of this remarkable institution and its role in establishing separate standards for Islamic finance.

ISLAMIC INTEGRATION: THE CREATION OF AAOIFI

The Accounting and Auditing Organization for Islamic Financial Institutions (AAOIFI) is a private self-regulatory body created to promulgate accounting and auditing standards for Islamic banks. AAOIFI was initiated by an alliance of the largest domestic and transnational Islamic banks and a supranational body, the Islamic Development Bank (IDB). The idea to fashion an alternative set of accounting standards different from those laid out by the International Accounting Board (IAB) was first taken up at the annual meetings of Islamic banks organized under the auspices of the IDB in 1987. After extensive discussions that included at various times Islamic bank officials, Islamic legal scholars, academics, accountants, and regulators, the idea of a standard-setting body for Islamic financial institutions was endorsed in the IDB Islamic bank meeting two years later in 1989. The Financial Accounting Organization for Islamic Banks and Financial Institutions (FAOIBFI)—which later became AAOIFI when auditing standards were added to its agenda—was finally registered in Bahrain in 1991.

The push for specific standards tailored to Islamic finance, then, came not from state regulators but from the banks themselves. The fact that private sector institutions took the lead in their own regulation is unusual; although some private sector actors have pushed for greater regulation (most notably the Mexican financial sector), this is relatively rare, and exceedingly so in the Middle East.[8] The alternative faced by these banks, however, was not to be left unregulated, but rather to be forced to adhere to conventional banking regulations as interpreted by their central banks.

It is difficult to understand the creation of AAOIFI without first appreciating the attitude of state regulators toward Islamic finance. In my own research I found those charged with regulating banks to be very conformist in their beliefs and eager to enforce international norms and standards. They were mostly educated in Western institutions and took seriously their role in enforcing economic orthodoxy. In many cases they viewed Islamic finance as an aberration and an embarrassment. They also resented the special treatment of Islamic financial institutions that often left

[8] The unusual nature of the enterprise is noted by Abdel Karim 1995b.

the latter outside of their full control; as one bank official in the United Arab Emirates stated to me, "Why should a bank having the word 'Islamic' in its name mean we treat it any differently?"[9] Even in states that were supportive of Islamic finance, such as Kuwait, the central bank was unaccommodating. And in those states that did not recognize Islamic finance, such as Saudi Arabia, separate consideration was impossible. At best, then, state regulators were ignorant and indifferent to the special needs of Islamic finance; at worst they were openly hostile to its claims of cultural exception.

The first secretary general of AAOIFI has stated directly that the motivation behind the creation of AAOIFI was the anxiety individual Islamic banks felt about the actions of their respective governments; specifically they feared that central banks and stock exchanges would force the Islamic banks to implement the standards set down for conventional banks by international regulatory bodies such as the IAS and Basel Committee in a way detrimental to their interests.[10] In a pre-emptive measure to avoid this regulation by conventional bodies, they agreed to form their own standard-setting organization charged with adapting regulations specifically for Islamic finance. This gave the banks an independent transnational institutional base from which they could—in the words of the secretary general—"mobilize more power to resist pressures from their environments"[11] and win special consideration for the industry.

In doing this, however, the individual Islamic banks faced considerable obstacles to collective action. The Islamic banking industry up until this time had a poor record in organizing, primarily due to the immaturity of the industry, the reality of business competition, and personal rivalries among its leading members. The banks also operate in a number of different countries and could not rely on national authorities to help in organizing. Furthermore, no banks like to be regulated, and some of the smaller, locally-oriented Islamic banks were enjoying the ambiguity of regulation in the current situation. It was the banking groups such as al-Baraka, which are present in several different countries, that suffer from the lack of uniform regulation most acutely. Therefore, it was up to these large globally-present Islamic banks to overcome their differences and take the initiative in organizing.[12] Indeed, the budget for the standard-setting

---

9 Interviews with Farooq A. Ashraf, Banking Supervision and Examination Department, UAE Central Bank, January 2001; Salah Kohli, assistant manager, Supervision Department, Kuwait Central Bank, November 1999; discussion with Abdel Razaq Abdul Khalik Abdulla, internal audit manager, Bahrain Islamic Bank, January 2001, on its early dealings with the Bahrain Monetary Authority.

10 Abdel Karim 1990: 302.

11 Ibid., 303.

12 This outcome is consistent with collective action theory, which suggests that market makers are willing to take on the added costs of organizing. See Olsen 1965: 29-31.

organization was paid through contributions from the IDB and the four largest institutions in the industry: the Faisal Group of Islamic Banks, the Al-Baraka Group of Islamic Banks, Al-Rajhi Banking and Investment Corporation, and Kuwait Finance House.[13]

From its inception, AAOIFI has been fighting on two fronts: (1) with its own constituents, to force an improvement in transparency and compliance with its regulations, and (2) with global institutions and central banks, to obtain recognition of Islamic finance's unique attributes and need for appropriately tailored regulations. As suggested above, the efforts to bring cohesion and consensus within the industry are challenging. Islamic finance incorporates companies from some thirty-seven countries, many with very different practices. Differences are particularly pronounced between the two axes of the industry; the Gulf being more conservative, and Malaysia more liberal in its Islamic legal *(shari'a)* interpretations. Due process procedures for drafting standards are thus both lengthy and complex. The initial committees argue for a long time to get a base set of proposals that are then sent to AAOIFI's *shari'a* committee and to the Acting Board before being issued as an exposure draft which goes out to about three hundred institutions. After receiving comments and review at a public hearing, the draft has to go back to the board for the amendments and to pass again through the *shari'a* committee.[14] This lengthy due process procedure guarantees broad input from the industry and prevents any individual or clique from controlling the process. The committees themselves are chosen strategically to bring in individuals with widespread influence and respect, and to incorporate views from across the industry (both ideologically and geographically). Although working slowly, AAOIFI has now succeeded in issuing fifty standards in the areas of accounting, auditing, governance, ethics, and *shari'a* rulings.[15]

Ultimately, of course, the standards will only be effective to the degree that the institutions adopt them, or at least look to them as a base. Here AAOIFI has faced the same difficulties as other standard-setting bodies that rely on voluntary adoption. Thus far only three states (Bahrain, Sudan, and Qatar) have adopted AAOIFI's standards in full, although others (Saudi Arabia, Malaysia, Jordan) are studying them or are looking to adapt them, and some individual banks turn to them on their own.[16] Clearly then, AAOIFI faces a fundamental dilemma. Its very existence is attributable to the conviction that Islamic banks will not get a fair hearing from their central banks. Yet because these banks operate in government-driven

---

[13] Abdel Karim 1995a: 121.

[14] Related in an interview with Rifaat Ahmed Abdel Karim, secretary general of AAOIFI, Bahrain, December 11, 2000.

[15] AAOIFI 2004.

[16] Malaysia's current debate over accounting standards for Islamic banks was recently discussed on an Islamic investors' website. *See* Hafizah 2001.

economies, the only way to get AAOIFI standards fully implemented by recalcitrant banks is through the directives of these same government institutions![17] It is for this reason that the sympathy and support of the IFIs is so important to AAOIFI's success. The IFIs yield enormous influence over central banks in the region, and support from them would have the effect of legitimizing the enterprise of Islamic finance. AAOIFI's strategy, then, has been to lobby over the heads of the national governments in the hope that they can bring the IFIs to their cause and through them the central banks. A flow chart of this dynamic is displayed below:

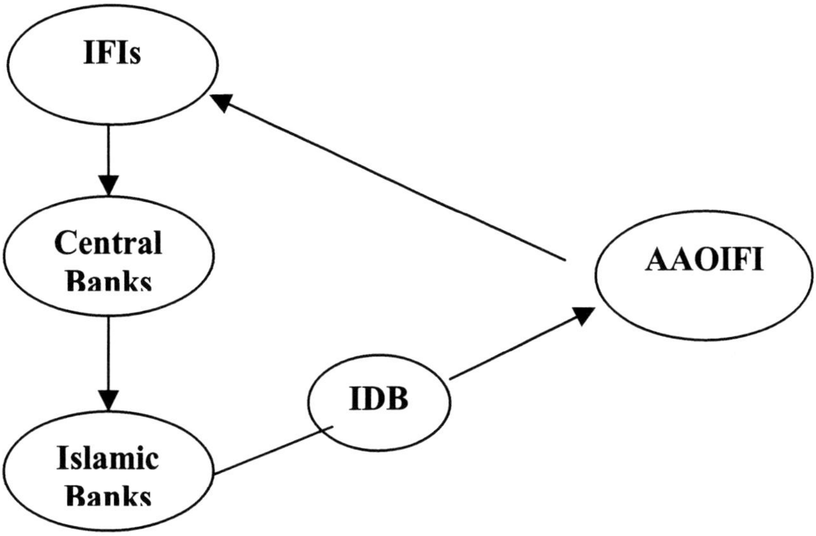

FIGURE 1.

Once constituted, then, AAOIFI began an all-out campaign to gain the recognition and backing of IFIs such as the International Accounting Board (IAB) and the Bank for International Settlements (BIS) which issues standards on capital adequacy through its Basel Committee. To gain the sympathy of these IFIs, AAOIFI lobbied them directly, but also began an assiduous courting of a most important mediator, the International Monetary Fund (IMF).

The IMF had become aware of Islamic finance through its member countries, particularly those that were attempting to implement from the top down a fully Islamic financial system. Its first operational involvement was with Iran, which was seeking to issue Islamically acceptable treasury bills. Later, the IMF also assisted the Sudan in developing an Islamic financial

[17] The need for the central bank support is duly noted by Abdel Karim 1990: 304-305.

instrument for absorbing liquidity from the market. These initial forays into Islamic finance were complemented by some studies through the IMF research department into the effects of Islamic finance on government and monetary policies.[18] Yet another working paper was commissioned in 1998 to look at issues of prudential regulations and supervision in Islamic finance.[19] Still these engagements could be characterized as ad-hoc and did not constitute a significant visible engagement with the industry.

This more substantial interaction came through the persistence of AAOIFI, which succeeded in convincing the IMF to cosponsor a conference on the regulation of Islamic financial institutions held in Bahrain in February 2000. This conference received heavy participation from IMF officials, who presented papers on a wide variety of regulatory issues. A review of the papers, however, reveals that there was still not much intellectual engagement with the specific needs of Islamic finance; most of them merely reviewed the standing international regulations and urged Islamic banks to come into compliance with these conventional regulations—a point that was coldly received by the participating Islamic bankers.

Nonetheless, this conference did mark a gathering momentum in the interest and full engagement of IFIs in Islamic finance. It is fair to say that the IMF did not fully appreciate the consequences of its participation; as David Marston, the IMF Division Chief of Banking Supervision and Regulation, noted (tongue in cheek) he was "conned" into participation by AAOIFI Secretary General Rifaat Abdel Kareem, and was drawn into even deeper involvement in negotiations over the regulation of the Islamic finance industry after that. In these initiatives, he characterized the IMF as a "facilitator" and freely credited AAOIFI as being the "prime mover." The following September at the annual meetings in Prague, the IMF issued invitations to the central bank governors of eighteen countries to set up a working group to consider specific regulations for Islamic banks. The outcome of these negotiations was the establishment of the Islamic Financial Services Board (IFSB) in April 2002, with AAOIFI Secretary General Rifaat Abdel Karim as director. The goal is for the IFSB, which now has fifty-two members including fifteen regulatory bodies, is to have responsibility for the regulation and supervision of the Islamic financial services industry, with duties including (1) setting and disseminating standards and core principles for supervision and regulation; (2) cooperating with other standard-setters in the areas of monetary and financial stability; and (3) promoting good practices in risk management through research, training, and technical assistance.

The creation of the IFSB backed by the credibility of the IMF is the crowning achievement of AAOIFI and a testament to its success in defying

[18] Khan and Mirakhor 1991; Ul Haque and Mirakhor 1998.
[19] Errico and Farahbaksh 1998.

the trend toward the elimination of separate standards. AAOIFI's alliance with the IMF also gave it added clout in approaching other IFIs, and AAOIFI scored an impressive string of successes in gaining acknowledgment for Islamic finance. Rifaat Abdel Karim got the IAS to recognize Islamic accounting, and scored a seat on the Standards Advisory Council (SAC) of the International Accounting Standards Board (IASB) which provides advice to the IASB on priorities in setting standards and informs the board of the implications of proposed standards for both users and producers of financial accounts. Even more significantly, the establishment of the IFSB, which secured the influence of large state monetary authorities such as Saudi Arabia and Malaysia, finally persuaded the notoriously reluctant Basel Committee to support AAOIFI's initiatives on the grounds of making "more robust" its stated goal of adapting standards to local conditions.

The acceptance of AAOIFI and the IFSB are concrete manifestations of the success of the Islamic finance industry in gaining international acceptance of Islamic finance and acknowledgment of the need for separate consideration of its regulation. In gaining this recognition, however, the industry has had to pay the cost of relinquishing some of its authority in standard setting back to governmental bodies, both state and international. This serves the goal of achieving greater standardization within the industry. However, Islamic banks also have an interest in negotiating standards to their best interests and in seeing that their particular interpretation of international standards predominates. The question still remains: Can these new transnational Islamic institutions—and the argument for cultural exception more generally—be instrumentalized to yield concrete gains for the industry? The outcome of the negotiation between central bank governors, the IFIs, and the Islamic banks themselves can only become apparent by delving into the arcane minutiae of financial prudentials. To better understand the economic stakes in the battle taking shape, I will look in more detail at the arguments surrounding one such area: capital adequacy standards for Islamic banks.

THE POLITICS OF STANDARD SETTING: THE CASE OF CAPITAL ADEQUACY REGULATIONS

In the previous section I focused on "how" the Islamic finance industry is seeking to maintain its distinction and represent its interests on the global level through the creation of institutions like AAOIFI. In this section, I will focus on the "why": more specifically, why is it in the interest of Islamic finance to lobby for its own standards? Standard setting is a rather technocratic area of study. My goal here is not to give an exhaustive account of these procedures, but simply to provide enough background to show why having separate Islamic standards may work to the benefit of the Islamic financial industry, and thus why it may want to use the argument of cultural exception in its negotiations with the IFIs.

One of the key new components of international banking regulation aimed at increasing the strength and stability of the international financial system has been in the area of capital regulation. The main idea behind this regulation is to ensure adequate capitalization, given a bank's risk portfolio, to protect a bank from collapse. This area has received a lot of attention from IFIs as adequate capitalization is seen as a first line of defense in preventing banking failure and insulating the overall financial system from contagion. Enforcing minimal capital adequacy requirements is likewise a means to diminish a source of competitive inequality between international banks. Increasing capital reserves makes a bank more stable, but also diminishes its profitability; thus the existence of differing regulations results in an uneven playing field.

The agreed framework for measuring capital adequacy and the minimum standards to be achieved were laid out by the Basel Committee on Banking Supervision in the Basel Accords that were implemented in 1992. The Basel Committee is formed under the auspices of the Bank of International Settlements, which serves as a "central bank for central bankers" and is dominated by the G-10 countries. The accord sets a minimum ratio of a bank's capital to its risk weighted assets of 8 percent. Capital is further differentiated into two categories: Tier 1 and Tier 2, with restrictions placed on their relative size and relations to assets. Assets are assigned different risk-weightings based on a risk grid that weights more heavily for bank business with the private sector (vs. central government) and for non-OECD countries (vs. OECD):

Table 5. Basel Capital Adequacy Ratio and Risk Grid

Basel Capital Adequacy Requirement (CAR):

$$\frac{\text{Banks Capital (Tier 1+Tier 2)}}{\text{Risk-weighted Assets}} \geq 8\%$$

Sample Risk Grid (showing risk-weightings):

	Central Govt	Public Sector	Bank	Non-Bank
OECD	0%	20%	50%	100%
Non-OECD	20%	40%	70%	120%

Thus for example a bank doing a lot of business with the private sector of a developing country would have a higher risk portfolio of assets than one working predominately with European governments, and would consequently be required by the Basel capital adequacy requirement (CAR) to hold more capital reserves. The basic concept, then, is to rate the riskiness of a bank's assets and to ensure an adequate amount of capital to cover that risk.

Islamic banks have been slow to warm to this system, and have questioned its applicability to Islamic financial institutions. In a 1988 interview, one of the leading Islamic banks, Kuwait Finance House, forcefully pointed out the "irrelevance" of what it called the "traditional" capital-adequacy ratio of commercial banks. The secretary general of AAOIFI shared this view in nearly identical language nearly a decade later.[20] Still, with regulators keen to push for these ratios—and the private sector turning to them as an important criterion as well—the industry and its standard-setting body felt it necessary to engage the CAR and make their case on their own terms. Their argument is based on the need to "adjust the framework to cater to the unique characteristics of Islamic banks."[21] The main difficulties in adapting the framework are twofold and are basd on both the asset and capital mobilization sides of the accounts.

As reviewed earlier, the most prominent distinction of Islamic banking is that it does not rely on interest-based instruments, and it does not deal in debt. This effectively shuts Islamic banks out of one class of assets that figures significantly in many banks, especially in developing countries: government bonds. Because these instruments are interest-based, Islamic banks are not in the business of lending money to the public or borrowing from it. At the same time, the most important set of assets for Islamic banks—namely *murabaha* facilities—are directed almost exclusively at the private sector. According to the Basel framework, these kinds of investments show a higher risk-weighting—100 percent or more—which means that under the Basel Accord, Islamic banks would be required to maintain higher capital reserves to offset these risks. This trend is exacerbated by the higher risk weighting for dealing in non-OECD businesses, which comprise a notable portion of Islamic bank asset portfolios.

Thus an initial reading of the Basel CAR would assign a higher risk to Islamic banks' assets and this would require them to set aside a larger portion of the banks' capital, cutting into bank profits.[22] This poses a grave problem for many Islamic banks because in their mobilization of funds, many are pursuing a strategy of aggressively pursuing profit-sharing investment accounts and keeping equity capital to a minimum.[23] Thus far,

[20] Quoted in Abdel Karim 1996: 32.
[21] Ibid., 33.
[22] The IMF report studying the application of prudential regulations to Islamic banks even suggests *increasing* the recommended Basel CAR to above 8 percent.
[23] KFH Annual Report 2001; or see graph in Abdel Karim 1996: 39.

then, the interaction between the prevailing norms on capital adequacy regulation and the different instruments used on the asset side of the balance sheet in Islamic banks works to the disadvantage of Islamic financiers. It is then to the liability side of the balance sheet that the Islamic finance industry turns to argue for special treatment and turn the difference of Islamic finance to its advantage.

The primary means Islamic banks use for mobilizing funds is through profit-sharing investment accounts (PSIA). PSIAs are uniquely structured to reward depositors if the bank profits, but to show losses if the bank's investments do not pay off. In practical terms, however, competitive pressures push the Islamic banks to reward PSIA account holders at rates nearly equal to prevailing conventional deposit interest rates. Islamic banks are also loath to lose depositors' money, and cases of this in the history of the industry are extremely rare. Still, the Islamic finance industry—through AAOIFI—has argued that PSIAs are fundamentally different from normal deposit accounts, and that this difference must be integrated into the CAR.[24]

The basic argument put forth by the industry is that since PSIAs bear risk in ways similar to equity capital, allowing the banks to absorb operating losses while staying in business, they should be used to augment the bank's capital calculations. The secretary general of AAOIFI suggests remedying this situation by allowing Islamic banks to deduct PSIAs from their risk-weighted assets. This would allow the Islamic banks to satisfy the core capital requirements stipulated by the Basel framework, while continuing to pursue a low-equity capital strategy that allows bank shareholders to maximize profits at no extra risk.[25] Therefore, this acknowledgment of the unique attributes of Islamic finance capital mobilization on the part of regulators would yield real financial benefits to Islamic financiers, and would offset the negative impact of CAR rules on risky assets.

AAOIFI has aggressively pursued its interpretation of capital adequacy standards on behalf of the industry, despite the fact that this is outside of its original mandate of adapting accounting and auditing standards. And it has had some success in arguing for the risk-bearing nature of Islamic deposits. In 2001, the Bahrain Monetary Authority (BMA) accepted AAOIFI's argument at least in part, allowing Islamic banks in Bahrain in calculating the CAR to subtract 50 percent of their PSIA deposits from their risk-weighted assets. This has the effect of freeing up bank capital for investment, thereby increasing potential profits for Islamic banks. Furthermore, there is no question that AAOIFI's bold entry into the area of capital adequacy standards forced state regulators to take up the issue; the concerns of state regulators about the industry writing its own regulations were one of the motivating factors behind the establishment of the IFSB. The IFSB has yet to issue its regulations on capital adequacy

[24] This argument is laid out in Abdel Karim 1996: 32-44.
[25] Ibid., 39.

standards, but since former AAOIFI secretary general Rifaat Abdel Karim is now heading the IFSB, he is in a prime position to argue the industry's case, and early indications are that his argument will be accepted, at least in part.

These significant successes have been tempered by resistance from another set of international decision makers that have been less receptive to the Islamic finance industry's arguments: the ratings agencies. In June 2004, a revised framework for the international convergence of capital measurement and capital standards—known as Basel II—was published. Basel II gives much more authority to ratings agencies in determining the riskiness of banks and their assets. Thus a quick look at the relationship between Islamic banks and ratings agencies is in order; especially as it is revealing of the broad range of actors one must convince in gaining market acceptance and of some of the pitfalls in pursuing difference. The recent creation of an *Islamic* ratings agency also provides a window to exploring the rationale for and consequences of the expansion of a separate financial architecture for Islamic finance.

THE PROBLEM OF RATINGS AGENCIES AND THE CREATION OF THE IIRA

The case of capital adequacy standards shows clearly how the Islamic finance industry can use its difference strategically to negotiate to its advantage within the conventional financial architecture. Sustaining this advantage proves difficult, however, as such claims require acceptance by a wide array of actors and agencies. One class of actors that has been particularly bothersome to the Islamic finance industry is the ratings agencies. This is of concern due to the important market position of these institutions; the ratings agencies essentially signal to the market the credibility/riskiness of countries and institutions, and poor ratings can therefore limit one's access to international capital and global business.[26] The lower ratings consistently given to Islamic banks by the large ratings houses leave these banks paying higher spreads to raise money abroad; for example, KFH would currently pay higher rates in borrowing from Citibank (through Islamic instruments, of course) than would a Jamaican bank. And as stated above, ratings are to gain even more importance as the new Basel regulations come into force; then poor ratings will affect the capital adequacy requirements of these banks as well.

[26] In some sense Islamic banks are less vulnerable to ratings agencies because they are not on the bond market (ratings affect the bond prices for a bank). Still, the ratings affect their business in letters of credit and trade facilities, and there are general reputational costs as some banks are unwilling to accept dealings with lower rated banks.

The poor relationship with ratings agencies also deprives Islamic banks of a powerful market force for industry-wide standardization and acceptance. For example, one of the smaller ratings agencies sanctioned the Faisal Islamic Bank for not using AAOIFI accounting standards;[27] if such support for AAOIFI standards were widespread among ratings agencies they could become a powerful force for promoting AAOIFI and the unification of the industry. Unfortunately, however, the relations with the larger ratings agencies are more contentious, with the prevailing attitude toward the Islamic banks being "meet conventional standards or suffer the consequences."[28]

The ratings agencies claim simply that the Islamic banks have weaker internal controls and so earn lower ratings.[29] Yet they privately acknowledge that higher ratings tend to come to those banks that are at the heart of global finance. The professionalism looked for by the ratings agencies derives from dealing with Western banks, and becoming socialized in the same milieu; insular banks always tend to attract lower ratings. One agent confessed to me that although objective criteria are paramount, dealing with the raters is in some sense a confidence game where presentation and socialization count for a lot.[30] It is not surprising then that Islamic banks that aim for a separate and distinctive socialization of their own would be easily dismissed by these global arbiters. And it is understandable to see why the Islamic banks are now searching for a way to be judged by an institution closer to their worldview.

To this end, the International Islamic Ratings Agency (IIRA) was established in October 2002, and became operational in 2003. The IIRA is intended to be an independent body charged with rating Islamic banks and products by a uniform set of standards tailored to the requirements of Islamic finance. Still, from its inception there have been concerns about its independence and objectivity. The original conception of the IIRA called for strong participation from existing regional and international ratings agencies, which were to supply 50 percent of its financing while the Islamic banks would fund 35 percent and the IDB the remaining 15 percent of capital. Yet at the time of its launch, the IIRA received the bulk of its paid up capital—over 80 percent—from the IDB and the Islamic banks themselves. This lends greater credence to questions about its independence and objectivity. Although acknowledging a problem with the conventional ratings agencies, David Marston of the IMF expressed concerns about the

[27] Capital Intelligence rating of Faisal Islamic Bank-Egypt, 1998.
[28] Interview with David Marston, IMF Division Chief of Banking Supervision and Regulation, May 2002.
[29] Interview with Andrew Cunningham, Moody's Ratings Agency, London, September 14, 2002.
[30] Interview with Andrew Cunningham, September 14, 2002.

moral hazard inherent in IIRA's link to industry in saying: "There is a risk in me telling myself I am handsome."[31]

More broadly, the creation of the IIRA reflects another danger with the whole strategy of creating an alternative financial architecture for Islamic finance. Although these institutions are necessary for the healthy functioning of Islamic finance on a global level, they can easily lead to its marginalization from global finance. The Moody's rater for the Middle East, Andrew Cunningham, stressed that this danger will become more pronounced with the shift from Basel I to Basel II. The new structure will encourage market players to employ a much more quantitative approach to judging banks, which will leave even less room for difference and explanation. He contends:

> One may argue for exceptions, but will anyone take the time to listen? This seems likely only for those organizations large enough and important enough to demand exception, and Islamic banks are still a small industry in the general scheme of global finance. The problem goes beyond convincing the IMF or the Central Banks; the market itself will ignore you.[32]

Stated another way, the creation of a separate market framed by distinct regulation and supervision will be in vain if there are not sufficient players to enter that market; as one trenchant observer of the Islamic finance industry noted, "You need products before you can have a market."[33] The Islamic finance industry—and its new state allies—have been attempting to address this problem by moving beyond building the regulatory framework of Islamic finance to addressing the dearth of products. This effort is epitomized in two new institutions based in Bahrain—the International Islamic Financial Market (IIFM) and the affiliated Liquidity Marketing Center (LMC).

MAKING A MARKET: THE INTERNATIONAL ISLAMIC FINANCIAL MARKET (IIFM) AND LIQUIDITY MANAGEMENT CENTER (LMC)

AAOIFI, the IFSB, and the IIRA mark concrete achievements in improving the regulation and supervision of Islamic finance. But making a market requires more than a regulatory framework. There is a need for a standardization of the contracts underlying the financial products, which in

[31] Interview with David Marston, May 2002.
[32] Interview with Andrew Cunningham, September 14, 2002.
[33] Interview with Taha Al-Tayeb, director of the Islamic Banking Program, Bahrain Institute of Banking and Finance (BIBF), June 23, 2002.

turn requires consistency in *shari'a* rulings. There is a need for greater openness and cooperation between companies and with government authorities. And there is a distinct need for more engagement from government authorities in helping banks to manage their liquidity. With this greater standardization and participation, a deepening and maturing of the market becomes possible through the creation of secondary markets.

The expansion and growing credibility of the Islamic marketplace has indeed attracted the attention of state authorities in the Gulf. This has given the industry an opportunity to enhance its product offerings by convincing monetary authorities to develop Islamically-acceptable treasury products. The fruits of these efforts are the new International Islamic Financial Market (IIFM) and the related Liquidity Management Center (LMC), both based in Bahrain.

The agreement to establish the IIFM was signed in November 2001 in Paris by Malaysia, Indonesia, Bahrain, Sudan, and the IDB. All of these states have a financial interest in seeing the growth of the Islamic financial industry. Their cooperation in achieving this growth, however, is complicated due to the competition between the two leading state proponents of Islamic finance: Bahrain and Malaysia. Both states have invested heavily in their offshore financial markets, and both have ambitions to be the center of the Islamic finance industry. It is a favorable sign, however, that they were able to compromise and clear the way for the establishment of the IIFM; Bahrain was selected as the headquarters of the venture, but the first chief executive officer selected, Abdel Rais Abdel Majid, is a Malaysian banker. The geographical distance between the two hubs is actually an asset, as both believe they can contribute to generating a twenty-four hour market for the industry.

The IIFM is set up as a company with the five country central bank governors and the IDB on board as shareholders. It is often advertised in ambitious terms as the new Islamic bond market, where governmental and non-governmental Islamic bonds can be issued, and a secondary market can be generated through the trading of these bonds. In reality its initial tasks are much more modest; the real goal of the IIFM is not to develop a competitive market to the existing one, but rather to ride on the existing infrastructure while providing the necessary incentives and support for bringing more Islamic products on the global market.[34]

As mentioned earlier, Islamic finance suffers from its inability to access the interest-denominated interbank market and likewise the market for government bonds.[35] This leaves the banks with few options for managing their short-term liquidity. The solution has been to turn to

---

[34] Interview with Abdel Rais Abdul Majid, chief executive officer of the International Islamic Financial Market, Manama, Bahrain, June 23, 2002.

[35] The exception to this has been Malaysia, which issues Islamic government bonds, but the legal basis for this is contested in the more conservative Gulf.

contracts with conventional banks for short term commodity purchases—a device known in the industry as a commodity *murabaha*—but these vehicles give very little profit, leaving Islamic banks at a disadvantage against their conventional competitors. They are also disliked by *shari'a* scholars who have approved them only reluctantly with the expectation that the industry will eventually develop a more Islamically sound liquidity management vehicle.

Islamic and conventional financial institutions are working to do just that, but there is little cooperation and coordination between them. Instead each institution incurs expenses in developing the specialized contracts to pass through *shari'a* regulations, and thus sees these contracts/products as proprietary. Thus the relationship between the banks is still very competitive, as each bank guards its specific *shari'a* approved products as company secrets, and competing *shari'a* boards often refuse to accept the rulings of competitors. This has left the market extremely fragmented, as each contract is designed on an ad hoc basis, with little standardization and information sharing.

The IIFM is addressing this problem primarily through the creation of a *shari'a* supervisory committee (SSC) that will monitor the products being issued on the market. The hope is that this global committee, drawn from a geographically diverse and universally respected set of *shari'a* scholars, will help to bring about more transparency and standardization of *shari'a* rulings. It is also hoped that the new IIRA will bring more openness and consistency to the industry. There are also plans to open an Arbitration and Reconciliation Center for Islamic Financial Institutions (ARCIFI) to curb the more damaging side effects of competition between Islamic banks.

At present, however, the IIFM is hindered by the lack of commitment from the industry. The initiating governments that have a financial stake in seeing Islamic finance develop have contributed to the start-up costs of the IIFM, but the competing banks and financial institutions have not yet done so. This has left the IIFM with very modest resources; reportedly the IIFM began its work with a mere $100,000, barely enough to make it through its first year. Unless things change, with such minimal financial commitment, the CEO of the IIFM is reduced to the role of fundraiser, promoter, and agitator; having no resources on his own for product development, he can only persuade industry players of the importance of their development and encourage information sharing between them.

Due to the IIFM's limited resources, the initiative for product development has been taken up in earnest by its sister institution in Bahrain, the Liquidity Management Center (LMC), whose stated goal is to develop an active secondary market for short-term *shari'a* compliant treasury products. As an initial step in this process, the Bahrain Monetary Authority in June 2002 became the first state authority in the Gulf to issue Islamic government bills on a monthly basis. In August of the same year, the BMA announced the release of five-year Islamic leasing bonds to address the requirements of Islamic financial institutions for medium and long-term investment opportunities. On their own, these two releases are small—the Islamic government bill issue was only $25 million, and the Islamic leasing bonds issue was $100 million—but they marked a first step toward adding tradeable investment products for the Islamic market.

The actions taken by BMA have led more government authorities to experiment in asset-backed Islamic government bonds that are known in the industry as *sukuk*. Since the initiative taken by Bahrain, the IDB, Malaysia, Qatar, and the German state of Saxony-Anhalt have all issued international *sukuk,* and they are currently under consideration by the Central Bank of Kuwait as well. The IIFM and LMC are betting that financial institutions, conventional and Islamic, will likewise be attracted to the capital mobilization potential of Islamic finance, and will see the opportunity in creating a wider array of Islamic investments and products. In any case, the entrance into the Islamic market of many governments that were once ignorant of or hostile to Islamic finance is a further reflection of the growing acceptance of Islamic finance in the Islamic world.

ISLAM IN THE CONVENTIONAL GLOBAL MARKETS: A "FINANCIAL CLASH OF CIVILIZATIONS"?

This paper has provided an overview and analysis of the underlying institutions of the newly emerging global Islamic financial market. It is worth reflecting on the political implications of this incipient act of market creation. Although initiated for the express purpose of further integrating Islamic finance into global financial markets, these uniquely Islamic institutions clearly represent an alternative financial vision underpinned by its own norms and standards. Taken together with the growing mistrust and distance generated between the West and the Islamic world by the September 11 tragedy and its aftermath, one might ask if this signals a growing divide: a financial clash of civilizations? More specifically, can these newly established institutions be instrumentalized economically and politically to promote market divisions and create a regional market for capital mobilization and investment nurtured by an Islamic worldview?

Most Islamic bankers support using claims of cultural exception to negotiate to their advantage in the application of regulations; we have already seen this done successfully to alleviate the burden of capital adequacy on Islamic banks. Still others would like to wave the banner of cultural authenticity more broadly in an attempt to mobilize political loyalities with the intent of shifting business patterns. The CEO of the IIFM, Abdel Majid, speaks in ambitious terms of drawing Islamic money from the capital rich region of the Gulf to the product rich areas of Asia. The goal is to use Islamic solidarity as expressed through the IIFM to shift capital flow from the West to the East.[36] He sees an ideal opportunity for such an historic shift in the tension-filled atmosphere of post – September 11th West-Islamic relations.

There are clear signs that the poisonous atmosphere of the war on terrorism has strengthened the desire among many Muslims for Islamic solidarity in the financial realm. The director of the Islamic Banking Department at the State Bank of Pakistan noted that the current international situation has prompted a strong response, motivating many Muslims to shift to Islamic banking.[37] Also since September 11th there is growing unease over the arbitrary way in which regulatory authorities in the West have been acting against Islamic investment funds as well as conventional funds promoted by Arab banks. Some fund managers from the MENA (Middle-East North African) countries are considering relocating the domicile of their funds from Western jurisdictions such as Luxembourg to the growing Islamic financial centers of Bahrain and Labuan (Malaysia). Wealthy Arab investors have likewise been outraged by the freezing of Arab bank accounts, sometimes due to confusion over names, and many are looking to diversify their investments away from Western markets. There at least seems to be the potential to stem in part the capital flight from the Gulf and to generate a regional network for project finance and investment that would be small in global terms but quite significant for the region.

Such a shift still faces powerful economic impediments, however, in the form of small markets and political risk. Still, if political polarization with the West accelerates, then the political risk for Arab and Muslim investors may rise in the advanced industrial countries as well, making investment on the Islamic market more attractive.

The constitution of Islamic finance on the global level is the culmination of a strong desire on the part of many Muslims both to hold true to their religious principles and to express global Islamic solidarity. Whether this can be translated into greater financial independence and regional integration remains to be seen. But even in its incipient form, the evolving Islamic financial system has succeeded on a political level in constructing a concrete institutional manifestation of those aspirations.

---

36 Interview with Abdel Rais Abdel Majid, June 23, 2002.

37 Mentioned in a talk by Pervez Said, director of the Islamic Banking Department, State Bank of Pakistan, before the Sixth Harvard University Forum on Islamic Finance, May 8-9, 2004.

References

Abdel-Fadil, Mahmoud. 1989. *Al-Khadi`a al-Maliyya al-Kubra: al-Iqtisad al-Siyasi li-Sharikat Tawzif al-Amwal*. al-Qahira: Dar al-Mustaqbal al-'Arabi.

Abdel Karim, Rifaat Ahmed. 1996. "The impact of the Basel capital adequacy ratio regulation on the financial and marketing strategies of Islamic banks." *International Journal of Bank Marketing* 14(7): 32.

---------------. 1995a. "Financial Accounting and Reporting of Islamic Banks and Financial Institutes." *Encyclopedia of Islamic Banking*. London: Institute of Islamic Banking and Insurance.

---------------. 1995b. "The Nature and Rationale of a Conceptual Framework for Financial Reporting by Islamic Banks." *Accounting and Business Research* 25(100): 288.

---------------. 1990. "Standard Setting for the Financial Reporting of Religious Business Organizations: The Case of Islamic Banks." *Accounting and Business Research* 20(80): 302.

Abdul Barr, Muhammad Zaki. 1991. "Ta'liq." *Journal of King Abdulaziz University: Islamic Economics* 3: 61.

---------------. 1990. "Ra'yun Akhar fi Matl al-Madin, Hal Yulzam bi al-Ta`wid?" *Journal of King Abdulaziz University: Islamic Economics* 2: 155.

Accounting and Auditing Organization for Islamic Financial Institutions (AAOIFI). 2004. *Accounting, Auditing & Governance Standards for Islamic Financial Institutions*. 2003-2004 edition. Manama: AAOIFI.

---------------. 2003. *Shari'a Standards*. Manama/Bahrain: AAOIFI.

Ahmad, Ahmad Muhyi al-Din. 1996. *Fatawa al-Murabaha. Silsilat al-Fatawa al-Iqtisadiyya. al-Tab'a al-Ula*. Jidda: Dallat al-Baraka.

Algabid, Hamid. 1990. *Les banques islamiques*. Paris: Economics.

Allen, Steve L. 2001. *Financial Risk Management: A Practitioner's Guide to Managing Market and Credit Risk*. New York: Wiley.

al-Amine, Muhammad al-Bashir Muhammad. 2001. “The Islamic Bond Market: Possibilities and Challenges.” *International Journal of Islamic Financial Services* 3(1). Available at http://Islamic-finance.net/journal.html.

’Aniyyah, Jamal al-Din. 1986. “al-Bunuk al-Islamiyya Bayna al-Hurriyya wa al-Tanoim, al-Taqlid wa al-Ijtihad, al- Naoariyya wa al-Tanbiq.” *Kitab al-Ummah* 13. Duha: Ri’asat al-Mahakim al-Shar’iyya wa al-Shu’un al-Diniyya bi-Dawlat Qatar.

Archer, Simon, and Rifaat Ahmed Abdel-Karim. 2002. *Islamic Finance: Innovation and Growth*. London: Euromoney Books and AAOIFI.

al-Ashqar, Muhammad Sulayman. 1995. “Bay‘ al-Murabaha ka-ma Tajrihi al-Bunuk al-Islamiyya: `Aqd al-Salam wa `Aqd al-Istida’ wa-Imkaniyyat Istifadat al-Bunuk al-Islamiyya Minhuma.” In *Abhath Iqtisadiyya Shar’iyya*. Amman: Dar al-Nafa’is.

‘Attiyah, Jamal. 1990. “al-Jawanib al-Qanuniyah li-Tatbiq ’Aqd al-Murabaha.” *Journal of King Abdulaziz University: Islamic Economics* 2: 125.

al-Ba’li, ’Abdul Hamid Mahmoud. 1991. *al-Istithmar wa al-Riqaba al-Shar’iyya fi al-Bunuk al-Islamiyya wa al-Mu’assat al-Maliyya al-Islamiyya: Dirasa Fiqhiyya wa Qanuniyya wa-Masrafiyya.* Qubrus: Bank Faisal al-Islami.

Bälz, Kilian. 2004a. “Das islamische Recht als Vertragsstatut? *Shamil Bank of Bahrain vs. Beximco Pharmaceuticals Ltd. and Others,* London High Court vom 1. August 2003.” *Praxis des Internationalen Privat- und Verfahrensrechts* (in print).

---------------. 2004b. “A *Murabaha* Transaction in an English Court. The London High Court of 13th February 2002 in *Islamic Investment Company of the Gulf (Bahamas) Ltd. v. Symphony Gems N.V. & Ors*.” *Islamic Law and Society* 11: 117-134.

---------------. 2001. “Islamic Law as Governing Law under the Rome Convention: Inversalist *Lex Mercatoria* vs. the Regional Unification of Laws.” *Yearbook of Islamic and Middle Eastern Laws* 8: 73.

Bank for International Settlements (BIS), Basel Committee on Banking Supervision. 2003. *The New Basel Capital Accord.* Basel: BIS.

Basel Committee. 2003. *Position Paper on the Third Consultative Document Issued by the Basel Committee by Union Europeenne De L'Artisanat Et Des Petites Et Moyennes Entreprises*. Available at www.bis.org/bcbs/ cp3/ ueapme.pdf.

Basel Committee on Banking Supervision (BCBS). 2004. *International Convergence of Capital Measurement and Capital Standards: A Revised Framework.* Basel: BIS.

Berger, Klaus-Peter, et al. 2002. "Anwendung Transnationalen Rechts in der internationalen Vertrags- und Schiedspraxis - Hintergrund, Methode und ausgewählte Ergebnisse einer Umfrage des Center for Transnational Law (CENTRAL)." *Zeitschrift für vergleichende Rechtswissenschaft* 101: 12-37.

Buhayri, Muhammad 'Abd al-Wahhab. 1974. *al-Hiyal fi al-Shari`a al-Islamiyya wa-Sharh ma Warada Fiha min al-Ayat wa al-Ahadith aw Kashf al-Niqab 'an Mawqi' al-Hiyal min al-Sunna wa al-Kitab.* al-Qahira.

Chapra, M. U., and Tariqullah Khan. 2000. *Regulation and Supervision of Islamic Banks*. Jedda: Islamic Development Bank.

Collins, Lawrence (ed.). 2000. *Dicey and Morris on the Conflict of Laws.* Volume 2. 13th ed. London: Sweet & Maxwell.

al-Dareer, al-Siddiq Muhammad al-Amin. 1993a. "Ta'liq." *Journal of King Abdulaziz University: Islamic Economics* 5: 69.

---------------. 1993b. "Ta'liq." *Journal of King Abdulaziz University: Islamic Economics* 5: 63.

---------------. 1985. "al-Ittifaq 'ala Ilzam al-Madin al-Mu'sir bi-Ta'wid Darar al-Mumatala." *Journal of Research in Islamic Economics* 3(1): 111.

DiFonzo, Luigi. 1983. *St. Peter's Banker: Michele Sindona.* New York: Franklin Watts.

Elgari, M. A., M. N. Siddiqi, and M. A. Zarqa. 1993. "Qanun al-Masarif Sigha Muqtaraha li-Tanzim Qita' Masrafi Islami." *Review of Islamic Economics* 2(2): 67.

Errico, Luca, and Mitra Farahbaksh. 1998. *Islamic Banking: Issues in Prudential Regulations and Supervision*. Washington: International Monetary Fund.

Fabozzi, Frank J., and Franco Modigliani. 2002. *Capital Markets: Institutions and Instruments*. Upper Saddle River, New Jersey: Prentice Hall.

Fayyaa, 'Aniyya. 1999. *al-Tabiqat al-Masrafiyya li-Bay' al-Murabaha fi Daw' al-Fiqh al-Islami*. al-Qahira: Dar al-Nashr lil-Gami'at.

Fox, Lawrence J. 2000. "The Future of the Profession: A Symposium on Multidisciplinary Practice." *Minnesota Law Review* 84 (June): 1097.

Goode, Roy. 1995. *Commercial Law*. 2nd ed. London: Penguin Books.

Griffith-Jones, Stephany, et al. 2002. *Basel II and Developing Countries: Diversification and Portfolio Effects*. Available at http://www.ids.ac.uk/ids/global/finance/pdfs/FINALBasel-diversification2.pdf.

Hafizah, Sharifah. 2001. "IAS: A Milestone for Malaysia's Islamic Banking Sector." *IslamiQ Islamic News*. Available at www.islamiq.com.

Hallaq, Wael B. 2001. *Authority, Continuity, and Change in Islamic Law*. New York: Cambridge University Press.

Hammad, Nazeeh Kamal. 1985. "al-Mu`ayyidat al-Shar'iyah li-Haml al-Madin al-Mumatil `ala al-Wafa' wa-Butlan al-Hukm bi al-Ta`wid al-Mali `an Darar al-Mumatala." *Journal of Research in Islamic Economics* 3(1): 101.

al-Harran, Saad, ed. 1995. *Leading Issues in Islamic Banking and Finance*. Selangor, Malaysia: Pelanduk Publications.

Hayes, Simon, et al. 2002. "The impact of the new Basel Accord on the supply of capital to emerging market economies." *Financial Stability Review* 101. Available at www.bankofengland.co.uk/fsr/ fsr13art4.pdf.

Henry, Clement, and Rodney Wilson. 2004. *The Politics of Islamic Finance*. Edinburgh: Edinburgh University Press.

Hooper, Judge C. A. 1933. "Majalat ASl-Akham al-Adliyah." *The Civil Law of Palestine and Trans-Jordan,* Volumes 1-2. Reprinted in 4 *Arab Law Quarterly* (August 1986).

Hummud, Sami Hasan Ahmad. 1976. *Tanwir al-A`mal al-Masrifiyya bi-ma Yattafiqu wa al-Shari`a al-Islamiyya.* al-Qahira: Dar al-Ittihad al-'Arabi li l-Tiba'a.

Ibn Anas, Malik. 2000. *al-Muwatta* (Mohamed Rahimuddin, trans.). 5th ed. New Delhi: Kitab Bhavan.

Ibn Qayyim al-Jawziyya, Muhammad ibn Abi Bakr. 1998. *I`lam al-Muwaqqi`in `an Rabb al-`Alamin.* Bayrut: Dar al-Kitab al-'Arabi.

Ibn Taymiyya, Taqi al-Din. 1987. *Al-Fatwa al-Kubra Majmu'at Fatawa Shaykh al-Islam Taqi al-Din Ibn Taymiyya al-Harrani, al-Tab'a al-Ula.* Volume 3. Bayrut: Dar al-Qalam.

Ishak, Dato Othman Hj. 1997. "Developing Dha'wa Ta'ajjal in Structuring Islamic Instruments." Presented at International Capital Market Conference, Kuala Lumpur, July 15-16, 1997.

Islamic *Fiqh* Academy. 2000. *Resolutions and Recommendations of the Council of the Islamic Fiqh Academy 1985-2000.* Jedda: Islamic Development Bank.

---------------. 1988. Second Resolution of the Fifth Conference of the Islamic *Fiqh* Academy, Kuwait, December 10-15, 1988.

Janahi, Abdul Latif. 1995. *Islamic Banking: Concept, Practice and Future.* 2nd ed. Manama: Bahrain Islamic Bank.

al-Kaff, Habib Hamid Abdul Rahman. 1993. "Ta'liq." *Journal of King Abdulaziz University: Islamic Economics* 3: 63.

Kamali, Hashim. 2000. *Islamic Commercial Law An Analysis of Futures and Options*. Cambridge: Islamic Texts Society.

Kazarian, Elias. 1993. *Islamic versus Traditional Banking: Financial Innovation in Egypt.* Boulder: Westview Press.

Khan, Mohsin, and Abbas Mirakhor. 1991. *Islamic Banking*. Washington: IMF.

Khan, Tariqullah, and Habib Ahmad. 2001. *Risk Management: An Analysis of Issues in Islamic Financial Industry 103*. Jedda: Islamic Development Bank.

Lannoo, Karel. 1995. *Corporate Governance in Europe*. Center for European Policy Studies (CEPS) Working Paper No. 12. Brussels: CEPS.

Lew, Julian D. M., et al. 2003. *Comparative International Commercial Arbitration*. The Hague, London, and New York: Kluwer Law International.

Malaysian Securities Commission. 2002. *Resolutions of the Securities Commission Syariya Advisory Council*. Kuala Lumpur.

Massachusetts Bankers Association. 2003. Comments submitted to Federal Deposit Insurance Corporation (FDIC) on November 3, 2003. Available at www.fdic.gov/regulations/laws/federal/03cmassbankers.html.

McMillen, Michael J. T. 2001. "Islamic *Shari'a*-Compliant Project Finance: Collateral Security and Financing Structure Case Studies." *Fordham International Law Journal* 24: 1184.

Misri, Rafiq. 2001. *Buhuth fi al-Masarif al-Islamiyya: Nahwa Iqtisad Islami*. Dimashq: Dar al-Maktabi.

al-Najjar, A. 1993. *Harakat al-Bunuk al-Islamiyya: Haqa'iq al-Asl wa Awham al-Sura*. al-Qahira.

Nyazee, Imran Ahsan Khan. 1995. *The Concept of Riba and Islamic Banking*. Available at http://islamic-finance.net/islamic*fiqh*/islbanks/conc*riba*.pdf .

Olsen, Mancur. 1965. *The Logic of Collective Action*. Cambridge: Harvard University Press.

al-Omar, Fuad, and Mohammed Abdel-Haq. 1996. *Islamic Banking: Theory, Practice and Challenges*. London: Zed Books.

Parigi, Stéphanie. 1989. *Des Banques Islamiques*. Paris: Ramsay.

Pettit, Philip. 1997. *Equity and the Law of Trusts*. London: Butterworths.

Potts, Mark, Nicholas Kochan, and Robert Whittington. 1992. *Dirty Money: BCCI: The Inside Story of the World's Sleaziest Bank*. Washington: National Press Books.

al-Qaradawi, Y. 1987. *Bay' al-Murabaha li al-Amir bi al-Shira' ka-ma Tujrihi al-Masarif al-Islamiyya: Dirasa fi Daw' al-Nusus wa al-Qawa'id al-Shar'iyya*. al-Qahira: Maktabat Wahba.

Qasim, Yusuf. 1988. *Usul al-Ahkam al-Shar'iyya.* al-Qahira: Dar al-Nahaa al-'Arabiyya.

Riyaa, Mohammad. 1996. *Usul al-Fatwa wa al-Qaaa' fi al-Madhhab al-Malik.* al-Dar al-Bayaa': Manba'at al-Najah al-Jadida.

al-Roobi, Rabi'. 1992. "Ta'liq." *Journal of King Abdulaziz University: Islamic Economics* 4: 67.

Rosly, Saiful Azhar, and Mahmood M. Sanusi. 1999. "The Application of *bai-al-inah* and *bai-al-dayn* in Malaysian Islamic Bonds: An Islamic Analysis." *International Journal of Islamic Financial Services* (online), 1 (no. 2): 3-11.

al-Sadr, M. Baqir. 1969. *al-Bank al-la-Rabawi fi al-Islam: Utruha li al-Ta`wid `an al-Riba wa-Dirasa li-Kaffat Awjuh Nashatat al-Bunuk fi-Daw' al-Fiqh al-Islami.* Kuwait: al-Matba'a al-'Asriyya.

Saeed, Abdullah. 1999. *Islamic Banking and Interest. A Study on the Prohibition of Riba and its Contemporary Interpretation.* Leiden, Boston, and Cologne: Brill.

Saidenberg, Marc, and Til Schuermann. 2003. *The New Basel Capital Accord and Questions for Research.* Available at http://papers.ssrn.com/sol3/papers.cfm?abstract_id=410322#PaperDownload.

Saleh, Ibn al-Haj Mohammad. 2002. "al-Ta`wid `inda al-Ta'khir fi al-Sidad Bayna al-Mu'aradah wa al-Ta'id." *Majallat al-Masarif* (Khurtum) 1.

Saleh, Nabil. 1986. *Unlawful Gain and Legitimate Profit in Islamic Law.* Preface. Cambridge: Cambridge University Press.

Schacht, Joseph. 1982. *An Introduction To Islamic Law.* Oxford: Clarendon Press.

Securities Commission. 2002. *Resolutions of the Securities Commission* (March 2002). Syriah Advisory Council. Kuala Lumpur: Securites Commission.

al-Shanibi, Ibrahim ibn Musa. 2000. *al-Muwafaqat fi Usul al-Shari`a.* Bayrut: al-Maktaba al-'Asriyya.

al-Shaybani, Muhammad ibn al-Hasan. 1997. *Risalatan fi al-Kasb,* ed. 'Ali ibn al-Labudi and Suhayl Zakkar. Bayrut: Dar al-Fikr lil- Tiba'a wa al-Nashr wa al-Tawzi'.

Simmons, Mark R. 1997. "What You Should Know about Conflict of Interest." *Articles on Internal Auditing and Fraud Investigation*. Available at www.dartmouth.edu/~msimmons/fraud-investigation/coiknow.htm.

Smith, Kristin. 2004. "The Kuwait Finance House and the Islamization of Public Life in Kuwait." In Clement Henry and Rodney Wilson (eds.), *The Politics of Islamic Finance*. Edinburgh: Edinburgh University Press.

State Bank of Pakistan. 2004. "State Bank's *Shari'a* Board Approves Essentials and Model Agreements for Islamic Modes of Financing" (press release). Available at www.sbp.org.pk/press/2004/Islamic_modes. pdf.

Sundararajan, V., and Luca Errico. 2002. *Islamic Financial Institutions and Products in the Global Financial System: Key Issues in Risk Management and Challenges Ahead.* IMF Working Paper, WP/02/192.

Taylor, John B. 2004. "Understanding and Supporting Islamic Finance: Product and Differentiation and International Standards." Sixth Harvard University Forum on Islamic Finance, Cambridge, Massachusetts, 2004.

Temple, Peter. 2001. *Hedge Funds: Courtesans of Capitalism*. New York: Wiley.

Udovitch, Abraham L. 1970. *Partnership and Profit in Medieval Islam*. Princeton University Press.

Ul Haque, Nadeem, and Abbas Mirakhor. 1998. *The Design of Instruments for Government Finance in an Islamic Economy; IMF Working Paper*. Washington: IMF.

Union of Arab Banks. 2004. "The Role of Islamic Banking in Resource Mobilization in the Arab World." Conference held in Beirut, December 4-6, 2004. Available at www.uabonline.org/UABWeb/Conference/2004/Islamic %20Banking%20Conference/new/backgrounden.htm.

---------------. 2003. *The Basel II Capital Accord: Where Do Arab Banks Stand?* Available at www.ratingdevelopments.com/nphotiades/UAB%20 Basel%20II%20Study%20August%202003.doc.

Usmani, Muhammad Taqi. 2002. *An Introduction to Islamic Finance*. The Hague: Kluwer Law International.

---------------. 2000a. "Bay 'al-Dayn wa al-Awraq al-Maliyah wa-Bada'iluha al-Shar'iyah." *Dirasat Iqtisadiyah Islamiyah* (Jedda) 7(1): 7.

---------------. 2000b. *The Historic Judgement on Interest Delivered in the Supreme Court of Pakistan*. Karachi: Idaratul Maarif.

Vickers, Douglas. 1997. *Economics and Ethics*. Westport, Connecticut: Praeger.

Vogel, Frank E., and Samuel L. Hayes. 1998. *Islamic Law and Finance. Religion, Risk and Return*. The Hague, London, and Boston: Kluwer Law International.

Von Bar, Christian, and Peter Mankowski. 2003. *Internationales Privatrecht*. Volume 1. Munich: C.H. Beck.

Wagner, Gerhard. 2002. "Germany." In *Practitioner's Handbook on International Arbitration*, ed. Frank-Bernd Weigand; pp. 685-829. Munich: C. H. Beck; Copenhagen: DJOF.

Warde, Ibrahim. 2002. "Faiseurs de krach boursier." *Le Monde diplomatique.*

---------------. 2000. *Islamic Finance in the Global Economy*. Edinburgh: Edinburgh University Press.

---------------. 1998. "Le système bancaire dans la tourmente." *Le Monde diplomatique.*

Wichard, Johannes Christian. 1996. "Die Anwendung der UNIDROIT-Prinzipien für internationale Handelsverträge durch Schiedsgerichte und staatliche Gerichte." *Rabels Zeitschrift für ausländisches und internationales Privatrecht* 60: 262.

Wilson, Peter W. 1991. *A Question of Interest: The Paralysis of Saudi Banking*. Boulder: Westview Press.

Wilson, Rodney. 2002. "Islamic Capital Flight." Third Mediterranean Social and Political Research Meeting, Florence, March 20-24, 2002.

al-Zanjani, Mahmud ibn Ahmad, and Muhammad Adib Salih. 1987. *Takhrij al-Furu` `Ala al-Usul*. Bayrut: Mu'assasat al-Risala.

al-Zarqa, Mohammad Anas, and Mohammad Ali Elgari. 1991. "al-Ta`wid `an Darar al-Mumatala fi al-Dayn Bayn al-Fiqh wa al-Iqtisad." *Journal of King Abdulaziz University: Islamic Economics* 3: 25.

al-Zarqa, Mustafa Ahmed. 1985. "Hal Yuqbal Shar`an al-Hukm `ala al-Madin al-Mumatil bi al-Ta`wid `ala al-Da'in?" *Journal of Research in Islamic Economics* 2(2): 89.

Zions Bancorporation. 2003. Comments submitted to FDIC. Available at www.fdic.gov/regulations/laws/federal/03cZIONSbanc.html.

Zubeida, Sami. 1997. "Is Iran an Islamic State?" In Joel Beinin and Joe Stork, eds., *Political Islam: Essays from Middle East Report.* Berkeley: University of California Press.

Zweigert, Konrad, and Hein Kötz. 1987. *An Introduction to Comparative Law*. 2nd ed. Oxford: Clarendon Press.

Glossary

ajr — stipend/ wage/ reward

al-asl fi al-umur al-ibaha — principle that the default judgment regarding human actions is permissiveness

al-ghunm bi-al-ghurm — profit sharing comes with risk sharing

al-hawl — one lunar year during which a taxable property remained in one's possession

al-kharaj bi-al-daman — profit comes with liability

amana — the status or duty of a trusted person *(amin)*; one of two basic relationships toward property, which entails absence of liability for loss except in breach of duty; compare *daman*

'ayn — an existent, tangible thing considered as unique and individual; a thing (Latin, *res*) as opposed to its usufruct *(manfa'a)*; thus, antonyms include genus, *dayn*, fungible, and usufruct; present coins.

azima — the *hukm* under normal circumstances

bay' — sale

bay' al-dayn — sale of obligation/debt

bay' al-'ina — a transaction where the seller sells an asset to the buyer on a spot payment basis and the buyer immediately sells it back to the seller at a higher price on a deferred payment basis

bay' al-istisna' — manufacturing contract with or without advance payment

bay' al-kali' bi-al-kali' — sale of one debt for another

bay' al-mu'ajjal — deferred sale

bay' al-murabaha — cost-plus sale contract (also known as mark-up sale contract)

bay' al-salam/salaf — purchase with deferred delivery

bay' al-wafa' — sale with a right in the seller to repurchase (redeem) the property by refunding the purchase price

bay' bi-thaman 'ajil — deferred credit sale with mark up

daman — (1) contract of guarantee (also called *kafala*); (2) one of two basic relationships toward property, entailing bearing the risk of its loss; compare *amana*

darurat — basic needs

dayn — generic property; property defined or contracted for only by its genus, species, and other characteristics (usually fungibles); any property, not an *'ayn*, that a debtor owes, either now or in the future; such property when due in the future; compare *'ayn*; debt

dirham — principal monetary unit of a number of Muslim countries in the past and present

fa'ida — profit

faqih — legal scholar/ jurist

faskh — termination; cancellation, rescission

fatwa (pl. *fatawa*) — an authoritative legal opinion issued by a scholar of *fiqh*

fiqh — Islamic jurisprudence

fisq — grave sin

fitra — instinct

fuqaha' — experts in Islamic law

gharar — uncertainty

gharar fahish — excessive uncertainty

hadith — lit., report; historical account of a saying, act, or omission of the Prophet or, secondarily, of an esteemed figure among his companions and early Muslim generations

hajat — additional needs

halal — allowed; lawful

Hanafi — one of the four Sunni schools of law

Hanbali — one of the four Sunni schools of law

haqq Allah — rights of Allah on his creation

haram — prohibited; unlawful

hiba — contract of gift

hikma — rationale/ wisdom

hila — juristic stratagem

hila ja'iza — allowable stratagem

hisas — shares

hisba — the principle that social authority is empowered to take the steps necessary to protect public interest

hiyal (sing., *hila*) — legal artifices or stratagems

hukm (pl., *ahkam*) — judgment; value assigned by *fiqh* to an act

'ibadat — acts of worship; compare *mu'amalat*

ifta' — institution/practice of seeking a *fatwa*

ijara — operating lease

ijara wa iqtina' — financial lease

ijara muntahiya bi-tamlik — lease ending with purchase

ijma' — unanimous agreement of all qualified *fiqh* scholars of an age; one of the four roots *(usul)* of *fiqh*

'ina — double-sale by which the borrower and the lender sell and then resell an object between them, once for cash and once for a higher price on credit, with the net result being a loan with interest

istisna' — contract providing for the manufacture and purchase of a specified item

ji'ala — service charges/ wage

khiyar al-ru'ya — option to inspect

khiyarat — options

khulta — lexically "mix"; In fiqh, a mix of properties that belong to 2 or more parties, such as when 4 sheep owned by Zayd and 5 owned by `Amr are allowed to mingle in one flock.

li'an — imprecation

madhhab — school of thought

mafsada — harm

mahr — Islamic dowry

makharij al-shar'iyya — lawful devices used by jurists to find alternative bases for permitting certain acts that appear to violate *shari`a* rules

makruh — reprehensible

Maliki — one of the four Sunni schools of law

maqasid al-shari'a — objectives of *shari'a*

maslaha — benefit

mu'amalat — dealings or transactions among human beings; compare *'ibadat*

mudaraba — (also called *qirad*) a form of partnership to which some of the partners contribute only capital and the other partners only labor (some schools do not treat it as a partnership but as a contract *sui generis*)

mudarib — a partner contributing labor in a *mudaraba*

mufti — an Islamic jurisconsult

muhallil — a third party who serves as an intermediary to avoid a prohibition

mujtahid — a jurist who exerts his legal talents to find the proper interpretation of the law

mukallaf — person to whom a judgment applies

mulaffiq — person seeking *talfiq*

mumathala — delay in payment of a debt incurred in a credit purchase

murabaha — sale at a percentage markup; one of the sales *(bay')* in which the price is stated in terms of the sale object's cost to the seller, the others being sale at cost *(tawliya)* and sale at discount *(wadi'a)*

murabaha li-amir bi-al-shira' — lit., sale by markup to one commissioning a purchase; a transaction involving two sales: A promises B that, if B buys for A certain specified goods, A will repurchase them from B by *murabaha*, i.e., at a markup

musharaka — equity participation contract

musharaka mutanaqisa — diminishing *musharaka*

mu'sir — insolvent

mustafti — person seeking a *fatwa*

mustawriq — person seeking *tawarruq*

nikah — marriage

qaradan — beneficence loan

qawa'id — principle, general rule, maxim

qiyas — analogy; one of the four roots *(usul)* of *fiqh*

rabb al-mal — lit., the owner of the property; a partner who contributes capital

raf' — lifting, raising or removal [of hardship]

riba — usury as forbidden in the Qur'an; interpreted in classical *fiqh* as including interest and various other forms of gain in contract

riba al-jahiliyya — compensation/increase for deferring a due debt

rukhas manduba — recommended exceptional dispensations

rukhas mubaha — dispensations that are neither recommended nor reprehensible

rukhas wajiba — mandatory exceptional dispensations

rukhsa (pl., *rukhas*) — exemption/permission

sadd al-dhara'i — prevention of stratagems to achieve illegal ends through legal means

sakk — check/Islamic bond

salam — sale with deferred delivery

salat al-janaza — the funeral prayer

sanadat — more conventional term for "bonds"

Shafi'i — one of the four Sunni schools of law

shahadat al-dayn — evidence of a debt

shar' — legal/law

shari'a — the divine law known from the Qur'an and Sunna

shirkat al-milk — joint ownership of property/noncontractual partnership

shubha — doubt and uncertainty about the permissibility of an act under Islamic law

sukuk — Islamic bonds and certificates

sukuk al-ijara — Islamic bond based on an *ijara* asset

sukuk al-istithmar — Islamic bond based on an investment

sukuk al-salam — Islamic bond based on a *salam* contract. Islamic T-Bill introduced by the Bahrain Monetary Agency

Sunna — the Prophet Muhammad's normative example, as known from the *ahadith*; one of the four roots *(usul)* of *fiqh*

tahayul — dishonesty

takhfif — to make light, easy

talfiq — biased amalgamation of previous opinions to circumvent a prohibition

taslim — capable of delivery

tawarruq — a practice by which a needy person buys something on credit and at once sells it for cash to a third party in a separate transaction

usul al-fiqh — principles of legal reasoning

wa'd — promise

wa'd al-amir bi-al-shira' — a promise by the one who ordered/requested the initial purchase

zagha wa 'azagha — to go astray and cause others to go astray

zakat — the third pillar of Islam; obligatory alms-giving that every well-off Muslim is required to relinquish to the Islamic authority for distribution to the poor and needy

zina — sex outside of marriage

Guide to Contributors

BÄLZ, KILIAN
Partner, Gleiss Lutz; Frankfurt, Germany
Kilian Bälz is among the pioneers of Islamic finance in Germany and has published widely on issues related to Islamic banking and other topics of Islamic and Middle Eastern law. He specializes in international M&A and capital markets with a particular focus on the MENA region. Gleiss Lutz is one of the leading German corporate law firms with international reach. Before joining the firm, Bälz taught law at the University of Frankfurt. Bälz studied law and Middle East studies at the University of Freiburg. He has also studied at universities in Berlin (Dr. jur.), Damascus, Cairo, and London (LL.M., SOAS).

EL-GAMAL, MAHMOUD A.
Professor of Islamic Economics, Finance, and Management, Rice University; Houston, Texas
Mahmoud A. El-Gamal is Professor of Economics and Statistics at Rice University, in Houston, Texas, where he holds the endowed Chair in Islamic Economics, Finance, and Management. Prior to joining Rice in 1998, he had been an associate professor at the University of Wisconsin at Madison, and an assistant professor at Caltech and the University of Rochester. He also served in 1995-96 as an Economist at the Middle East Department of the International Monetary Fund, and for June through December 2004 as the first Scholar in Residence on Islamic Finance at the U.S. Department of Treasury. He has published extensively in the areas of econometrics, experimental economics, Islamic law and finance, and economics of the Middle East.

HANEEF, MOHAMED RAFE MD.
Head of Islamic Finance, ABN AMRO Bank N.V.; Dubai, United Arab Emirates
Mohamed Rafe Haneef is Head of Islamic Finance at ABN AMRO Bank in Dubai. Prior to that he was associate director of HSBC Amanah, Dubai responsible for originating Islamic cross-border transactions from Asia with a focus on Islamic debt securities. His association with HSBC began in 1999 in its London office, as a core member of the Islamic cross-border

financing team. Haneef graduated from the International Islamic University, Malaysia in 1994 with a Bachelor of Laws degree in Common Law and Shari`a. He obtained an LL.M. in 1997 from Harvard Law School, where he specialized in international finance. He was admitted to the Malaysian Bar in 1995 and qualified for the New York Bar in 1997. Haneef practiced law in Malaysia, specializing in Islamic banking, before moving to HSBC.

HEGAZY, WALID

International Consultant, Fulbright & Jaworski; Houston, Texas

Walid Hegazy is currently working as counsel at Fulbright & Jaworski LLP in Houston, Texas and is currently writing a dissertation on the theory and practice of Islamic finance. His thesis focuses on the theory of *daman* and the practice of Islamic finance. He holds LL.M. degrees from Harvard Law School and Paris IX University. Hegazy worked for the law firm of White & Case in New York City and for Baker & McKenzie in Saudi Arabia. He is admitted to the Cairo Bar Association and has been a member of the Egyptian Bar Association since 1991 and the American Bar Association since April 2003.

HENRY, CLEMENT M.

Professor of Government, University of Texas, Austin; Austin, Texas

Clement M. Henry currently specializes in the Middle East and North Africa at the University of Texas, Austin, where he has researched political parties, the engineering profession, and financial institutions. He has lived more than twelve years in the field and taught in Algiers, Beirut, Cairo, and Rabat. From 1973 to 1980, he taught at the University of Michigan. Henry received his A.B., *summa cum laude*, and his Ph.D. in political science from Harvard University, and his MBA from the University of Michigan. His most recent work with Rodney Wilson, co-edited *The Politics of Islamic Finance* (Edinburgh Univeristy Press, 2004). He has written, co-authored, and co-edited ten books, and contributed over three dozen articles to other publications, including the *American Political Science Review*. One of his recent noteworthy publications co-authored with Robert Springborg, is *Globalization and the Politics of Development in the Middle East* (Cambridge University Press, 2001). In July 1999, Henry guest-edited a special double issue of the *Thunderbird International Business Review* on Islamic banking.

McMILLEN, MICHAEL J. T.

Partner, King & Spalding; New York, New York

Michael J. T. McMillen is a partner in the New York office of King & Spalding, where he focuses on Islamic finance and international and domestic project finance, leasing, and structured finance. He was formerly a partner with White & Case and spent three years in Jedda with the law office of Hassan Mahassni. He is an international project financing expert and has worked on some of the largest and most innovative project financing deals in well over twenty countries. McMillen has extensive transactional experience in the field of Islamic finance, and has developed many Islamic financial products in Saudi Arabia and the Gulf. He developed the first *istisna'-ijara* (construction contract-lease) construction and mini-perm finance structure for United States real estate. He has particular expertise in the electricity generation, petrochemical, mining, paper milling, and natural gas sectors. McMillen received his BBA from the University of Wisconsin, his M.D. from the Albert Einstein College of Medicine, and his J.D. from the University of Wisconsin.

SHAKIL, MANSOOR
Manager, HSBC Amanah; Dubai, United Arab Emirates
Mansoor Shakil is Manager at HSBC Amanah. He completed his LL.M. at Harvard Law School, where he specialized in international financial systems. He holds another Master of Law (commercial law) from the University of Cambridge, and a Bachelors in Shari`a and Law from International Islamic University, Islamabad, Pakistan. He has worked for a year in the corporate division of a premier law firm in Karachi, where he was involved in the structuring, drafting, and negotiation of banking, financial, and leasing transactions. He also handled the documentation for the first Islamic banking branch of a major commercial bank in Pakistan.

SIDDIQI, M. NEJATULLAH
Independent Researcher; Milpitas, California
M. Nejatullah Siddiqi is a visiting fellow at the University of California at Los Angeles and the president of the International Association for Islamic Economics. Prior to this, he was Professor of Economics at the Center for Research in Islamic Economics at King Abdulaziz University. He was formerly Professor of Islamic Studies and Director of the Institute of Islamic Studies at Aligarh Muslim University. Siddiqi has a Ph.D. in economics from Aligarh Muslim University. He has supervised Ph.D. dissertations at Aligarh Muslim University, Umm al-Qura University, Imam Muhammad bin Saud University, and Sokoto University. Siddiqi has been the recipient of the King Faisal Islamic International Prize for Islamic Studies. He is the author of dozens of books, including *Muslim Economic Thinking*, *Banking without Interest*, and *Role of the State in the Economy: An Islamic Perspective*.

SMITH, KRISTIN
Qatar Postdoctoral Fellow, Center for Contemporary Arab Studies, Georgetown University, Washington D.C.
Kristin Smith is completing her Ph.D. from the Department of Government at Harvard University where her dissertation is on the political economy of Islamic Finance in the Arab Gulf. Research for this project took place in

Kuwait, Bahrain, and the United Arab Emirates and resulted in the publication of a chapter on the political aspects of Islamic banking in Kuwait in the book *The Politics of Islamic Finance* (Edinburgh: Edinburgh University Press, 2004). Smith has also published "Kuwait in the Balance: Islamist-Liberal Politics in the wake of September 11th" in *Middle East Policy* (September 2002). She is currently teaching a seminar course on Arab Gulf politics at Georgetown University.

WARDE, IBRAHIM
Research Affiliate, Center for International Studies, Massachusetts Institute of Technology; Cambridge, Massachusetts
Ibrahim Warde is a research affiliate at MIT's Center for International Studies as well as an international consultant specializing in global financial issues. He was previously a research fellow at the Berkeley Roundtable on the International Economy, where he did extensive research on the Silicon Valley economy and business practices. Warde has a B.A. from the Universite Saint-Joseph, an MBA from École des Hautes Études Commerciales, and a Ph.D. in Political Science from the University of California at Berkeley. Warde is the author of *Islamic Finance in the Global Economy* (Edinburgh University Press, 1999) and has written more than thirty monographs and articles on international finance.

Index